Emerging Markets and Financial Resilience

Emerging Markets and Financial Resilience

Decoupling Growth from Turbulence

Edited by

Chee-Wooi Hooy
Senior Lecturer, Universiti Sains Malaysia

Ruhani Ali
Professor of Finance, Universiti Sains Malaysia

and

S. Ghon Rhee
Shidler Distinguished Professor of Finance, University of Hawaii

palgrave
macmillan

First published 2013 by
PALGRAVE MACMILLAN

Palgrave Macmillan in the UK is an imprint of Macmillan Publishers Limited, registered in England, company number 785998, of Houndmills, Basingstoke, Hampshire RG21 6XS.

Palgrave Macmillan in the US is a division of St Martin's Press LLC, 175 Fifth Avenue, New York, NY 10010.

Palgrave Macmillan is the global academic imprint of the above companies and has companies and representatives throughout the world.

Palgrave® and Macmillan® are registered trademarks in the United States, the United Kingdom, Europe and other countries

ISBN 978-1-349-44139-2 ISBN 978-1-137-26661-3 (eBook)
DOI 10.1057/9781137266613

This book is printed on paper suitable for recycling and made from fully managed and sustained forest sources. Logging, pulping and manufacturing processes are expected to conform to the environmental regulations of the country of origin.

A catalogue record for this book is available from the British Library.

A catalog record for this book is available from the Library of Congress.

Contents

Part IV Foreign Direct Investments and Equity Investments

Part V Corporate Finance and Banking

List of Tables

List of Figures

Appendix

Notes on Contributors

ABU MANSOR Shazali is a professor at the Faculty of Economics and Business, Universiti Malaysia Sarawak. His research interests include corporate governance, international trade and development economics. To date, he has published more than 30 articles in international refereed journals. He is very active in economics and business consultancy works.

AHMAD Rubi is an associate professor of finance and banking and is currently head of the Department of Finance and Banking, University of Malaya. Her research interests are banking, corporate finance and microfinance. She co-authored several chapters in four books and a number of journal articles, which include *Journal of International Money and Finance, Investment Management and Financial Innovations, Asia-Pacific Financial Markets, Multinational Finance Journal* and *Asian Journal of Business and Accounting*.

ALI Ruhani is a professor at the Graduate School of Business, Universiti Sains Malaysia. Her research interests are corporate finance and investment. She has held a visiting scholar position at the University of Western Australia and the University of Connecticut. She is the founding editor and editor-in-chief of the *Asian Academy of Management Journal of Accounting and Finance*. She is a board member of the Asian Finance Association and also serves on the editorial committee of *Capital Markets Review*, the official journal of the Malaysian Finance Association.

AMIR Khairunnisa was an MBA student of Professor Catherine Ho and is a graduate of Arshad Ayub Graduate Business School, Universiti Teknologi MARA.

ANG Wei-Rong is a master student at the School of Social Sciences, Universiti Sains Malaysia. His thesis concerns socially responsible investing funds under the supervision of Associate Professor Dr. Lean Hooi Hooi.

ANUSAKUMAR Shangkari V. is a doctoral candidate under the supervision of Professor Datin Ruhani Ali and Dr. Chee-Wooi Hooy at the School of Management, and is currently also a research officer at the

Graduate School of Business, Universiti Sains Malaysia. Her research interests include behavioral finance and investments.

BAHARUMSHAH Ahmad Zubaidi is a professor in the Department of Economics, Faculty of Economics and Management, Universiti Putra Malaysia. His areas of interest are international finance, time series econometrics and macroeconomics. He has published a book with Ashgate, several book chapters, and more than 80 research articles in such publications as *Applied Economics, China Economic Review, Economic Modelling, Economics Letters, International Review of Economics and Finance, Journal of Policy Modeling* and *Journal of Post Keynesian Economics*.

CHAN Tze-Haw is presently at the Graduate School of Business, Universiti Sains Malaysia. He was the founder of the Centre of Globalization and Sustainability Research at Multimedia University, and was the holder of the Prime Minister's Perdana Research Fellowship over 2009–12. His research interests are international finance and financial econometrics. He has 25 articles in journals which include *Applied Economics, Japan and the World Economy, Bulletin of Economic Research, Global Economic Review* and *Global Finance Journal*.

HARON Razali is an assistant professor at the International Islamic University Malaysia. His research interests are corporate finance and portfolio management. He has published in many journals, which include *Global Business Review, International Review of Business Research Papers, Journal of Policy and Business Research, International Journal of Commerce and Management, International Journal of Accounting and Finance, Journal of International Business and Entrepreneurship, International Journal of Economics and Management* and *IIUM Journal of Economics and Management*.

HO Catherine Soke-Fun is a professor of finance and head of the Centre for Finance, Insurance, Economics and Islamic Banking Studies at the Faculty of Business Management, Universiti Teknologi MARA. Her areas of specialization are international finance, Islamic finance, banking and corporate structure. She is vice president of the MFA and a member of the Asian Finance Association. She has published in many journals, including *Applied Economics, Global Finance Journal, International Journal of Trade, Economics and Finance* and *International Journal of Banking and Finance*.

HOOY Chee-Wooi is a senior lecturer at the School of Management, Universiti Sains Malaysia. He is a life member of the Malaysian Economic

Association and MFA, and has been a visiting scholar at Columbia University, Monash University and Chinese University of Hong Kong. He has published 3 books and 50 academic papers in refereed journals, including *Asian Economic Journal, Emerging Market Review, Journal of Policy Modeling, Journal of the Asia Pacific Economy* and *The Manchester School.*

IBRAHIM Izani is a professor at the Graduate School of Business, Universiti Kebangsaan Malaysia. His research interests are econometrics, derivatives and investment. He has published in many journals, which include *Corporate Ownership and Control, Journal of Current Research in Global Business, Investment Management and Financial Innovation, Jurnal Analisis, Journal of International Trade and Economic Development, Jurnal Pengurusan, Capital Markets Review* and *Global Business Review.*

IBRAHIM Khairunisah is a lecturer at the International Islamic University Malaysia and has published her work in *Global Business Review, International Review of Business Research Papers, Journal of Policy and Business Research* and *ICFAI Journal of Corporate Governance.* Her research interest is in the area of corporate finance.

IBRAHIM Mansor is a professor at the International Centre for Education in Islamic Finance (INCEIF), Kuala Lumpur, Malaysia. His research interests are macroeconomics, monetary economics and financial economics. His articles appear in various journals, including *Asian Economic Journal, Journal of the Asia-Pacific Economy, Journal of Applied Economics, Developing Economies, Global Economic Review, International Economic Review, Economic Changes and Restructuring* and *Journal of Forecasting.*

ISMAIL Hamizun is a senior lecturer at Universiti Kebangsaan Malaysia. His research interests are in open macroeconomics, time series analysis and Islamic finance. He has published in several economic journals, including *Empirical Economics, Journal of Economic Studies, Sains Malaysiana,* and *Jurnal Pengurusan.*

LAW Siong-Hook is an associate professor of economics in the Department of Economics, Universiti Putra Malaysia. Currently, he is a visiting scholar at the University of California. His research interest is in financial economics. His has published in many journals, which include *Journal of Development Economics, Economics Letters, Economic Modelling, International Economic Journal, International Journal of Finance* *and Economics, Asian Economic Journal, Journal of Economic Inequality,* and *Economics of Governance.*

LEAN Hooi Hooi is an associate professor at the School of Social Sciences, Universiti Sains Malaysia. Her research interests are financial economics, energy economics, Asia Pacific and Chinese economics. She has published more than 60 articles in journals which include *Applied Economics, Economics Letters, Energy Economics, Journal of Financial Markets* and *Pacific Basin Finance Journal.*

LIEW Venus Khim-Sen is an associate professor at the Faculty of Economics and Business, Universiti Malaysia Sarawak. His research interests are in financial econometrics and forecasting. He has published a book and over 60 research articles in refereed journals, which include *Economic Modeling, Global Economic Review, International Review of Economics and Finance, Applied Economics Letters, Bulletin of Economics Research, Open Economies Review, Economics Bulletin,* and *Journal of Business Economics and Management.*

MAT NOR Fauzias is a professor at the Graduate School of Business, Universiti Kebangsaan Malaysia. She has a strong interest in the areas of corporate finance and investment. Her research articles have been published in journals such as *Jurnal Pengurusan, International Journal of Management Studies, The Journal of Accounting, Management and Economics, Asian Academy of Management Journal, Banks and Banks System, Corporate Ownership and Control,* and *The Journal of American Academy of Business.*

MATEMILOLA Bolaji Tunde is a PhD candidate at Universiti Putra Malaysia, from which he received an MBA.

MOHD SALLEH Norlida Hanim is a postgraduate student in the Faculty of Economics, Universiti Kebangsaan Malaysia. Her research interests include economics, environment and sustainability issues.

NASARUDDIN Linda Sia was an MBA candidate supervised by Professor Catherine Ho. She is a graduate of Arshad Ayub Graduate Business School, Universiti Teknologi MARA.

PUAH Chin-Hong is an associate professor and deputy dean at the Faculty of Economics and Business, Universiti Malaysia Sarawak. His research interests are applied macroeconomics and monetary economics.

He has over 50 journal articles in such publications as *Journal of Business Economics and Management, Global Economic Review, Journal of Economic Computation and Economic Cybernetics Studies and Research, Economic Issues* and *Economics Bulletin.*

RHEE S. Ghon is Shidler Distinguished Professor of Finance at the University of Hawai'i. He is the managing editor of the *Pacific-Basin Finance Journal* and is a board member of the Asian Finance Association. He has published over 90 academic papers in journals which include *Journal of Finance, Review of Financial Studies, Journal of Financial and Quantitative Analysis, Journal of Banking and Finance* and *Journal of International Money and Finance.*

SARMIDI Tamat is an associate professor of economics at the School of Economics, Universiti Kebangsaan Malaysia. His research interests are natural resource management, human capital and international finance. He has published many academic papers in journals publications such as *Journal of Asia Pacific Economy, International Economic Journal, International Journal of Economics and Management, Asian Academy of Management Journal, Capital Market Review, International Journal of Management Studies, Jurnal Ekonomi Malaysia* and *Jurnal Pengurusan.*

SOON Siew-Voon is a PhD candidate at the Department of Economics, Faculty of Economics and Management, Universiti Putra Malaysia. Her areas of interest are in macroeconomics and international finance. She has published several articles in refereed journals, which include *Applied Economics, Emerging Markets Finance and Trade,* and *Journal of International Financial Markets, Institutions and Money.*

WONG Shirly Siew-Ling is a PhD candidate at the Faculty of Economics and Business, Universiti Malaysia Sarawak. Her research area includes business cycle study and macroeconomics forecasting. She has received several research poster awards at both national and international level conferences.

WONG Yuen-Meng is a PhD candidate at the University of Malaya. His research interests are foreign exchange and international finance. He is currently a treasury manager at a real estate investment trust (REIT) management company. Prior to the start of his PhD programme in 2009, he spent four years as a foreign exchange trader with a foreign commercial bank in Malaysia.

ZAINAL ABIDIN Nurain Farahana was an MBA student supervised by Professor Catherine Ho. She is a graduate of Arshad Ayub Graduate Business School, Universiti Teknologi MARA.

Preface and Acknowledgments

Emerging Markets and Financial Resilience: Decoupling Growth from Turbulence aims to present a picture of the current financial research on emerging markets as presented at the 14th Malaysian Finance Association (MFA) Conference held at the Pearl of the Orient, Penang, Malaysia, from 1–3 June 2012. The MFA conferences are annual events that provide an avenue for scholarly interaction among finance researchers, professionals, industry practitioners and policy regulators. The 2012 conference was jointly hosted by the MFA and Graduate School of Business of Universiti Sains Malaysia.

The conference provided a forum for both theoretical and empirical works to address the issue of financial resilience in emerging markets. This multi-contributor book is timely because emerging countries are faced with unique challenges as they continue to contribute and drive regional, as well as global economic growth. The biggest challenge is to find ways of sustaining its current trajectory, while taking a more decisive role in shaping the global financial architecture to ensure sustainable growth. Eleven of the presentations that best addressed these issues were selected and included in the book.

The target audience of this book includes researchers, postgraduate students, practitioners and regulators in finance-related areas. Topics include financial markets and development, international finance, foreign direct investment, portfolio management, corporate finance and banking. We hope that the book will serve as a source of new information as well as for further research.

We would like to convey our appreciation to all the contributors and to thank the reviewers whose insightful feedback and comments helped improve the book. In addition, our deepest appreciation goes to Professor Fauzias Mat Nor, former president of MFA, and Professor Datin Hasnah Haron, former Dean of Graduate School of Business, Universiti Sains Malaysia, for their support. Finally, our special thanks to Aimee Dibbens and Tom Earl from Palgrave Macmillan, for their kind support and effort in bringing this book to fruition.

Chee-Wooi Hooy, Ruhani Ali and S. Ghon Rhee
October 2012

Part I
Introduction

1
Emerging Markets and Financial Resilience

Chee-Wooi Hooy, Ruhani Ali and S. Ghon Rhee

Research in financial markets which have special focus on emerging markets has gained momentum since the early 1990s. Today, the role of emerging countries in the world economy is significant. In the year 2010, more than 50 per cent of world output expansion at purchasing power parity (PPP) was contributed by emerging markets, the largest being China, 25 per cent, followed by India, 10 per cent, and Brazil, 4 per cent; and, given the uptrend of economic growth in these emerging markets, the figures are still rising.

Recently, we have seen a series of financial crises that originated from both developed and emerging markets. Unlike the emerging market crises that have little impact on the developed markets, the recent subprime mortgage crisis that originated from the developed markets (and the crisis's aftermath, which is still ongoing) has affected their emerging counterparts. Malaysia, as one of the leading emerging markets, has no escape from these turbulences. Given the new financial landscape in the emerging markets over the last decade, there is a need to revisit and further explore existing theory and issues established on the basis of developed markets.

This book is a collection of papers that were presented at the 14th Malaysian Finance Association Annual Conference 2012, held at the Pearl of the Orient, Penang, Malaysia, over 1–3 June, with the conference theme: 'Emerging Markets and Financial Resilience: Decoupling Growth from Turbulence'. This edited compilation adopts the same theme as the conference title. We collected 11 articles that shed light on the above issue.

The first section, 'Financial Market Development and Business Cycle', begins with the chapter entitled 'Social Capital and Financial Market Development' by Siong-Hook Law and Mansor Ibrahim. The chapter emphasizes the role of social capital in financial development. The authors first indicate that social capital does affect financial development, although the impact is weaker than that of formal institutions. Their further examination reveals that social capital and formal institutions are actually complementing each other in ensuring the development of the financial market. Nonetheless, the role of social capital becomes significant in facilitating the development of the financial market when the quality of the country's formal institutions are low.

Tamat Sarmidi, Siong-Hook Law and Norlida Hanim Mohd Salleh further discuss the issue of financial development in the second chapter of this section: 'Resource Curses Finance, Can Humans Stop It?' The authors shed light on the relationship between natural resources and financial development by considering the human development channel. The chapter presents the notion that the relationship between resource abundance and financial development is non-monotonic, since many relationships between economic variables are not linear throughout time or space due to natural cycle of economic forces. Instead, human development contributes positively to financial development. The authors further suggest that the existence of a natural resource curse hypothesis in the finance–resource nexus depends on the level of resource dependency. Low–resource-dependent economies experience the positive contribution of natural resources to financial development, but this relationship is not applicable for high–resource-dependent economies. Interestingly, the study finds that too much reliance on natural resources could spoil the positive contribution of human capital to financial development.

This section ends with the chapter, 'Forecasting Malaysian Business Cycle Movement', by Shirly Wong, Shazali Abu Mansor, Chin-Hong Puah and Venus Liew. At the beginning of this chapter, the authors argue that early detection of a turning point in a business cycle is crucial, as information about the changing phases in business cycles enables policymakers and investors to cope better with unexpected events in the economy. In this chapter, empirical analysis has been conducted to evaluate the forecasting performance of the Malaysian composite leading indicator (CLI) in tracing the movement in the business cycle. Albeit the findings indicated that CLI is able to trace closely the business cycle and offer advanced detection of its turning points, it is evident that the lead times of CLI has been diminishing. This has significantly weaken the fundamental function of CLI as a leading indicator to signal economic vulnerability.

The subsequent section, 'Regional Financial Market Integration', begins with the chapter by Tze-Haw Chan and Ahmad Zubaidi Baharumshah, entitled, 'Financial Integration between China and Asia-Pacific'. The chapter presents a joint investigation of the international parity conditions between China and its major trading partners in the Asia-Pacific over the globalization era. The authors claim that purchasing power parity (PPP) and real interest rate parity (RIP) are partially true among APEC-China. Both parities are time-varying and tend to hold better in the recent years, which is attributed not only to the financial liberalization process among APEC economies, but also to Chinese trade policy and the regional commitment for ASEAN+3+2+1 cooperation. However, China and APEC have improved their ability to absorb regional shocks, especially when the post-Asia crisis era is included.

The next chapter, 'Budget Deficits and Current Account Balances', by Ahmad Zubaidi Baharumshah, Siew-Voon Soon and Hamizun Ismail, examines the relevance of the twin deficits hypothesis and financial integration in 13 Asian countries. The chapter's findings reveal that budget balance plays a significant role in the determination of a current account balance, and there is strong evidence supporting the Keynesian view of the twin deficits. Next, investment has a notable impact on current account balance and is in line with the theoretical prediction. Lastly, the authors point out that the Feldstein–Horioka puzzle seems to be valid in most of the countries, even after allowing for a break in the data. This chapter suggests that financial integration remains weak in most of the Asian countries, as is evident from the degree of international capital mobility and that certain of the economies (China and India) appear to be effectively closed.

The last chapter of this section, 'Asia-Pacific Currency Excess Returns', by Yuen-Meng Wong, focuses on the potential profits opportunity by exploiting the failure of the forward unbiasedness hypothesis in the Asia-Pacific foreign exchange markets. The chapter shows that the forward bias puzzle is not a severe problem in most of the Asia-Pacific foreign exchange markets. Nevertheless, the failure to reject the forward unbiasedness hypothesis in the Asia-Pacific foreign exchange markets is predominantly due to the huge standard error of estimates. However, domestic stock markets' excess returns are shown as the main driving force to the currency excess returns from the Asia-Pacific foreign exchange markets. Instead, the common risk factors such as the U.S.

stock market excess returns and the U.S. inflation rate have little impact in explaining the excess returns of the Asia-Pacific currency markets. Last, but not least, Wong finds a general absence of calendar effect in the Asia-Pacific currency excess returns.

The third section, 'Foreign Direct Investments and Equity Investments', begins with the chapter by Catherine Ho, Khairunnisa Amir, Linda Nasaruddin Sia and Nurain Farahana Zainal Abidin: 'Openness, Market Size and Foreign Direct Investments'. This chapter tends to determine the significant relation between trade openness, market size and foreign direct investment (FDI) in fast-emerging countries, including Brazil, Russia, India, China, South Africa (given the acronym BRICS) and Malaysia. The authors innovatively investigate a new factor, index of economic freedom from the Heritage Foundation, in the analysis on FDI. The authors indicate that market size, interest rate and infrastructure quality are the critical factors in determining FDI inflows for this group of emerging countries. In this chapter, the authors suggest that empirical findings should provide authorities in emerging countries with policy recommendations to further accelerate development through foreign investments.

The next chapter, by Shangkari V.Anusakumar, Ruhani Ali and Chee-Wooi Hooy, is titled 'Momentum and Contrarian Strategies on ASEAN Markets'. This chapter emphasizes the profitability of momentum and contrarian strategies in four emerging ASEAN stock markets. The authors demonstrate that there is no momentum in Malaysia and Thailand, although negative momentum is found in the Philippines and Indonesia. Long-term contrarian strategy is highly profitable in the ASEAN markets but only marginally significant in Malaysia. The authors further indicate that the highest returns were found for ranking and holding periods of not more than 48 months. Moreover, the findings are generally unaffected by the January seasonality and the global financial crisis. Nevertheless, survivorship bias seems to influence momentum and contrarian returns, particularly for the Malaysian market. In sum, the authors give us the notion that investors would be able to generate significant profit by implementing a contrarian strategy in the ASEAN stock market.

This section ends with 'Socially Responsible Investing Funds in Asia-Pacific', by Wei-Rong Ang and Hooi Hooi Lean, who shed light on socially responsible investing (SRI) funds which are growing rapidly throughout the world. Statistics from the European Sustainable Investment Forum (Eurosif) 2010 report showed that 0.82 per cent of the total SRI assets are from the Asia-Pacific region. The Asia-Pacific region is still in the process of developing this alternative investment instrument. This chapter attempts to analyze the performance of SRI funds that were invested in the Asia-Pacific region from January 2003 to June 2010. Ang and Lean employ the standard reward-to-volatility ratios, that is, the Sharpe ratio, Treynor ratio and Jensen's alpha as well as the Fama-French model and Carhart model for the analysis. A positive monthly return of 0.26 per cent on average is found, which is better than the U.S. T-bill. This infers that SRI funds are still profitable, although they are restricted from investing in certain sectors. Consistent with previous literature, Ang and Lean find no significant difference in the performance of SRI funds against the conventional benchmarks. Moreover, SRI funds are conservative funds with respect to the markets. There is no small size effect but growth effect and momentum effect are found in the funds. Hence, this chapter suggests that SRI funds can be developed as an attractive alternative investment instrument in the Asia-Pacific region.

The final section, 'Issues in Corporate Finance and Banking', begins with the chapter by Razali Haron, Khairunisah Ibrahim, Fauzias Mat Nor and Izani Ibrahim: 'Capital Structure of Southeast Asian Firms'. The authors argue that inconclusive results in capital structure studies are still unresolved to date. Various possibilities and justifications are being put forward by researchers past and present to rationalize their inconsistent findings. Different leverage definitions used in the studies are identified as being among the main factors that lead to inconsistent results recorded in the literature. Different leverage definitions serve differently according to the needs of the study and this leads to inconclusive findings. Different models employed also played a significant role in this issue of inconsistencies. Different natures of models employed greatly influence the results in capital structure studies throughout. This chapter proves that inconsistent results reported within Malaysia, Thailand and Singapore are due to the different definitions of leverage (six leverage measures used) as well as the different models (the static and dynamic models) employed. Inconsistencies are more rampant in the use of different leverage definitions with the same model as compared to different models with the same leverage definition. The Fixed Effect Model and Partial Adjustment Model are employed representing the static and dynamic models respectively. Therefore, the capital structure studies still need one universally accepted leverage definition and also one appropriate model to satisfy the needs of in-depth understanding of the relationship between capital structure decisions and the value of a firm.

The last chapter in this section, 'Determinants of Bank Profits and Net Interest Margins', by Rubi Ahmad and Bolaji Tunde Matemilola, focuses on the investigation of the determinants of bank profits in the post–Asian crisis era, using panel regression analysis. The findings indicate that capital adequacy, management efficiency, credit quality, GDP growth, inflation and concentration ratio are important determinants of bank profits. Conversely, size, liquidity, capital adequacy and management efficiency are important determinants of the net interest margin. In sum, the authors conclude that bank-unique factors such as capital adequacy and management efficiency are consistent determinants of bank profits and net interest margins.

Over the last turbulent decade, policy makers and regulators in emerging markets have taken many measures to improve their economic systems, especially on the depth, efficiency and transparency of their financial markets. Their aim is to allow investors, both local and foreign, to make more informed choices. However, like the body of a human being, the financial sector cannot be strengthened overnight. With a high degree of globalization, the world financial market today is extremely integrated and interrelated. Thus, we need to know and understand the common threats to emerging markets. This is to ensure that a collective prudent system can be built in the near future to withstand stiff challenges ahead. Furthermore, emerging markets are by nature more vulnerable to economic and financial crises. It is unwise and unrealistic to think or assume that the policy framework from the Western developed markets can be easily installed to avert turbulence. We hope that what this book has put in place can offer the parties concerned – especially policy makers, regulators and investors – a bigger picture of what emerging markets should pay attention to during their further development and evolution. This would aid in establishing a more resilient financial sector to decouple its economic growth from the turbulence ahead.

Part II

Financial Market Development and Business Cycle

2

Social Capital and Financial Market Development

Siong-Hook Law and Mansor Ibrahim

1 Introduction

In the 1990s, institutions became an important area of focus when investigating the process of financial development and the success or failure of financial reforms. This was partly a consequence of the failure of many developing countries that had liberalized their financial systems to realize the expected benefits from such reforms. For example, Demetriades and Andrianova (2004) argue that the strength of institutions, such as financial regulation and the rule of law, may determine the success or failure of financial reforms. Chinn and Ito (2006) also suggest that financial systems with a higher degree of legal/institutional development tend to benefit more from financial liberalization than do those with a lower degree. Mishkin (2009) points out that a legal system that enforces contracts quickly and fairly is a prerequisite for supporting strong property rights and financial development. Thus, eliminating corruption is essential to strengthening property rights and the legal system, which will further enhance the healthy functioning of economic and financial systems.

Another recent strand of the literature has focused on the relationship between informal institutions (or 'social capital') and financial development. Social capital is often defined as shared norms that promote cooperation between two or more individuals (Coleman, 1988; Fukuyama, 1999; Ostrom, 2000).[1] Shared norms facilitate the functioning of a society by fostering trust and reducing the incentive to cheat. At the same time, people in the society may rely more on others keeping their promises due to the moral attitude imprinted upon individuals through education. Trust increases people's perception that others will cooperate. Thus, trust can play an important role in supporting cooperation in large organizations, such as the government and large firms (La Porta et al., 1997), or simply in large markets. Numerous studies have been conducted to analyse the role of trust-based social capital and economic performance. Among others, Knack and Keefer (1997), Beugelsdijk and Schaik (2005), Dinda (2008), and Dearmon and Grier (2009) have found a positive association between the level of trust and economic growth. Nevertheless, empirical evidence on the influence of social capital on financial market development remains relatively thin. To our knowledge, only Calderon et al. (2001) and Guiso et al. (2004) have investigated the roles of trust and social capital in financial development, and Guiso et al. (2008) examine the link between trust and stock market participation.

How can social capital affect financial development? Since financial contracts are the ultimate trust-intensive contracts, social capital should have a major effect on the development of financial markets. A financial contract is an exchange of a sum of money for a promise of more money in the future, which can only take place to the extent that the financier trusts the borrower. Adequate enforcement of formal contracts and of additional clauses, such as collateral requirements, may lend credibility to such promise. Therefore, trust is especially important when legal institutions are inadequately designed or enforced. Guiso et al. (2004) point out that, since social capital is an important determinant of the level of trust, it should also affect the level of financial development. Stulz and Williamson (2003) and Garretsen et al. (2004) also show that other informal institutions, namely societal norms and culture, help to explain differences in cross-country financial development.

This study examines the role of social capital in influencing financial development using cross-country analysis. After the corporate scandals and the financial crisis of 2007–08, many politicians, economists and business commentators argued that investors were deserting the financial markets because they had lost their confidence in the markets themselves. Despite the popularity of this interpretation, the financial economics literature has thus far largely ignored the role of trust-based social capital in explaining financial development. In addition, there has been no comprehensive study of the macroeconomic effects of social capital – that is, the degree of social capital's contribution to financial development. Thus, it is important to fill this gap by addressing the determinant of financial development from a social capital perspective, since recent literature has pointed out that institutions tend to promote financial development.

Three motivations give rise to this study. First, testing the role of social capital in financial development requires data on social capital. Such data are taken from the World Value Survey (WVS), which covers only a limited amount of developed countries; however, recently, Lee et al. (2011) constructed a social capital index for 72 countries by extracting the principal components from 44 variables. We utilize this dataset to test the link between social capital and financial development. Second, we also evaluate whether social capital and formal institutions are complementary in enhancing financial development. Third, using threshold regression, this study also investigates whether the effect of social capital on financial development is subject to the level of development of the country's formal institutions. For example, when institutional quality in a country is low, trust may play a greater role in ensuring the progress of financial development, and when trust in a country is low, institutional quantity may has greater role in fostering financial development.

Examining the link between social capital and financial development in the case of Italy, Guiso et al. (2004) find a strong connection between social capital and financial development. In particular, higher levels of trust are correlated with: lower levels of household investment in cash; higher investment in stock and more use of checks; higher access to institutional credit; and less informal credit. Guiso et al. (2004) also point out that trust is especially important where legal enforcement is weaker. Calderon et al. (2002) investigate the link between trust and financial development by focusing on a sample of 48 developed and developing countries. They find a positive and large impact of trust in the size and activity of financial intermediaries, in the efficiency of commercial banks, and in the extent of stock and bond market development. They also conclude that trust appears to be a key complement of formal institutions when a society has little regard for the rule of law.

With respect to the link between social capital and stock market development, Guiso et al. (2008) demonstrate that lack of trust can explain why individuals do not participate in the stock market even in the absence of any other friction. Differences in trust across individuals and countries helps to explain why some invest in stocks while others do not. They also argue that differences in trust across individuals and countries helps to explain why some invest in stocks while others do not. In addition, culture plays an extremely important role in shaping beliefs and preferences, where people decide whether to participate depending on their expectations about how honest other people are.

The remainder of this study is organized as follows. The next section describes the empirical model and econometric methodology. The third section explains the data employed in the analyses, and the fourth section reports on and discusses the estimation results. The final section presents a summary and conclusions.

2 Empirical model and econometric estimation

The empirical specification is aimed at explaining the determinants of financial development by testing the role of social capital. Thus, the empirical model employed in the analysis is as follows:

$$\begin{aligned} ln\ FD_i = \beta_0 + \beta_1\ ln\ SC_i + \beta_2\ ln\ INS_i + \beta_3\ ln\ RGDPC_i + \beta_4\ ln\ TOPEN_i \\ + \beta_5\ FOPEN_i + \beta_6\ Legal\ Origin_i + \varepsilon_i \end{aligned} \quad (1)$$

where *FD* is financial development, *SC* is social capital, and *INS* is formal institutions, *RGDPC* is real income per capita (a proxy for demand for financing), *TOPEN* is trade openness, *FOPEN* is financial openness, and *Legal Origin* consists of three legal origin dummy variables, namely British common law, French civil law and German law, and ε_i is the error term.

We control for formal institutions because it has been found to promote financial development by La Porta et al. (1997, 1998), Mayer and Sussman (2001), Beck et al. (2003) and Pagano and Volpin (2001) among others. The real GDP per capita is included in the specification to capture the effect of increased demand for financial services in line with the theoretical literature on financial development, as demonstrated by Patrick (1966),[2] Colombage (2009), Demetriades and Hussein (1996), Calderon and Liu (2002) and Yang and Yi (2008) among others. We control for trade openness and financial openness as suggested by Rajan and Zingales (2003), Law (2008, 2009), Baltagi et al. (2009), Svaleryd and Vlachos (2002), Huang (2006), Chinn and Ito (2006) and Braun and Raddatz (2008). Finally, we also control for the origin of a country's legal system, as shown by La Porta et al. (1998).[3]

If a higher degree of social capital improves financial development, then β_1 is expected to be positive. Financial systems with better institutional development tend on average to enhance financial market development; therefore, β_2 is expected to be positive. Moreover, β_3, β_4 and β_5 are expected to be positive, since greater demand for financing and openness in terms of trade and capital accounts leads to financial development. We also perform the F-statistic to analyse the joint significance between social capital and institutions in influencing financial development.

2.1 Robust standard errors and without outlier robust estimations

It is well known that heteroskedasticity is prevalent in cross-sectional data sets, and the estimation is inefficient and biased if the outlier is present. In this study, we also report outlier robust regressions, as the sample has a number of outliers, both positive and negative (see Figures 2.1a–2.1d). The inclusion or exclusion of outliers, especially if the sample size is small, can substantially alter the results of regression analysis. Therefore, Equation (1) is estimated using (a) the OLS estimation with standard errors, which are robust to arbitrary heteroskedasticity, and (b) robust estimation without outliers.

The DFITS statistic of Welsch and Kuh (1977) is used to detect outliers. The statistic identifies observation with a high combination of leverage and residual (see Figure 2.2). The statistic is

$$DFITS_i = r_i\sqrt{\frac{h_i}{1-h_i}} \tag{2}$$

where r_i are the studentized residuals. Thus, large residuals increase the value of DFITS, as do large values of leverage, or h_i. Following Belsley et al. (1980), an observation is considered as an outlier if the absolute DFITS statistic is greater than $2\sqrt{k/n}$, where k denotes the number of explanatory variables and n the number of countries.

2.2 Threshold regression

To test the effect of social capital on financial development is depends on a country's level of institutions, we argue that the following Equation (3) is particularly well suited to capture the presence of contingency effects. The model, based on threshold regression, takes the following form:

$$FD_i = \begin{cases} \beta_0^1 + \beta_1^1 SC_i + \beta_3^1 X_i + e_i, & \text{INS} \le \lambda \\ \beta_0^2 + \beta_1^2 SC_i + \beta_2^2 X_i + e_i, & \text{INS} > \lambda \end{cases} \tag{3}$$

where *FD* is financial development, *SC* is social capital, *X*is the vector of control variables, *INS* (i.e., level of institutional development) is the threshold variable used to split the sample into regimes or groups and λ is the unknown threshold parameter. This type of modeling strategy allows

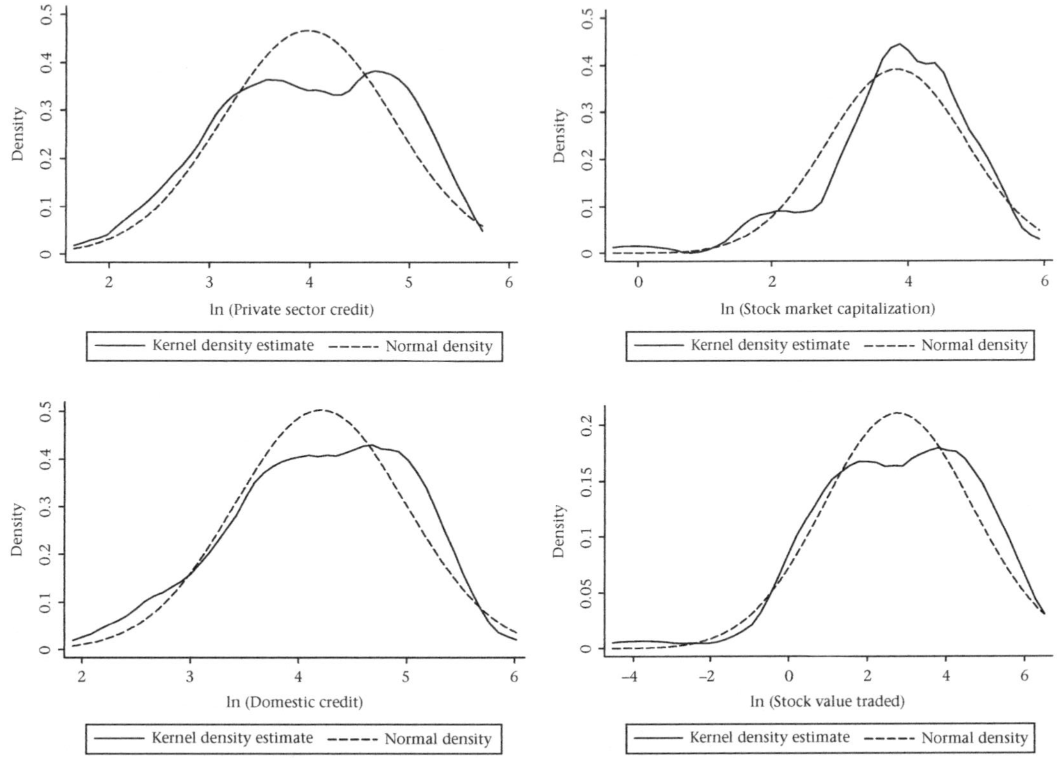

Figure 2.1 (a) Distribution of private sector credit variable; (b) Distribution of domestic credit variable; (c) Distribution of stock market capitalization variable and (d) Distribution of share value traded variable

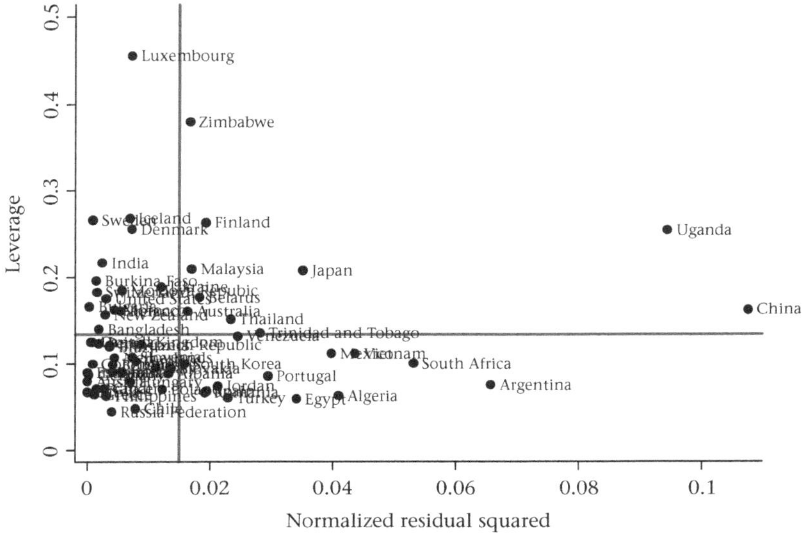

Figure 2.2 Scatter plot of leverage and residual squared

the role of social capital to differ depending on whether institutions are below or above some unknown level of λ. In this equation, institutions act as sample-splitting (or threshold) variables. The impact of social capital on growth will be β_1^1 and β_1^2 for countries with a low or high regime, respectively. It is obvious that under the hypothesis $\beta^1 = \beta^2$, the model becomes linear and reduces to (1).

The first step of our estimation was to test the null hypothesis of linearity H_0: $\beta^1 = \beta^2$ against the threshold model in Equation (3). Since the threshold parameter λ was not identified under the null, this became a non-standard inference problem and the Wald or LM test statistics, therefore, did not carry their conventional chi-square limits (see Hansen, 1996, 2000). Instead, inferences were implemented by calculating a Wald or LM statistic for each possible value of λ and subsequently basing inferences on the supremum of the Wald or LM across all possible λs. The limiting distribution of this supremum statistic is non-standard and depends on numerous model-specific nuisance parameters. Since tabulations were not possible, inferences were conducted via a model based on bootstrap whose validity and properties were established by Hansen (1996). Once an estimate of λ was obtained (as the minimizer of the residual sum of squares computed across all possible values of λ), estimates of the slope parameters followed trivially as $\hat{\delta}(\hat{\lambda})$.

3 The data

In this study, to estimate Equation (1) we employ two data sets corresponding to the two different measures of financial development indicators – banking sector development and stock market development.

The first measure of financial development (*FD*) contains two banking sector development indicators – private sector credit and domestic credit, where both are collected from World Development Indicators (WDI). The private sector credit is defined as the value of financial intermediary credits to the private sector, whereas domestic credit comprises private credit as well as credit to the public sector (central and local governments as well as public enterprises). These two banking sector development indicators samples are collected from 68 countries[4] for the period of 1995–2008 and are expressed as ratios to GDP. The second measure of financial development comprises two stock market development indicators – stock market capitalization and total stock traded. The market capitalization is the value of listed companies' shares on domestic exchanges, and the stock traded is the total value of shares traded during the period. The data is gathered from WDI and is collected from 63 countries for the period 1995–2008.

Two social capital indicators are employed in the analysis. The first social capital variable is obtained from Lee et al. (2011), who constructed an index for 72 countries by extracting the principal components from 44 variables. The index incorporates four main components of social capital – social trust, norms, networks and social structure. Using this index, Lee et al. (2011) find that social capital is significantly related to various social and economic indicators, including income per capita, education, infant mortality, regulatory quality and happiness. The second social capital is called the *Trust* indicator, an indicator compiled by Knack and Keefer (1997) using data from the World Values Surveys (World Values Study Group, 1999). This variable is constructed from the survey results of the following question: 'Generally speaking, would you say that most people can be trusted, or that you can't be too careful in dealing with people?' Trust is the percentage of respondents in each nation who replied that 'most people can be trusted' after eliminating the 'don't know' response.

The formal institutions (*INS*) dataset employed was gathered from the *International Country Risk Guide* – a monthly publication of Political Risk Services (PRS). Five PRS indicators were used to measure the overall institutional environment: (a) corruption, (b) rule of law, (c) bureaucratic quality, (d) democratic accountability and (e) government stability. These five variables were scaled from 0 to 10, with higher values implying better institutional quality, and lower values implying lesser institutional quality. The institutions indicator was obtained by summing these five indicators.[5]

Annual data on real GDP per capita (*RGDPC*) was obtained from the WDI based on 2000 U.S. dollar constant prices, whereas the trade openness (*TO*) indicator employed in the analysis is proxied by total trade (the sum of exports and imports) over GDP. Both variables are obtained from the WDI. The financial openness (*FO*) indicator is from Lane and Millesi-Ferretti (2007). This indicator is defined as the volume of a country's foreign assets and liabilities (per cent of GDP). This measure provides a useful summary of a country's history of capital account openness. The country legal origin was obtained from the Global Development Network Growth Database, World Bank.

Table 2.1 presents the descriptive statistics of the variables employed in the analysis. Figure 2.3 depicts a matrix graph among the private sector credit (as a financial development indicator) and other variables. As shown in this figure, the correlations among private sector credit, social capital, real GDP per capita and institutions are positively correlated. This figure also confirms the linear relationship between financial development and social capital. Figures 2.4 and 2.5 present the scatter plot between financial development indicator and social capital for private sector credit and stock market capitalization. As shown in these tables, countries that are rich in social capital tend to have higher levels of financial development.

4 Empirical results

The empirical results of Equation (1) are presented in Table 2.2, utilizing banking sector development and stock market development indicators. Models 1a–1d are estimated using robust standard errors, whereas Models 2a–2d are estimated using robust regressions without outliers. The social capital has a positive coefficient but weak significant determinant of banking sector development – namely, private sector credit in Models 1a and 2a. Social capital, however, is insignificant in the stock market development regressions. The institutions variable, on the other hand,

Table 2.1 Descriptive statistics

Variable	Mean	Standard deviation	Minimum	Maximum	Unit of measurement	Sample period	Source
Financial Development							
Private sector credit	73.69	54.86	7.21	221.13	% of GDP	1995–2008	WDI
Domestic credit	87.63	61.64	9.21	302.58	% of GDP	1995–2008	WDI
Market capitalization	68.18	56.60	0.97	271.23	% of GDP	1995–2008	WDI
Total value traded	54.66	77.13	0.02	320.77	% of GDP	1995–2008	WDI
Social Capital							
Social capital index	5.00	1.71	1.62	8.29	Index	1995–2008	Lee et al. (2011)
Social trust	0.31	0.15	0.05	0.62	Percentage	1990–2000	Knack and Keefer (1997)
Real GDP per capita	10760.14	12069	246.7	50924.79	Constant 2000 US dollar	1995–2008	WDI
Trade openness	88.50	47.42	25.16	290.6	% of GDP	1995–2008	WDI
Financial openness	314.95	1057.58	36.19	8963.89	% of GDP	1995–2008	Lane and Milesi-Feretti (2007)
Institutions	27.19	7.03	18.36	48.61	Scale 1–50	1995–2008	ICRG

List of Countries: Algeria, Argentina, Australia, Austria, Bangladesh, Belarus, Belgium, Brazil, Bulgaria, Burkina Faso, Canada, Chile, China, Colombia, Croatia, Cyprus, Czech Republic, Denmark, Egypt, Estonia, Finland, France, Germany, Greece, Hungary, Iceland, India, Indonesia, Ireland, Italy, Japan, Jordan, Kyrgyzstan, Latvia, Lithuania, Luxembourg, Macedonia, Malaysia, Malta, Mexico, Moldova, Morocco, Netherlands, New Zealand, Peru, Philippines, Poland, Portugal, Romania, Russia, Serbia, Slovakia, Slovenia, South Africa, South Korea, Spain, Sweden, Switzerland, Thailand, Trinidad and Tobago, Turkey, Uganda, Ukraine, United Kingdom, United States, Venezuela, Vietnam and Zimbabwe.

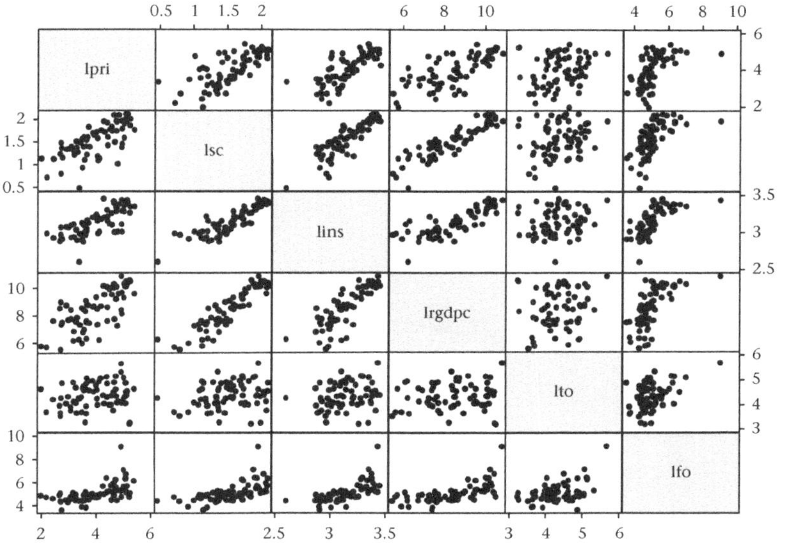

Figure 2.3 Matrix graph

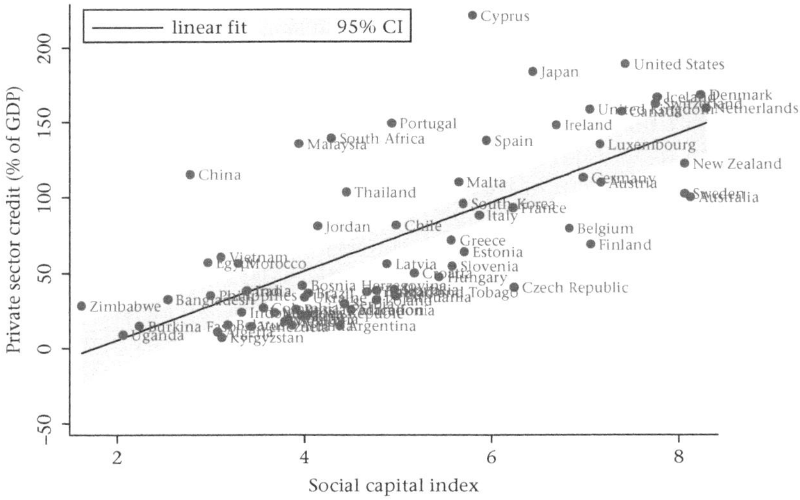

Figure 2.4 Private sector credit and social capital (68 Cross-country, 1995–2008)

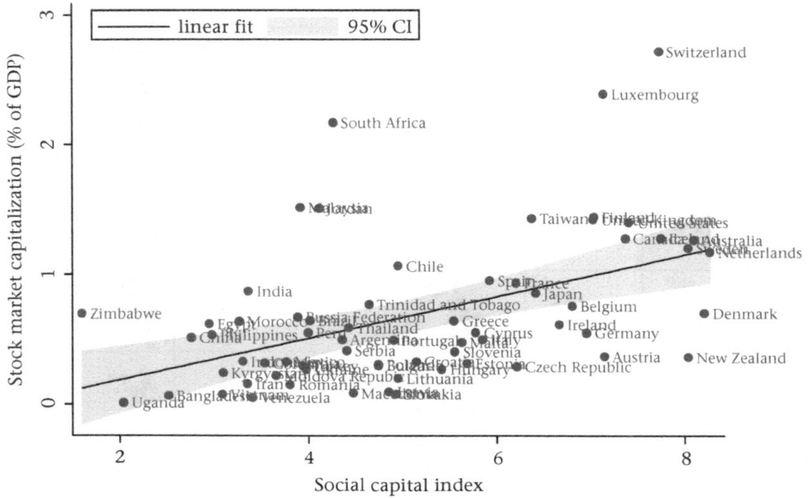

Figure 2.5 Stock market capitalization and social capital (63 Cross-country, 1995–2008)

is statistically significant determinant of private sector credit at the 5 per cent level, indicating that formal institutions play a greater role than social capital in promoting financial development. The findings also demonstrate that different financial development measures respond differently to social capital and institutions, where both variables have a much greater association with banking sector development than stock market development.

Next, turning to the hypothesis of interest, the F-statistics for the joint hypothesis are statistically significant at the 5 per cent and 1 per cent levels in Models 1a and 2a, respectively, where the financial development indicator is private sector credit. This finding reveals that social capital and institutions are complementary in promoting financial development especially banking sector. With respect to the control variables, the real GDP per capita has a robust positive effect on financial development using the robust estimation (without outliers) in Models 2a and 2c. The British common law dummy variable is positive and significant in determining private sector credit and domestic credit. This result is consistent with La Porta et al. (1997), who find that British common law protected small investors much better than did French law, which is conducive to the development of financial markets.

Table 2.2 OLS regression results with robust standard errors and outlier (sample period: 1995–2008, cross-country). Dependent variable: Financial development; Social capital: Social capital index from Lee et al. (2011)

	OLS with robust standard errors				Robust regressions (without outliers)			
	Banking sector		Stock market		Banking sector		Stock market	
	(Model 1a) Private sector credit	(Model 1b) Domestic credit	(Model 1c) Stock market capi-talization	(Model 1d) Total value traded	(Model 2a) Private sector credit	(Model 2b) Domestic credit	(Model 2c) Stock market capi-talization	(Model 2d) Total value traded
Constant	−4.39	−2.70	1.58	−5.45	−5.21	−1.82	3.47	−6.75
	(−2.02)	(−1.09)	(0.41)	(−0.83)	(−2.49)	(−0.81)	(1.17)	(−1.15)
ln SC	0.09	−0.10	0.47	1.03	0.34	0.07	0.31	0.38
	(1.69)*	(−0.15)	(0.45)	(0.52)	(1.78)*	(0.12)	(0.43)	(0.23)
ln INS	1.89	1.49	−0.37	2.48	2.22	1.08	−0.26	3.34
	(2.15)**	(1.47)	(−0.20)	(0.82)	(2.80)***	(1.31)	(−0.22)	(1.44)
ln RGDPC	0.16	0.23	0.25	0.40	0.03	0.20	0.09	0.13
	(2.23)**	(1.61)	(1.92)*	(0.86)	(2.21)**	(1.62)	(2.49)**	(0.33)
ln TOPEN	0.10	0.03	0.11	0.52	0.14	0.12	0.61	0.94
	(0.59)	(0.16)	(0.31)	(0.81)	(1.02)	(0.74)	(2.64)**	(2.08)**
ln FOPEN	0.06	0.01	0.23	−0.38	0.17	0.04	0.59	0.39
	(0.49)	(0.03)	(0.85)	(−0.66)	(1.32)	(0.28)	(3.80)***	(1.10)
D_{Common}	0.51	0.53	0.01	0.13	0.38	0.64	0.30	0.16
	(2.00)**	(2.04)**	(0.04)	(0.24)	(1.74)*	(2.63)**	(1.08)	(0.35)
D_{French}	0.03	0.15	−0.17	−0.58	0.10	0.11	−0.37	−0.64
	(0.10)	(0.56)	(−0.45)	(−0.84)	(0.43)	(0.43)	(−1.09)	(−1.10)
D_{German}	0.13	0.16	−0.58	−0.93	0.17	0.08	−0.56	−1.14
	(0.51)	(0.62)	(−1.56)	(−1.57)	(0.82)	(0.37)	(−1.01)	(−1.26)

Continued

Table 2.2 Continued

	OLS with robust standard errors				Robust regressions (without outliers)			
	Banking sector		Stock market		Banking sector		Stock market	
	(Model 1a) Private sector credit	(Model 1b) Domestic credit	(Model 1c) Stock market capi-talization	(Model 1d) Total value traded	(Model 2a) Private sector credit	(Model 2b) Domestic credit	(Model 2c) Stock market capi-talization	(Model 2d) Total value traded
Joint Test	4.08**	1.31	0.10	0.81	4.99***	1.01	0.10	1.15
ln SC & ln FINS	(0.0220)	(0.2772)	(0.9030)	(0.4516)	(0.0104)	(0.3715)	(0.9046)	(0.3252)
F-stat (p-value)								
R^2	0.64	0.53	0.38	0.41	0.72	0.65	0.55	0.55
Observations	68	68	63	63	63	61	58	57

Notes: The figures in parentheses are t-statistics except for joint test, which are p-values. *, ** and *** denote significant at 10%, 5% and 1%, respectively.
Model 2a: Outliers are Zimbabwe, China, Japan, Finland and Uganda.
Model 2b: Outliers are Zimbabwe, China, Japan, Finland, Uganda, Venezuela and Trinidad & Tobago.
Model 2c: Outliers are Zimbabwe, India, China, Venezuela and Uganda.
Model 2d: Outliers are Zimbabwe, India, China, Venezuela, Uganda and Luxembourg.

Table 2.3 OLS regression results with robust standard errors and outlier (sample period: 1990–2000, cross-country). Dependent variable: Financial development; Social capital: *Trust* variable from World Value Survey (WVS)

	OLS with robust standard errors				Robust regressions (without outliers)			
	Banking sector		Stock market		Banking sector		Stock market	
	(Model 3a) Private sector credit	(Model 3b) Domestic credit	(Model 3c) Stock market capi-talization	(Model 3d) Total value traded	(Model 4a) Private sector credit	(Model 4b) Domestic credit	(Model 4c) Stock market capi-talization	(Model 4d) Total value traded
Constant	−4.49	−1.82	−1.84	−9.41	−5.91	−2.38	−3.33	−10.19
	(−2.24)	(−0.78)	(−0.46)	(−1.51)	(−2.30)	(−0.94)	(−1.35)	(−1.61)
ln SC	0.34	0.66	0.25	2.62	0.35	0.57	0.23	1.70
	(1.75)*	(0.96)	(0.33)	(1.92)*	(1.83)*	(0.85)	(0.34)	(1.47)
ln INS	2.03	1.55	1.97	3.74	2.63	1.61	3.02	3.58
	(2.38)**	(1.59)	(1.13)	(1.39)	(2.35)**	(1.53)	(1.77)*	(1.24)
ln RGDPC	0.14	0.09	0.11	0.35	0.11	0.12	0.22	0.34
	(2.12)**	(0.79)	(0.46)	(0.93)	(2.19)**	(1.16)	(2.01)*	(0.92)
ln TOPEN	0.18	0.03	0.17	0.25	0.12	0.09	0.38	0.04
	(0.78)	(0.13)	(0.42)	(0.36)	(0.45)	(0.37)	(1.13)	(0.05)
ln FOPEN	0.02	0.01	0.33	−0.83	0.03	0.05	0.33	0.32
	(0.16)	(0.13)	(1.51)	(−1.40)	(0.24)	(0.41)	(1.90)*	(0.57)
D_{Common}	0.56	0.57	0.07	0.64	0.54	0.55	0.24	0.40
	(1.92)*	(1.91)*	(0.22)	(0.93)	(1.82)*	(1.88)*	(0.74)	(0.60)
D_{French}	0.08	0.22	−0.27	0.24	0.20	0.32	−0.10	0.33
	(0.25)	(0.73)	(−0.66)	(0.34)	(0.57)	(0.96)	(−0.41)	(0.47)
D_{German}	0.55	0.64	−0.08	0.45	0.62	0.44	0.07	0.15
	(0.85)	(1.33)	(−0.16)	(0.44)	(1.27)	(1.49)	(0.23)	(0.26)

Continued

Table 2.3 Continued

	OLS with robust standard errors				Robust regressions (without outliers)			
	Banking sector		Stock market		Banking sector		Stock market	
	(Model 3a) Private sector credit	(Model 3b) Domestic credit	(Model 3c) Stock market capi-talization	(Model 3d) Total value traded	(Model 4a) Private sector credit	(Model 4b) Domestic credit	(Model 4c) Stock market capi-talization	(Model 4d) Total value traded
Joint Test	3.99**	2.17	0.65	3.32*	3.92**	1.41	1.60	1.54
ln SC & ln FINS	(0.0288)	(0.1315)	(0.5280)	(0.0502)	(0.0305)	(0.2610)	(0.2163)	(0.2355)
F-stat (p-value)								
R^2	0.71	0.60	0.35	0.52	0.71	0.60	0.53	0.59
Observations	40	40	38	38	39	37	32	33

Notes: The figures in parentheses are t-statistics except for joint test, which are p-values. *, ** and *** denote significant at 10%, 5% and 1%, respectively.
Model 4a: Outlier is Zimbabwe.
Model 4b: Outliers are Japan, Venezuela and Zimbabwe.
Model 4c: Outliers are Austria, Bangladesh, South Africa, Switzerland, Venezuela and Zimbabwe.
Model 4d: Outliers are Austria, Luxembourg, Switzerland, Venezuela and Zimbabwe.

Table 2.3 repeats the same analysis but using the *Trust* variable by Knack and Keefer (1997) as a proxy for social capital. The results are broadly similar to those reported in Table 2.2, where social capital remains positive in all models and a significant determinant of private sector credit at the 10 per cent level in Models 3a and 4a. The only notable difference is that the trade openness appears insignificant in Models 4c and 4d, where the financial development indicators are stock market capitalization and total share value traded. Again, the joint hypothesis results also indicate that both social capital and institutions are jointly significant determinants of private sector credit. This finding suggests that social capital and institutions are complementary in promoting financial development, especially banking sector development, even using other social capital measures.

The above findings suggest that the positive link between social capital and financial development exists when private sector credit is utilized, but such a relationship vanishes when stock market development indicators are chosen. This implies that social capital has a greater influence on bank-based than on market-based financial structure. Since banks can provide borrowers with valuable services and establish close relationships with their customers, improvements in social trust will boost banking sector development. In addition, banks ameliorate moral hazards through effective monitoring and form long-term relationships with customers or firms to ease asymmetric information distortions. The strength of social capital will facilitate these processes, where the transaction costs will be reduced and banks will have greater funds to channel to investors. In contrast, the stock market has tighter regulations and competition than the banking sector. Competitive stock markets play a positive role in aggregating diffuse information signals and effectively transmitting this information to investors, where the function of social capital is minimal in the stock market.

Table 2.4 reports the results of threshold Equation (3) using institutional quality variables – namely, institutions and rule of law. The statistical significance of the threshold estimate is evaluated by p-value calculated using the bootstrap method with 1,000 replications and 15 per cent trimming percentage. As shown in Models 5 and 6, the bootstrap p-values indicate that the test of no threshold effect can be rejected. Thus, the sample can be split into two regimes. For example, referring to Models 5 and 6, the empirical results favor a threshold model, regardless of whether the institutions are aggregate institutions or rule of law. The point estimate of the threshold value of institutions is 3.0946 for Model 5, which implies that countries with threshold values of less

Table 2.4 Regression results using institutions as a threshold variable. Dependent variable: financial development (Private sector credit)

	Threshold (Model 5a) Institutions (INS)		Threshold (Model 5b) Rule of Law (ROL)	
	Regime 1 INS < 3.0946	**Regime 2 INS > 3.0946**	**Regime 1 ROL < 1.4630**	**Regime 2 ROL > 1.4630**
Constant	−1.5007	−4.6897	0.2298	1.3268
	(0.5129)	(−2.3278)	(0.2289)	(1.9366)
Social capital	1.3417	1.2647	1.1173	0.8752
	(1.7436)*	(2.7244)***	(1.6486)*	(1.9706)**
Institutions	1.5779	2.1679	–	–
	(1.5757)	(3.2083)***	0.1311	0.1664
Rule of Law	–	–	(1.0816)	(2.3992)**
RGDPC	0.3474	0.4579	0.1930	0.4743
	(2.7305)***	(4.2241)***	(2.4880)**	(4.9716)***
Trade openness	0.0606	0.0193	0.1466	0.2482
	(0.3082)	(0.1387)	(0.8664)	(1.5425)
Financial openness	0.1471	0.0201	0.4487	0.0965
	(0.6993)	(0.1923)	(1.2168)	(1.1855)
$D_{CommonLaw}$	0.8656	0.3048	0.8443	0.1950
	(3.2124)***	(2.4542)**	(3.7894)***	(2.0586)**

R-sq	0.5139	0.7453	0.5606	0.7459
No. observations	26	37	34	29
Correlation: Social Capital and Institutions	0.5085	0.7589	0.2921	0.5796
	Threshold estimates of institutions (INS)			
First sample split				
LM test for no threshold	15.786	17.325		
Bootstrap p-value	0.0480	0.0030		
Threshold estimate	3.0946	1.4567		
95% confidence interval	(3.0168, 3.0946)	(1.0955, 1.4631)		
Second sample split				
LM test for no threshold	12.2629	10.8934		
Bootstrap p-value	0.2090	0.1490		

Notes: The standard errors are reported in parentheses * (White corrected for heteroskedasticity). Results correspond to trimming percentage of 15%. *** and ** indicate significance at 1% and 5% levels, respectively. The null hypothesis of LM test is no threshold effect.

than 3.0946 are classified into the low-INS group (i.e., low institutional quality), while those with greater values are classified in the high-INS group (high institutional quality). We also tested whether the high-INS group could be split further into sub-regimes. The bootstrap p-values are insignificant for the second sample split, which suggests that only the single threshold in Equation (3) is adequate for all models.

Having established the existence of an institutional quality threshold, the next question is how institutions affect the relationship between social capital and financial development. Turning first to Model 5a, the coefficient estimate of social capital is significant at the 10 per cent level when institutions (INS) fall below the threshold level. In contrast, above the threshold level of the institutions, the effects of social capital and institutions on financial development are significant and positive. When the institutions variable is measured by rule of law (ROL) in Models 6a and 6b, the results again reveal that below the rule of law threshold, social capital is positive and a significant determinant of financial development at the 10 per cent level; however, both social capital and institutions have significant effects on financial development for INS and ROL above the threshold level. These findings demonstrate that social capital is especially important when institutional quality or ROL is weaker. This result is consistent with Calderon et al. (2002), who find that trust appears to be a key complement of formal institutions when a society has little regard for the ROL.

5 Robustness checks

We also examine whether the results are robust to alternative measures of social capital – namely (a) the *News* variable, which is defined as the number of daily newspapers circulated per 1,000 people, and (b) the *Postal* variable, which is defined as the average number of letter-post items posted per inhabitant, divided by 1,000. Both datasets are taken from WDI and the Universal Postal Union, respectively.[6] Table 2.5 presents the summary results of the without-outlier robust regressions using different measurements of social indicators as well as other control variables.

As shown in Models 6a–9a, the empirical results demonstrate that the *News* variable is a statistically significant determinant of banking sector development, that is, private sector credit and domestic credit. Nevertheless, in terms of the relative importance of social capital and institutions, again, institutions play a greater role than social capital in promoting financial development. When the *Postal* variable is utilized as a proxy

Table 2.5 Summary of robustness checks Estimation method: Robust regression (without outliers)

Model	Financial development	Social capital measurement	Social capital	Institutions	Joint test	R^2	No. of observations
	(1) Other social capital measures model specification: $ln\ FD_i = \beta_0 + \beta_1 ln\ SC_i + \beta_2\ ln\ INS_i + \beta_3\ ln\ RGDPC_i + \beta_4\ ln\ TOPEN_i + \beta_5\ FOPEN_i + \beta_6\ Legal\ Origin_i + \varepsilon_i$						
6a	Private sector credit	*News*	2.52 (2.20)**	3.32 (4.54)***	15.35 (0.0000)***	0.7442	40
7a	Domestic credit	*News*	2.18 (1.86)*	1.83 (2.07)**	4.06 (0.0279)**	0.6712	38
8a	Stock market capitalization	*News*	1.22 (0.72)	0.27 (0.24)	0.28 (0.7567)	0.4102	36
9a	Total share value traded	*News*	2.02 (0.80)	1.44 (0.61)	0.61 (0.5536)	0.6080	34
6b	Private sector credit	*Postal*	0.07 (0.15)	1.18 (1.94)*	1.95 (0.1603)	0.7808	39
7b	Domestic credit	*Postal*	0.17 (0.49)	0.50 (0.70)	0.48 (0.6247)	0.7301	39
8b	Stock market capitalization	*Postal*	0.41 (0.61)	0.75 (0.36)	0.19 (0.8280)	0.4621	33
9b	Total share value traded	*Postal*	0.22 (0.18)	1.44 (0.48)	0.14 (0.8661)	0.6495	32
	(2) Include financial reforms index as a control variable (drop financial openness) model specification: $ln\ FD_i = \beta_0 + \beta_1 ln\ SC_i + \beta_2\ ln\ INS_i + \beta_3\ ln\ RGDPC_i + \beta_4\ ln\ TOPEN_i + \beta_5\ FINREFORM_i + \beta_6\ Legal\ Origin_i + \varepsilon_i$						
10	Private sector credit	Social capital Lee et al. (2011)	0.27 (0.43)	2.84 (4.02)***	9.82 (0.0003)***	0.7324	49

Continued

Table 2.5 Continued

Model	Financial development	Social capital measurement	Social capital	Institutions	Joint test	R^2	No. of observations
11	Domestic credit	Social capital	0.17	1.53	1.93	0.6372	49
		Lee et al. (2011)	(0.26)	(1.96)**	(0.1590)		
12	Private sector credit	Trust	0.67	2.52	3.89	0.7149	38
		K&K (1997)	(0.81)	(2.21)**	(0.0329)**		
13	Domestic credit	Trust	0.40	0.83	0.81	0.6370	32
		K&K (1997)	(0.61)	(0.94)	(0.4574)		
14	Private sector credit	*News*	3.08	2.37	12.31	0.7680	38
			(2.30)**	(4.48)***	(0.0001)***		
15	Domestic credit	*News*	2.48	1.54	4.04	0.6977	35
			(1.95)*	(1.86)*	(0.0303)**		
	(3) Include Culture Dummies as control variables (drop legal origin dummies) model specification: $ln\ FD_i = \beta_0 + \beta_1 ln\ SC_i + \beta_2\ ln\ INS_i + \beta_3\ ln\ RGDPC_i + \beta_4\ ln\ TOPEN_i + \beta_5\ FOPEN_i + \beta_6\ Religion_i + \varepsilon_i$						
16	Private sector credit	Social capital	0.36	2.55	10.86	0.7945	59
		Lee et al. (2011)	(0.62)	(3.66)***	(0.0001)***		
17	Domestic credit	Social capital	0.12	1.77	3.54	0.7305	59
		Lee et al. (2011)	(0.22)	(2.29)**	(0.0367)**		
18	Private sector credit	Trust	0.47	3.63	5.66	0.7402	36
		K&K (1997)	(0.57)	(3.29)***	(0.0091)***		
19	Domestic credit	Trust	0.37	1.90	2.69	0.6734	35
		K&K (1997)	(0.54)	(2.24)**	(0.0874)*		
20	Private sector credit	*News*	2.05	2.68	7.49	0.7457	37
			(1.58)	(3.31)***	(0.0025)***		
21	Domestic credit	*News*	2.06	2.24	5.09	0.6904	37
			(1.66)*	(2.39)**	(0.0130)**		

Notes: The figures in parentheses are t-statistics except for joint test, which are p-values. *, ** and *** denote significant at 10%, 5% and 1%, respectively.

for social capital, the results reveal that this indicator is insignificant in influencing financial development.

Some studies in the literature have also demonstrated that financial development is crucially shaped by the implementation of financial sector policies (Abiad & Mody, 2005; Ang & McKibbin, 2007; Ang, 2008). Therefore, we drop financial openness in the model specification and replace it with financial reform index constructed by Abiad et al. (2010). The empirical results as shown in Models 10–15 indicate that the financial reform index is significant at the 10 per cent level, where the financial development measure is private sector credit.[7] Again, institutions play a greater role than social capital except in Models 14–15, where the social capital proxy is the *News* variable.

Finally, we also control for the effects of religions in the specification, since Stulz and Williamson (2003) find that the religious composition of a country matters for financial development and that differences in culture (which are proxied by religion) cannot be ignored. Since culture proxies are correlated with legal origin (Stulz & Williamson, 2003), we replace the legal origins with four religion dummy variables – Catholic, Protestant, Muslim and Buddhist. The empirical results reported in Models 16–21 indicate that social capital is an insignificant determinant of financial development, except for Model 21, where the social capital proxy is the *News* variable. Again, institutions play a greater role than social capital in promoting financial development. Thus, it can be concluded that the weak social capital effect on financial development is robust to different measures of social capital and to the inclusion of financial reforms and culture variables, as well as to the estimation techniques.

6 Conclusion

Social capital in the form of generalized trust, network-generated trust, and cooperative norms may serve to reduce the uncertainties faced by investors and thus may promote greater financial development and spur economic growth. Arguing that there is a missing link between micro studies and macro studies of social capital, this study examines the effect of social capital on financial development using cross-country analysis. The social capital indicators employed were newness of construction proposed by Lee et al. (2011), social trust proposed by Knack and Keefer (1997) and other measurements used in the literature – namely, the number of daily newspapers circulated and the number of letter-post items posted. The empirical results from robust regression indicate that, in general, social capital has a weak significant effect on financial development.

Formal institutionals indicators appear to have a greater impact on financial development than does social capital; however, the joint effect of social capital and institutions is statistically significant, which suggests that social capital and institutions complement each other in promoting financial development.

Moreover, once we account for the role of institutions in mediating the effect of social capital and financial development, the impact of social capital on financial development appears. The findings indicate that social capital plays a greater role in enhancing financial development when institutional quality is low. When institutional quality is high, both social capital and institutions are complementary in promoting financial development, but again the roles played by formal institutions are greater than those played by informal institutions (social capital) in these processes. The empirical results also reveal that the role of social capital on financial development is more prevalent in banking sector development, especially private-sector credit. Stock market development, on the other hand, fails to establish a significant relationship between social capital and finance. The findings are robust to different measures of social capital and to the inclusion of other control variables.

Notes

1. Durlauf and Fafchamps (2005) define social capital as the informal forms of institutions and organizations that are based on the social relationships, networks and associations that create shared knowledge, mutual trust, social norms and unwritten rules. Bjornskov (2006) points out that there are at least three important dimensions of social capital: generalized trust, social norms and associational/network activity.
2. Patrick (1966) points out that the lack of financial markets and systems in developing countries is an indication of the lack of demand for their services – the so-called demand-following phenomenon. As the real side of the economy develops, its demands for various new financial services materialize. This implies that economic growth may increase the real sector's demand for financial services, thereby leading to financial market development.
3. La Porta et al. (1998) point out that common-law-based legal systems protect shareholders and creditors better than civil-law-based systems do, whereas within civil law tradition the French civil law group does worse than the German and Scandinavian ones. Over time, this has meant that British common law protected small investors much better than did French civil law, which is conducive to the development of capital markets.
4. The list of countries is presented in table 2.1.
5. Due to strong correlations among these separate indicators, with the consequent risk of multicollinearity, the five PRS variables were added to form an institutions index (Bekaert et al., 2005). Numerous studies have employed this

dataset in empirical analysis, including Easterly and Levine (1997), Hall and Jones (1999), Chong and Calderon (2000) and Clarke (2001).

6. Ishise and Sawada (2009) use *News* and *Postal* as a proxies of social capital in analysing the role of social capital on economic development. Since the data period is 1990–2000, the importance of the Internet should be minimal.
7. The results, however, are not reported here in order to save space.

References

Abiad, A., Detragiache, E. and Tressel, T. (2010) 'A New Database of Financial Reforms', IMF Staff Papers, 57(1), 281–302.

Abiad, A. and Mody, A. (2005) 'Financial Reform: What Shakes It? What Shapes It?' American Economic Review, 95(1), 63–88.

Ang, J. B. (2008) 'Are Financial Sector Policies Effective in Deepening the Malaysia Financial System?' Contemporary Economic Policy, 26(4), 623–35.

Ang, J. B. and McKibbin, W. J. (2007) 'Financial Liberalization, Financial Sector Development and Growth: Evidence from Malaysia', Journal of Development Economics, 84(1), 215–33.

Baltagi, B. H., Demetriades, P. and Law, S. H. (2009) 'Financial Development and Openness: Panel Data Evidence', Journal of Development Economics, 89(1), 285–96.

Beck, T., Demirguc-Kunt, A. and Levine, R. (2003) 'Law, Endowment and Finance', Journal of Financial Economics, 70(1), 137–81.

Bekaert, G., Harvey, C. R. and Lundblad, C. (2005) 'Does Financial Liberalization Spur Growth?' Journal of Financial Economics, 77(1), 3–55.

Belsley, D., Kuh, E. and Welsh, R. (1980) Regression Diagnostics. Wiley: New York.

Beugelsdijk, S. and Schaik, T. (2005) 'Social Capital and Growth in European Regions: An Empirical Test', European Journal of Political Economy, 21(1), 301–24.

Bjornskov, C. (2006) 'The Multiple Facets of Social Capital', European Journal of Political Economy, 22(1), 22–40.

Braun, M. and Raddatz, C. (2008) 'The Politics of Financial Development: Evidence from Trade Liberalization', Journal of Finance, 63(2), 1469–508.

Calderon, C., Chong, A. and Galindo, A. (2002) 'Development and Efficiency of the Financial Sector and Links with Trust: Cross-Country Evidence', Economic Development and Cultural Change, 51(1), 189–204.

Calderon, C. and Liu, L. (2002) 'The Direction of Causality between Financial Development and Economic Growth', Journal of Development Economics, 72(1), 321–34.

Chinn, M. and Ito, H. (2006). 'What Matters for Financial Development? Capital Controls, Institutions and Interactions', Journal of Development Economics, 81(1), 163–92.

Chong, A. and Calderon, C. (2000) 'Institutional Quality and Income Distribution', Economic Development and Cultural Change, 48(4), 761–86.

Clarke, G. (2001) 'How the Quality of Institutions Affects Technological Deepening in Developing Countries', Country Economics Department Working Paper No. (2603, (World Bank: Washington DC).

Coleman, J. S. (1988) 'Social Capital in the Creation of Human Capital', American Journal of Sociology, 94(1), 95–120.
Colombage, S. R. N. (2009) 'Financial Markets and Economic Performances: Empirical Evidence from Five Industrialized Economies', Research in International Business and Finance, 23(2), 339–48.
Dearmon, J. and Grier, K. (2009) 'Trust and Development', Journal of Economic Behavior and Organization, 71(1), 210–20.
Demetriades, P. and Andrianova, S. (2004) 'Finance and Growth: What We Know and What We Need to Know', in C. Goodhart (Ed.) Financial Development and Economic Growth: Explaining the Links, 38–65 (Basingstoke: Palgrave Macmillan).
Demetriades, P. O. and Hussein, K. (1996) 'Does Financial Development Cause Economic Growth? Time Series Evidence from 16 Countries', Journal of Development Economics, 51(1), 387–411.
Dinda, S. (2008) 'Social Capital in the Creation of Human Capital and Economic Growth: A Productive Consumption Approach', Journal of Socio-Economics, 37(5), 2020–33.
Durlauf, S. N. and Fafchamps, M. (2005) 'Social Capital', in Philippe, A. and Durlauf, S. (Eds) Handbook of Economic Growth, 1A, 555–677 (Amsterdam: North-Holland).
Easterly, W. and Levine, R. (1997) 'Africa's Growth Tragedy: Policies and Ethnic Divisions', Quarterly Journal of Economics, 112(4), 1203–50.
Fukuyama, F. (1999) The Great Disruption. Simon and Schuster: New York.
Garretsen, H., Robert, L. and Elmer, S. (2004) 'Growth, Financial Development, Societal Norms and Legal Institutions', Journal of International Financial Markets, Institutions and Money, 14(1), 165–83.
Guiso, L., Sapienza, P. and Zingales, L. (2004) 'The Role of Social Capital in Financial Development', American Economic Review, 94(2), 526–56.
Guiso, L., Sapienza, P. and Zingales, L. (2008) 'Trusting the Stock Market', Journal of Finance, 63(6), 2557–600.
Hall, R. and Jones, C. (1999) 'Why Do Some Countries Produce So Much More Output Per Worker Than Others?' Quarterly Journal of Economics, 114(1), 83–116.
Hansen, B. E. (1996) 'Inference When a Nuisance Parameter is Not Identified under the Null Hypothesis', Econometrica, 64(1), 413–30.
Hansen, B. E. (2000) 'Sample Splitting and Threshold Estimation', Econometrica, 68(2), 575–603.
Huang, W. (2006) 'Emerging Markets, Financial Openness and Financial Development, Bristol Economics Discussion Papers No. 06/588 (University of Bristol: United Kingdom).
Ishise, H. and Sawada, Y. (2009) 'Aggregate Returns to Social Capital: Estimates Based on the Augmented Augmented-Solow Model', Journal of Macroeconomics, 31(2), 376–93.
Knack, S. and Keefer, P. (1997) 'Does Social Capital Have an Economic Payoff? A Cross-Country Investigation', Quarterly Journal of Economics, 12(4), 1251–88.
Lane, P. R. and Milesi-Ferretti, G. M. (2007) 'The External Wealth Of Nations Mark II: Revised and Extended Estimates of Foreign Assets and Liabilities, 1970–2004', Journal of International Economics, 73(1), 223–50.

La Porta, R., Lopez-de-Silane, F., Shleifer, A. and Vishny, R. W. (1997) 'Legal Determinants of External Finance', Journal of Finance, 52(2), 1131–50.

La Porta, R., Lopez-de-Silane, F., Shleifer, A. and Vishny, R. W. (1998) 'Law and Finance', Journal of Political Economy, 106(6), 1113–55.

Law, S. H. (2008) 'Does a Country's Openness to Trade and Capital Flows Lead to Financial Development? Evidence from Malaysia', Asian Economic Journal, 22(1), 161–77.

Law, S. H. (2009) 'Trade Openness, Capital Inflows and Financial Development in Developing Countries', International Economic Journal, 23(2), 409–26.

Lee, D., Jeong, K. and Chae, S. (2011) 'Measuring Social Capital in East Asia and Other World Regions: Index of Social Capital for 72 Countries', Global Economic Review, 40(4), 385–407.

Levine, R. and Zervos, S. (1998) 'Stock Markets, Banks and Economic Growth', American Economic Review, 88(2), 537–58.

Levine, R. (2002) 'Bank-Based versus Market-Based Financial Systems: Which is Better?' Journal of Financial Intermediation, 11(4), 398–428.

Mayer, C. and Sussman, O. (2001) 'The Assessment: Finance, Law and Growth', Oxford Review of Economic Policy, 17(4), 457–66.

Mishkin, F. S. (2009) 'Globalization and Financial Development', Journal of Development Economics, 89(1), 164–69.

Ostrom, E. (2000) 'Social Capital: A Fad or a Fundamental Concept'. In Dasgupta, P. and Serageldin, I. (Eds) Social Capital: A Multifaceted Perspective, 172–214 (World Bank, Washington, D.C.).

Pagano, M. and Volpin, P. (2001) 'The Political Economy of Finance', Oxford Review of Economic Policy, 17(4), 502–19.

Patrick, H. T. (1966) 'Financial Development and Economic Growth in Under-developed Countries', Economic Development and Cultural Change, 14(1), 174–89.

Rajan, R. and Zingales, L. (2003) 'The Great Reversals: The Politics of Financial Development in the Twentieth Century', Journal of Financial Economics, 69(1), 5–50.

Rousseeuw, P. J. and Leroy, A. M. (1987) Robust Regression and Outlier Detection, John Wiley: New York.

Stulz, R. M. and Williamson, R. (2003) 'Culture, Openness and Finance', Journal of Financial Economics, 70(2), 313–49.

Svaleryd, H. and Vlachos, J. (2002) 'Markets for Risk and Openness to Trade: How are They Related', Journal of International Economics, 57(1), 369–95.

Welsch, R. E. and Kuh, E. (1977) 'Linear Regression Diagnostics', Technical Report 923–77, Cambridge, MA: Massachusetts Institute of Technology.

Yang, Y. Y. and Yi, M. H. (2008) 'Does Financial Development Cause Economic Growth? Implication for Policy in Korea', Journal of Policy Modeling, 30(5), 827–40.

3

Resource Curses Finance. Can Humans Stop It?

Tamat Sarmidi, Siong-Hook Law and Norlida Hanim Mohd Salleh

1 Introduction

Natural resource-rich countries shall enjoy better economic growth and socio-economic welfare than those that are less fortunate. Natural resources that have been endowed to these countries should be a genuine source of fortune and happiness. Surprisingly, everyday experiences and empirical studies show the reverse (Frankel, 2010). It seems that natural resource abundance is detrimental to economic growth. This puzzling phenomenon is known as the natural resource curse (NRC) hypothesis. In the past decades it has attracted voluminous research papers that try to empirically show the prevalence of the NRC and at the same time attempt to provide analytical explanations of why the NRC existed in the resource-abundant economies (Sachs & Warner, 1995; Leite & Weidmann, 1999; Gylfason, 2001; Gylfason & Zoega, 2006). In the literature, it is suggested that there are at least three theories explaining the NRC: 'Dutch disease' models (Sachs & Warner, 1999), rent-seeking phenomena (Tornell & Lane, 2000), and institutional explanations (Sachs & Warner, 1995, 2001). However, the empirical findings from these studies are still far from conclusive.

In this chapter we extend the debate on the NRC hypothesis by addressing three important issues. First, we focus on the relationship between natural resource dependence and financial development. Despite the large volume of literature discussing the issues of natural resources and economic growth, or financial development and growth, economists have not put much effort into studying the relationship between natural resources and financial development.

Resource dependence could directly jeopardise the intensity of financial development as well as economic growth through the 'crowding-out effect': that is, the productive means of economic activities are mainly channelled into the exploitation of resources to the neglect of other sectors. Unfortunately, there is little empirical literature that analyses the intricacies of the NRC paradox in the relationship between financial development and resource abundance (among the handful of papers that discuss the issue are those by Yuxiang & Chen, 2010; Nili & Rastad, 2007). Therefore, this chapter intends to extend the evidence by using the same dataset used by Sachs and Warner (1995, 2001).

Second, we further extend the investigation to the non-monotonicity relationship between resource dependence and financial development. Previous studies imposed an important a priori restriction so that the relationship between financial development and resource abundance is set to be linear and monotonic (Brunnschweiler & Bulte, 2008; Bhattacharyya & Hodler, 2010, among others). However, we argue that due to the natural cycle of economic forces the relationship between economic variables may not necessarily be linear throughout time or space. Therefore, it might be the case that, at a certain level, the effect of natural resource endowment to financial development is negative while, at another level of natural resource endowment, the effect might be positive. This phenomenon is commonly applicable to a bending-backward labour supply curve in a transitory economy (Guha, 1989), and in an economic growth carbon-emission analysis using the Environmental Kuznet Curve (Dinda, 2004; Narayan & Narayan, 2010). At the same time, the intricate relationship between financial development and natural resources raises other crucial questions: How much resources are to be exploited so that natural resources do have favourable effect on financial development and economic growth? What level of resource exploitation avoids the curse? This issue has never been addressed before, and that is why this chapter tries to determine the level of resources that is beneficial to financial development.

Third, this study attempts to provide an alternative solution to the NRC problem through social and human development channels. Empirical work by Gylfason and Zoega (2006) and Guiso et al. (2004) reaffirms the great importance of human capital in the process of empowering financial development. However, the process of developing human capital could be disadvantaged if a country has plenty of natural resources. It is because wealth and riches could divert the attention towards excellence in education. In the long run this situation could end up with lack of institutional reform and weak human capital (Gylfason, 2001).

Therefore, we suppose that a country can have resource abundance and, at the same time, experience good financial development if social capital is of a high quality. If so, policymakers should set certain human development levels that can nullify the resource curse paradox.

The purpose of this chapter is to examine the monotonicity relationship between natural resource and financial development while considering the human development channel. This study is expected to expand the natural resource curse literature by answering the following specific questions: (a) Does the NRC paradox exist in the resource dependence and financial development nexus? (b) Is the relationship between natural resources and financial development monotonic? (c) Does the development of social capital really nullify the curse of natural resources?

The remainder of the chapter is organized as follows: in the second section, we briefly discuss the theory and recent evidence of the NRC hypothesis and financial development. The next section describes the dataset used in the empirical analysis and the layout of the econometric procedures. The following section discusses the estimation results and, finally, the last section offers concluding remarks.

2 Natural resource, financial development and human capital

Economists generally agree that a certain level of financial development is needed to spur economic growth (Rajan & Zingales, 2003). Financial development functions as a mechanism that could accelerate efficient resource-allocation and productivity. However, countries which have an abundance of natural resources always have a tendency to sideline relatively less-important sectors, including finance (Looney, 1991; Kutan & Wyzan, 2005). As productive economic activities are limited, it is then presumed that the development of the financial sector, which serves to facilitate an efficient allocation of resources between real and financial sectors, will also be dampened. The situation is getting worse if national budget expenses are allocated proportionately, which leads to inefficiency in financial sectors. In some resource-dependent economies, even though tax revenue or investment are relatively high, the effect of investment to growth is marginal (Atkinson & Hamilton, 2003; Stevens & Dietsche, 2008). Nili and Rastad (2007) investigate this puzzling phenomenon and find that one of the root causes is less-developed financial institutions, which lead to imbalance and unsustainable economic growth.

At the same time, natural resource-rich developing economies tend to exploit and export large volumes of natural resources, such as oil, timber or valuable minerals (to name a few). This exposes the economy to instability because international resource prices are subject to price volatility (van der Ploeg & Poelhekke, 2010) and could inflate the value of local currency, which eventually would have serious repercussions for the domestic economy in the form of spending effects, irrespective of exchange-rate regimes. Resource-dependent economies with less-developed financial systems (which is very common) are seldom able to counter exchange-rate volatility or less competitiveness due to the inability to relax financial constraints and reduce institutional risk (Larrain, 2004).

Another important issue is that Leamer et al. (1999) argue that the complexity in the relationship between natural resources and financial development is subject to the level of human capital inherent in the economy. Appropriately skilled and highly competent labour forces are needed to accelerate evolutionary development paths of the resource-abundant economy, which usually start from

> labour-intensive extraction industries → capital-intensive extraction → resource-based manufacturing → capital-intensive manufacturing.

This view makes sense because at each stage, human capital is what fulfils all job requirements for the processes. Therefore, government's investment to educate the labour force to acquire required skills will pay off in the future. However, not many studies delve into this very important issue with respect to the natural resource curse hypothesis.

Glyfason (2001), among the handful of economists who study the above-mentioned issue, remarks that abundance of natural resources is not a root problem of the resource curse. It is the institutional and socio-economic nature, including human capital that nurtures the 'Dutch disease', rent seeking and the myopic problem of future development. A certain level of human capital development is required, by which the above-mentioned disease could be staved off and, at the same time, could lower transaction costs, promote cooperation among different parties and develop good trust for nations and joint ventures in the exploration for natural resources (Fukuyama, 2001; Gleason et al., 2002).

3 Empirical model

The empirical model is based on Bhattacharyya and Hodler (2010), in which the empirical linkages between financial development and natural resources use the following linear cross-country equation:

$$FD_i = \beta_0 + \beta_1 NR_i + \beta_2 HD_i + \beta_3 X_i + \varepsilon_i \tag{1}$$

where FD_i is the financial development indicator in country i, NR_i is the country's natural resource dependence, HD is human development, X is a vector of controls (political stability and economic growth), and ε_i is a noise term. Since we use logarithm, the effect of natural resources on financial development is expressed as elasticity.

To test the hypothesis outlined in the previous section, we argue that the following Equation (2) is particularly well-suited to capturing the presence of contingency effects and to offering a rich way of modelling the influence of human development on the impact of natural resources in financial development. The model, based on threshold regression, takes the following form:

$$FD_i = \begin{cases} \beta_0^1 + \beta_1^1 NR_i + \beta_2^1 HD_i + \beta_3^1 X_i + e_i, & \text{NR} \leq \lambda \\ \beta_0^2 + \beta_1^2 NR_i + \beta_2^2 HD_i + \beta_3^2 X_i + e_i, & \text{NR} > \lambda \end{cases} \tag{2}$$

where NR (i.e., level of natural resource dependency) is the threshold variable used to split the sample into regimes or groups, and λ is the unknown threshold parameter. This type of modelling strategy allows the role of human development to differ depending on whether natural resources are below or above some unknown level of λ. In this equation, the level of natural resource exploitation acts as sample-splitting (or threshold) variables. The impact of natural resources on financial development will be β_1^1 and β_1^2 for countries with a low or high regime, respectively. It is obvious that, under the hypothesis $\beta^1 = \beta^2$, the model becomes linear and reduces to (1).

The first step of our estimation is to test the null hypothesis of linearity H_0: $\beta^1 = \beta^2$ against the threshold model in Equation (2). We follow Hansen (1996, 2000), who suggests a heteroskedasticity-consistent Lagrange Multiplier (LM) bootstrap procedure to test the null hypothesis of a linear formulation against a threshold regression alternative. Since the threshold parameter, λ, is not identified under the null hypothesis of the no-threshold effect, the p values are computed by a fixed bootstrap method. Hansen (2000) shows that this procedure yields asymptotically correct p values. It is important to note that if the hypothesis of $\beta^1 = \beta^2$ is rejected and a threshold level is identified we should test again the threshold regression model against a linear specification after dividing the original sample according to the threshold thus identified.

This procedure is carried out until the null of $\beta^1 = \beta^2$ can no longer be rejected.

Even though natural resources may have a positive effect on financial development, the results may have been driven by resource-rich countries with high-quality human capital. In order to examine this possibility, Equation (2) is extended as follows to include an interaction term between human capital and natural resources:

$$FD_i = \beta_0 + \beta_1 NR_i + \beta_2 HD + \beta_3 (NR \times \mathrm{HD})_\mathrm{i} + \beta_4 X_i + \varepsilon_i \quad (3)$$

If β_3 is positive and statistically significant, this implies that the contingency positive financial development effect increases as human development improves. On the other hand, if β_3 is negative and significant, this indicates that the contingency negative financial development effect increases as the human development in the resource-dependent economy improves. Equation (3) is estimated using the threshold regression technique.

4 The data

This study employs cross-country estimations in order to estimate Equations (2 and 3). The number of countries is 75, and the sample period is from 1994 to 2000. Following Sachs and Warner (1995, 2001), Brunnschweiler (2008) and Brunnschweiler and Bulte (2008) we use primary exports over GDP (*sxp*) to measure resource dependency. We use secondary school enrolment to proxy for human capital, which is commonly used in the literature. The real GDP per capita is USD 2000 constant prices, and economic growth is an average of real GDP from 1994 to 2000. All datasets are obtained from World Development Indicators.

The financial development dataset employed in this study is extracted from the World Development Indicator (WDI) 2008 published by the World Bank. Two financial development indicators are used to measure the overall financial development which have been widely used by previous researchers: (a) ratio of bank credit over bank deposits; this measures banking sector development; the higher the ratio indicates higher development of the banking sector and expects that economic development is less dependent on resources; (b) ratio of stock market capitalization over GDP, which reveals the degree development in equity market. Countries with high market capitalization are expected to have more comprehensive economic-based activities and to be less dependent on natural resources.

To have a more meaningful and robust analysis, we exclude potential outlier observations by computing *DFITS* statistics proposed by Belsley et al. (1980). Figure 3.1 depicts simple regression between financial development and economic growth and natural-resource dependence. The result shows that natural resources have a negative relationship with financial development and economic growth, while financial development shows a positive relationship with economic growth. These initial findings are consistent with the literature for the resource

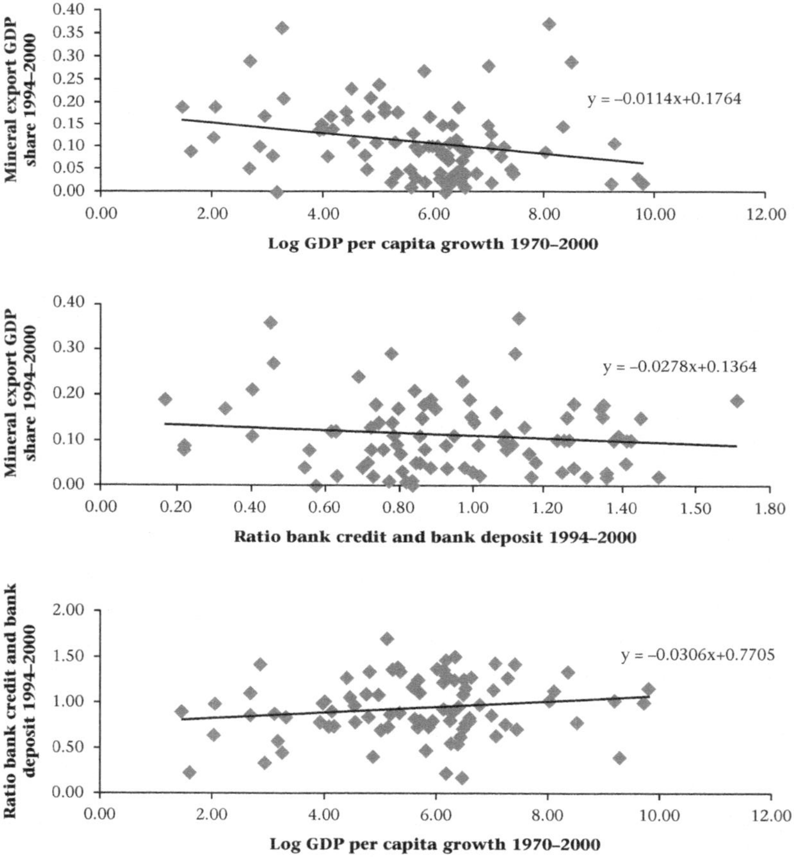

Figure 3.1 Relationship between natural resources dependence, financial development and economic growth

curse hypothesis (Sachs & Warner, 1995) and the growth–financial-development nexus (Demetriades & Law, 2006).

5 Results

Equations (2) and (3) have been estimated using two different models, depending on the financial development indicator (Model A: bank credit ratio; Model B: market capitalization ratio). The estimation results as presented in Tables 3.1 and 3.2 reveal several interesting findings. First, all the *p*-values of the hypothesis of no threshold effect as computed by a bootstrap method with 1,000 replications and 15 per cent trimming percentage are rejected at least at 5 per cent significant level (Model A: 0.001 and 0.03; Model B: 0.046 and 0.045). The finding clearly indicates that the relationship between financial

Table 3.1 Threshold estimates for Equation (2)

	Model A bank credit ratio			**Model B market capitalization**		
	Share of resource export to GDP					
	Linear	**≤ 8.07**	**> 8.07**	**Linear**	**≤ 8.37**	**> 8.37**
Constant	0.229	−0.300	1.76***	0.138	−0.503	1.98**
	(0.304)	(0.622)	(0.423)	(0.453)	(0.595)	(1.205)
GDP	−0.001	−0.002	−0.006	0.027	0.021***	0.121**
	(0.013)	(0.015)	(0.023)	(0.021)	(0.010)	(0.059)
Share of resource export to GDP	0.075**	0.132*	−0.088**	−0.054	0.063	−0.396***
	(0.038)	(0.0814)	(0.0501)	(0.061)	(0.076)	(0.145)
Human development	0.023*	0.033**	0.019	0.105***	0.047***	0.221***
	(0.015)	(0.0185)	(0.016)	(0.030)	(0.011)	(0.0481)
Political stability	0.096***	−0.058*	0.189***	0.148***	0.136***	0.047
	(0.043)	(0.037)	(0.0567)	(0.059)	(0.028)	(0.094)
Boot (p-value)	0.001			0.046		
R-sq	0.407	0.314	0.470	0.508	0.776	0.563
Het (p-value)	0.678	0.434	0.434	0.241	0.47	0.47
No. of Observations	70	27	43	53	24	29

Notes: The estimation of Equations 2 and 3 $\left(FD_i = \begin{cases} \beta_0^1 + \beta_1^1 NR_i + \beta_2^1 HD + \beta_3^1 X_i + e_i, & \text{NR} \le \lambda \\ \beta_0^2 + \beta_1^2 NR_i + \beta_3^2 HD_i + \beta_3^2 X_i + e_i, & \text{NR} > \lambda \end{cases}\right)$. The standard errors are reported in parentheses (White corrected for heteroskedasticity). Results correspond to trimming percentage of 15%. ***, ** and * indicate significance at 1%, 5% and 10% levels, respectively.

Table 3.2 Threshold estimates for Equation (3)

	Share of resource export to GDP					
	Model A bank credit ratio			**Model B market capitalization**		
	Linear	**≤ 7.76**	**> 7.76**	**Linear**	**≤ 8.89**	**> 8.89**
Constant	−0.537	−6.54***	0.772	0.704	−0.42	17.63***
	(0.596)	(1.484)	(1.153)	(0.629)	(0.518)	(6.62)
GDP	−0.009	−0.070***	−0.005	0.028	0.005	0.246***
	(0.015)	(0.018)	(0.015)	(0.021)	(0.017)	(0.092)
Share of resource export to GDP	0.174***	1.051***	0.021	−0.017	0.203**	0.428
	(0.0768)	(0.200)	(0.137)	(0.062)	(0.096)	(0.333)
Human development	0.163**	1.89***	0.086	0.165***	0.202**	1.155***
	(0.080)	(0.443)	(0.124)	(0.064)	(0.093)	(0.359)
Political stability	0.107***	−0.079***	0.195***	0.144***	0.187***	−0.074
	(0.041)	(0.026)	(0.053)	(0.058)	(0.037)	(0.143)
Interaction (Human development x share of resource export to GDP)	−0.016**	−0.247***	−0.007	−0.321*	−0.503*	−7.375***
	(0.009)	(0.058)	(0.014)	(0.226)	(0.324)	(2.870)
Boot (p-value)	0.030			0.045		
R-sq	0.428	0.663	0.377	0.515	0.666	0.643
Het(p-value)	0.262	0.582	0.582	0.270	0.181	0.181
No. of Observations	70	20	30	53	36	17

Notes: The estimation of Equations 2 and 3 $FD_i = \begin{cases} \beta_0^1 + \beta_1^1 NR_i + \beta_2^1 HD + \beta_3^1 X_i + e_i, & \text{NR} \leq \lambda \\ \beta_0^2 + \beta_1^2 NR_i + \beta_3^2 HD_i + \beta_3^2 X_i + e_i, & \text{NR} > \lambda \end{cases}$.
The standard errors are reported in parentheses (White corrected for heteroskedasticity). Results correspond to trimming percentage of 15%. ***, ** and * indicate significance at 1%, 5% and 10% levels, respectively.

development and natural resources is non-linear and, therefore, the imposition of a priori monotonic restriction on the relationship also can be very misleading. The finding provides a better explanation of a relationship between natural resources and financial development which are not uniform, depending on the degree of natural resource dependency.

Second, the presence of a threshold level also indicates that the analysis of financial development and natural resources can be split into two different groups, depending on the de facto level of natural resources dependency, that is, low resource-dependent and high resource-dependent economies. Any country that utilises natural resources less than the threshold value can be considered as low resource-dependent, while the one with greater than the threshold value can be classified as a high resource-dependent economy. Estimation of Equations (2) and (3) contingent on low and high resource dependency as shown in Tables 3.1 and 3.2 strongly reveal that the behaviour of the financial development-resource dependence relationship changes from positive significant to negative significant, or positive significant to insignificant, as resource dependency changes from low to high. For instance, the coefficient of the share of natural resource export over GDP is 0.132 for low resource-dependent economies and changes to −0.088 for high resource-dependent economies. This is to say that the utilization of resources before the threshold value is desirable for financial development but not beyond. The result is in line with the finding of Robinson et al. (2006) who find that over-extraction of resources could lead to a resource curse. The finding of this research is robust even if we replace the credit–ratio variable with market capitalization as a proxy for financial development. The result from Model B of Tables 3.1 and 3.2 shows a similar relationship. The coefficients of natural resources are positive 0.063 for a low resource-dependent economy and change to −0.396 for a high resource-dependent economy.

Next, the analysis shows that the human capital contributes to development of the financial sector. The coefficients are consistently positive ranges, from 0.23 to 1.89 for all models. Another interesting finding is that the regression's result from Equation (3) has provided new insight into the understanding of the financial development–natural resources nexus. The positive effect of human capital on financial development in a low resource-dependent economy can be nullified as resource dependence improves. For instance, for Model A, as resource dependence exceeds 7.65 the positive effect of (1.89) human capital contribution towards financial development is shattered. The result is consistent for Model B. This result shows that human development is an important ingredient for financial development. However, the positive effect of human development is reduced as the economy increases its reliance on natural resources. These cross-section regression estimations are econometrically valid since no heteroskedasticity problem is detected in the models.

6 Conclusion

In this chapter, we re-examined the well-known empirical puzzle of the resource curse hypothesis, using a threshold regression with reference to the financial development nexus. In particular, we endogenously determined the threshold level for low resource-dependent and high resource-dependent economies. Using the estimated threshold point, we empirically analysed the different effects of natural resources on financial development.

There are several major findings in this chapter. First, a priori monotonic restriction on the study of NRC-financial development could lead to a premature conclusion. In this study, we consistently failed to reject the presence of the threshold effect in the estimation, regardless of models. Second, the study highlights the different effect of natural resources on financial development, depending on the resource dependency. A low resource-dependent economy enjoys a positive relationship between resources and financial development while, for a high resource-dependent economy, the relationship is reversed. Finally, no doubt human development plays an important role in promoting financial development. However, the economy has to be wary of the evil effect of wealth resulting from extracting or exploiting natural resources too much, as this will divert the importance of human development. Excessive exploitation of natural resources may jeopardize present and future economic growth. Resources used should be well regulated and controlled, neither too much that ignites lavishness nor too little that deprives well-being. The exploitation of resources should not exceed the threshold point that is just enough to meet sustainable economic development. Therefore, this study tries to answer the question of how much resources should be exploited for the benefit of all. In summary, a nation desiring to have the full benefit from financial development should not excessively exploit its natural resources, as excessive use of resources may harm financial development and foster the resource curse even though the economy has very good human capital.

References

Atkinson, G. and Hamilton, K. (2003) 'Savings, Growth and the Resource Curse Hypothesis'. *World Development*, 31(11), 1793–807.

Belsley, D., Kuh, E. and Welsh, R. (1980) *Regression Diagnostics*. Wiley: New York.

Bhattacharyya, S. and Hodler, R. (2010) 'Natural Resources, Democracy and Corruption', *European Economic Review*, 54(4), 608–21.

Brunnschweiler, C. N. (2008) 'Cursing the Blessings? Natural Resource Abundance, Institutions, and Economic Growth', *World Development*, 36(3), 399–419.

Brunnschweiler, C. N. and Bulte, E. H. (2008) 'The Resource Curse Revisited and Revised: A Tale of Paradoxes and Red Herrings', *Journal of Environmental Economics and Management*, 55(3), 248–64.

Demetriades, P. and Law, S. (2006) 'Finance, Institutions and Economic Development', *International Journal of Finance and Economics,* 11, 245–60.

Dinda, S. (2004) 'Environmental Kuznets Curve Hypothesis: A Survey', *Ecological Economics,* 49(2004), 431–55.

Frankel, J. (2010) 'The Natural Resource Curse: A Survey', *Harvard Kennedy School Faculty Research Working Paper Series,* RWP10-005.

Fukuyama, F. (2001) 'Social Capital, Civil Society, and Development', *Third World Quarterly,* 22(1), 7–20.

Gleason, K. C., Chun, I. L. and Mathur, I. (2002) 'Dimensions of International Expansions by US Firms to China: Wealth Effects, Mode Selection, and Firm-Specific Factors', *International Review of Economics and Finance,* 11, 139–54.

Guha, A. (1989) 'Consumption, Efficiency and Surplus Labour', *Journal of Development and Economics,* 31(1), 1–12.

Guiso, L., Sapienza, P. and Zingales, L. (2004) 'The Role of Social Capital in Financial Development', *The American Economic Review,* 94, 526–56.

Gylfason, T. (2001) 'Natural Resources, Education, and Economic Development', *European Economic Review,* 45, 847–59.

Gylfason, T. and Zoega, G. (2006) 'Natural Resources and Economic Growth: The Role of Investment', *The World Economy,* 29(8), 1091–115.

Hansen, B. (1996) 'Inference When a Nuisance Parameter is Not Identified under the Null Hypothesis', *Econometrica,* 64, 413–30.

Hansen, B. (2000) 'Sample Splitting and Threshold Estimation', *Econometrica,* 68, 575–603.

Kutan, A. M. and Wyzan, M. L. (2005) 'Explaining the Real Exchange Rate in Kazakhstan, 1996 to 2003: Is Kazakhstan Vulnerable to the Dutch Disease?' *Economic Systems,* 29(2), 242–55.

Larrain, B. (2004) 'Financial Development, Financial Constraints, and the Volatility of Industrial Output', *Public Policy Discussion Paper 04–6,* Federal Reserve Bank of Boston.

Leamer, E. E., Maul, H., Rodriguez, S. and Schott, P. K. (1999) 'Does Natural Resource Abundance Increase Latin American Income Inequality?' *Journal of Development Economics,* 59, 3–42.

Leite, C. A. and J. Weidmann (1999) 'Does Mother Nature Corrupt? Natural Resources, Corruption, and Economic Growth', *IMF Working Paper* No. 99/85, Washington, DC: International Monetary Fund.

Looney, R. E. (1991) 'Diversification in a Small Oil Exporting Economy: The Impact of the Dutch Disease on Kuwait's Industrialization', *Resources Policy,* 17(1), 31–41.

Narayan, P. K. and Narayan, S (2010) 'Carbon Dioxide Emissions and Economic Growth: Panel Data Evidence from Developing Countries', *Energy Policy,* 38(1), 661–66.

Nili, M. and Rastad, M. (2007) 'Addressing the Growth Failure of the Oil Economies: The Role of Financial Development', *The Quarterly Review of Economics and Finance,* 46(5), 726–40.

Rajan, R. and Zingales, L. (2003) 'The Great Reversals: The Politics of Financial Development in the 20th Century', *Journal of Financial Economics,* 69, 5–50.

Robinson, J. A., Torvik, R. and Verdier, T. (2006) 'Political Foundations of the Resource Curse', *Journal of Development Economics,* 79(2), 447–68.

Sachs, J. D. and Warner, A (1995) 'Natural Resource Abundance and Economic Growth', Harvard Institute For International Development, *Development Discussion Paper No. 517.*

Sachs, J. D. and Warner, A. (1999) 'The Big Push, Natural Resource Booms and Growth', *Journal of Development Economics*, 59, 43–76.

Sachs, J. D. and Warner, A. (2001) 'Natural Resources and Economic Development: The Curse of Natural Resources', *European Economic Review*, 45, 827–38.

Stevens, P. and Dietsche, E. (2008) 'Resource Curse: An Analysis of Causes, Experiences and Possible Ways Forward', *Energy Policy,* 36(1), 56–65.

Tornell, A. and Lane, P. R. (1999) 'The Voracity Effect', *American Economic Review*, 89, 22–46.

van der Ploeg, F. and Poelhekke, S. (2010) 'The Pungent Smell of "Red Herrings": Subsoil Assets, Rents, Volatility and the Resource Curse', *Journal of Environmental Economics and Management,* 60(1), 44–55.

World Bank (2008) *World Development Indicators 2008*, Washington DC.

Yuxiang, K. and Chen, Z. (2010) 'Resource Abundance and Financial Development: Evidence from China', *Resources Policy,* In press, corrected proof.

4

Forecasting Malaysian Business Cycle Movement

Shirly Siew-Ling Wong, Shazali Abu Mansor, Chin-Hong Puah and Venus Khim-Sen Liew

1 Introduction

For years, economists have sought to summarize the visual evidence of cyclical oscillation in economic series to learn the characteristics of such cycles in real macroeconomic settings. The existence of various business cycle conceptions indeed shared a single objective, that is, to strengthen insight into the underlying thoughts behind recurring ups and downs in economic activity (Burns & Mitchell, 1946). However, the cyclical fluctuations in economic activity hardly follow a predictable pattern, as the size of expansion and contraction deviate across periods, each turning point in the business cycle presents certain crucial information that contains indications on future changing phases of the economy. Also, development in leading indicator analysis persuasively suggests that combinations of sets of leading series to form a unique composite index is generally better than any single series in explaining the cyclical movement.

Undeniably, attempts to track the business cycle may be undertaken under a composite leading indicator (CLI), since business cycles are widely characterized as broad-based co-movement among a set of economic series, which in turn reflect the future state of the economy. Since the pioneering works of Mitchell and Burns (1938) and Burns and Mitchell (1946), interest in leading indicator analysis has grown among national policymakers as well as the business community. This is evidenced by the fact that most of the industrialized economies seriously recognize the CLI as a signaling tool to enhance short-term economic forecasts (Cotrie et al., 2009). Unfortunately, there is little literature in this domain when we look at the developing nations. The application of the CLI approach in business cycle analysis in developing economies had only a short history. One of the great challenges is that the compilation of a CLI requires the use of a huge set of high-frequency macroeconomic data with long time series. Yet, the national statistical systems in most of the developing countries were unable to support the generation of a resilient CLI.

Malaysia is one of the fast-growing developing countries. However, growing under an increasingly dynamic and globalized economic environment, the Malaysian economy has always been remarkably open to external influences, which doubtless give rise to immense risk and uncertainty for the domestic economy. Such economic vulnerability has been proven in decisive moments demonstrated in the historical profile of the Malaysian business cycle during the period of the 1980s to the 2010s. For instance, the onslaught of the Asian financial crisis in 1997 has to some extent interrupted the notable growth in the economy. Given the availability of a publicly accessible CLI that is attributable to the national statistical institution of Malaysia, the present study presents a worthwhile opportunity to explore the experience in business cycle forecasting via CLI from the perspective of a fast-developing nation.

2 Indicator approach to business cycle forecasting

The underpinning work on business cycle analysis is credited to Burns and Mitchell (1946), who initiated a methodology in transforming the cyclical evidence of economic series in order to examine the characteristics of such cycles in the belief that the visual evidence of those economic series contains certain information about the economy. Their inspiration was the first venture into reality by the creation of the National Bureau of Economic Research (NBER) committee which is responsible for dating U.S. business cycles.

The Organization for Economic Co-operation and Development (OECD) characterizes a business cycle as a *recurrent sequence of alternating phases of expansion and contraction in the level of a time series*. Such an expression is widely termed as a "classical cycle". Alternatively, a "growth cycle" is described as *recurrent fluctuations in the series of deviation from trend*. In other words, a contraction phase represents a decline in the rate of growth in the economy, but not necessarily as a result of an absolute drop in economic activity (Everhart & Duval-Hernandez, 2000;

Yap, 2009). This study adopted a growth-cycle approach in characterizing the business cycle as, for Malaysia, growth cycle is indeed an appropriate characterization of the business cycle because the economy did not suffer from major oscillations in the level of general economic activity, but did experience fluctuations in the growth rates of economic activity (Zhang & Zhuang, 2002; Ahmad, 2003).

In order to monitor the cyclical fluctuations in the business cycle, the indicator approach utilizes a huge set of economic indicators that can be broadly classified into leading, coincident and lagging indicators. Among the three indicators, the CLI is the one designed to forecast business cycle turning points. The CLI is an aggregated unique series that encompasses a bundle of economic indicators that carry some leading attributes and possess significant anticipating elements about the future road map of the economy. As such, the individual leading series, when blended into a group, can form a CLI that is able to work as an early signalling tool in forecasting the business cycle.

In business cycle study, identification of an appropriate measure of business cycles is another key empirical concern. Yet, there is no general agreement on which series should be selected to represent the business cycle (European Central Bank, 2001). Some researchers regard real GDP (RGDP) to be a comprehensive measure of aggregate economy, while others favor using the Index of Industrial Production (IIP) to represent the business cycle. The latter argued that the IIP is usually publicly accessible and the degree of revision is less frequent compared to GDP series. In this study, RGDP will be adopted as a reference series following the NBER routine.

3 Data description

This study utilized monthly series' of RGDP and CLI for the period 1981–2010. The CLI data were compiled from Malaysian Economic Indicators published by the DOSM, while the consumer price index (CPI) and GDP[1] were extracted from the International Financial Statistics Yearbook (IFS). The ratio of GDP to CPI was then calculated to transform the GDP series into its real term. The CLI is constructed based on the Moore–Shiskin method by averaging the month-to-month growth rates of the index components[2] before standardizing them into the same unit. Then, the average growth rate is cumulated to obtain an index. Lastly, the index is adjusted to have the same average absolute percentage changes as the cyclical component of industrial production, and also the same average trend rate of growth as RGDP.

4 Empirical results and discussion

As noted by many macroeconomists, time series data are habitually non-stationary due to the existence of unit root. Thus, incorporating such an unstable series into regression estimates will yield an erroneous conclusion, as the inferences drawn from the regression estimates are based on spurious regression results (Engle & Granger, 1987). Therefore, most recent empirical works in time series analysis have accounted for the pre-testing of the time series properties. Hence, the time series properties of the CLI and RGDP were examined using the Augmented Dickey–Fuller (ADF) unit root tests developed by Dickey and Fuller (1979, 1981) and the Phillips–Perron (PP) and the Phillips–Perron (PP) unit root test proposed by Phillips and Perron (1988). The results of ADF and PP tests are presented in Table 4.1.

Both ADF and PP tests collectively show the existence of non-stationary CLI and RGDP at the level form of the series. However, both series appear to be stationary after first differencing. As the two variables own the same order of integration, that is $I(1)$, we can proceed to the cointegration test to examine the long-run co-movement between them. Before we proceed to the Johansen and Juselius (JJ) cointegration test proposed by Johansen and Juselius (1990), the Akaike Information Criterion (AIC) has been used to ascertain the optimal lag length for the VAR system. The finding indicates that the optimal lag length for the VAR system is 2.

The results for the JJ cointegration test, established on the basis of trace and maximum eigenvalue test statistics, are presented in Table 4.2.

Table 4.1 Unit root tests results

	ADF		PP	
Variables	**Constant/ No Trend**	**Constant/ Trend**	**Constant/ No Trend**	**Constant/ Trend**
Level				
LRGDP	−0.184	−2.971	−0.167	−3.226
LCLI	−0.391	−2.226	−0.378	−3.110
First difference				
ΔLRGDP	−5.583***	−5.575***	−7.232***	−7.210***
ΔLCLI	−25.186***	−25.154***	−24.348***	−24.322***

Notes: Asterisks (***) indicate statistically significant at 1% level. Lag lengths for ADF and PP tests have been chosen on the basis of Schwarz's Information Criteria (SC). LRGDP and LCLI denote natural logarithms of real GDP and CLI.

Table 4.2 Johansen and Juselius cointegration test results

Variables: LRGDP LCLI; k = 2, $r = 1$			
H_0	H_1	λ-trace	95% critical value
$r = 0$	$r \geq 1$	57.044*	15.495
$r \leq 1$	$r \geq 2$	0.259	3.841
H_0	H_1	λ−max	95% critical value
$r = 0$	$r = 1$	56.785*	14.265
$r \leq 1$	$r = 2$	0.259	3.841

Notes: Asterisks (**) denote significant at 5% level, k is the number of lag and r is the number of cointegration vector(s).

Table 4.3 Granger causality test results

Null hypothesis	Chi-square values (*p*-value)	ECT (t-statistics)
CLI does not Granger cause RGDP	8.636 (0.00)***	−0.094 [−7.447]***
RGDP does not Granger cause CLI	6.450 (0.011)**	−0.030 [−2.706]***

Note: Asterisks (***) and (**) denote statistically significant at the 1% and 5% levels, respectively.

Findings from both tests suggest that the null hypothesis of no cointegration can be firmly rejected at a 5 per cent level. Moreover, both test statistics consistently show the existence of only one cointegrating vector in the system. This confirms the presence of co-movement between CLI and RGDP in the long run, and these two variables share similar long-run equilibrium paths. Importantly, the presence of this long-run stable relationship ensures that we are more likely to own a higher degree of synchronized cyclical determinant between the CLI and business cycle.

As the cointegration test does not imply the direction of causality, we employed a vector error correction model (VECM) to examine the direction of causal effects between the CLI and business cycle. If a causal relationship in a Granger sense can be established, we can confirm that the CLI possesses predictive value or information content for the business cycle. The finding of causality test is presented in Table 4.3. The null hypothesis of CLI does not Granger causes RGDP is firmly rejected at a 1 per cent level. Likewise, the null hypothesis of RGDP does not Granger causes CLI also being rejected at 1 per cent level. These findings imply the existence of bidirectional causality between CLI and RGDP. Essentially, the existence of causality running from CLI to RGDP enables us to confirm that the CLI owns predictive content for the Malaysian business cycle as represented by RGDP. In this sense, the CLI can be regarded as a useful predictor to the Malaysian business cycle.

Next, we proceed to evaluate the forecasting ability of the CLI in tracing the turning points in the Malaysian business cycle. In order to study the cyclical movement of the CLI and RGDP, we decompose both time series to yield the cyclical component underlying the CLI and RGDP. For this purpose, the Hodrick–Prescott (HP) filter developed by Hodrick and Prescott (1980) has been employed to generate a smooth estimate of the long-run trend component of the CLI and RGDP. The HP filter is a widely applied de-trending framework used to decompose the seasonally adjusted time series into trends, besides providing a smooth trend to a minimized problem. The HP filter was first employed by Hodrick and Prescott in the early 1980s to study the business cycle for the United States. Thus far, it is one of the most commonly applied techniques to extract the cyclical component in business cycle analysis – see, for example, Everhart and Duval-Hernandez (2000), Kranendonk et al. (2005), Bascos-Deveza (2006), Zalewski (2009) and Polasek (2010).

After extracting the cyclical component CLI and RGDP from their long-term trends, we are able to analyze the Malaysian business cycle based on a growth-rate approach. The forecasting performance of the CLI to RGDP has been evaluated via turning-point analysis, and graphical presentation in Figure 4.1 serves as a means to examine the arrival of any

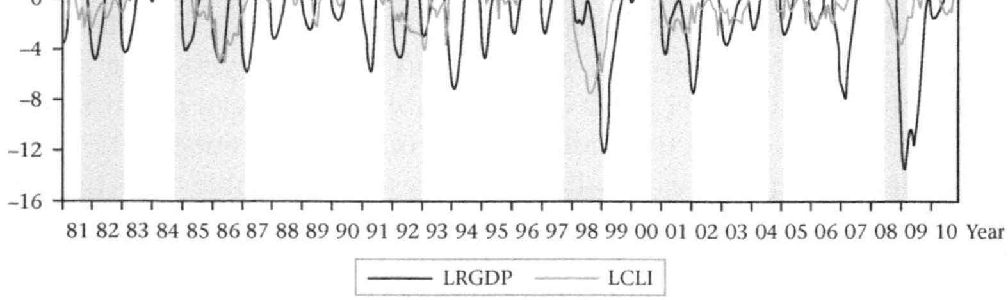

Figure 4.1 LRGDP versus LCLI, 1981: 01–2010: 12

critical turning point and to observe how the CLI traces the business cycle in Malaysia. In general, the presentation of cyclical oscillation in Figure 4.1 shows that the movement of the CLI is relatively coherent with the movement of the business cycle represented by RGDP. In chorus, the traced peaks and troughs from turning point analysis are fairly consistent with the historical profile of the Malaysian business cycle. Furthermore, from Figure 4.1, it is obvious that CLI moves in advance of RGDP most of the time, and the turning points in CLI consistently appear a few months earlier than the turning points in RGDP.

Then, following the procedure proposed by Bry and Boschan (1971), we establish an alternative chronology for the Malaysian business cycle and tabulate the amount of early signal provided by CLI in relation to the Malaysian business cycle in Table 4.4. Interestingly, we observe a decreasing trend of early signal offered by CLI. In other words, even though CLI traced the occurrence of turning point in an advanced time, the amount of signaling becomes smaller over time.

Moreover, another appealing finding can be witnessed through the comparative analysis presented in Table 4.5. The business cycle reference chronology marked in the present study is distinctively different from the officially published reference chronology. One obvious distinction in this context is largely due to the use of different reference series of the business cycle. The official reference chronology is marked by taking

Table 4.4 Reference chronology and the amount of early signals (1981–2010)

	Reference chronology of business cycle	Amount of early signals	Important events
Peak	Aug-1981	3 months	World recession
Trough	Mar-1982		
Peak	Oct-1984	7 months	Commodity shock
Trough	Mar-1987		
Peak	Sep-1991	6 months	Global recession
Trough	Jan-1993		
Peak	Oct-1997	5 months	Asian financial crisis
Trough	Jan-1999		
Peak	Sep-2000	4 months	U.S. technology bubble
Trough	Feb-2002		
Peak	Aug-2004	3 months	Oil price hikes
Trough	Feb-2005		
Peak	July-2008	3 months	Sub-prime mortgage crisis
Trough	Feb-2009		

Table 4.5 Comparative finding from turning point analysis (1981–2010)

	CLI v. RGDP (Present study)	CLI v. CCI (DOSM)	Important events
Peak	Aug-1981	–	World recession
Trough	Mar-1982	Nov-1982	
Peak	Oct-1984	Jan-1985	Commodity shock
Trough	Mar-1987	Jan-1987	
Peak	Sep-1991	Jan-1992	Global recession
Trough	Jan-1993	Jan-1993	
Peak	Oct-1997	Jan-1997	Asian financial crisis
Trough	Jan-1999	Jan-1999	
Peak	Sep-2000	Sep-2000	U.S. technology bubble
Trough	Feb-2002	Feb-2002	
Peak	Aug-2004	Apr-2004	Oil price hikes
Trough	Feb-2005	Dec-2004	
Peak	July-2008	Jan-2008	Sub-prime mortgage crisis
Trough	Feb-2009	Mar-2009	

the Composite Coincidence Index (CCI) built by the similar authority as the reference series. However, in the present study, RGDP serves as the reference series to the business cycle because it is regarded as an ideal representation of the Malaysian business cycle. Besides following the common practice of business cycle study, this selection is also supported by the finding of the Granger causality test reported in Table 4.3, which reveals that RGDP and CLI are indeed Granger causing each other, suggesting the existence of information content between these two series.

Another key finding we can draw from Table 4.5 is that the marked date of business cycle turning points obtained in the present study approach in advance of, or are analogous to, the one marked by the DOSM for 8 out of 13 turning points in the full sample period. On the other hand, the chronology marked by DOSM only owns 5 turning points that surpass the marked date of turning points obtained in this study. Hence, the one remarkable implication from this analysis is that business cycle forecasting is sensitive to the selection of an appropriate reference series of the overall economic activity besides the predictive power of the CLI per se.

5 Conclusion

Exploring the indicator approach furnished by the national statistical institution of Malaysia enables us to provide better insight into the applicability of the leading indicator approach to business cycle monitoring and forecasting for a developing nation whose progress is under a wave of economic dynamism. Empirical findings indicate that the CLI is cointegrated with RGDP, implying that the CLI and RGDP are synchronized along the period of the study. The evidence of synchronization serves as an important inference to strengthen the potential ability of the CLI as a predictor of the business cycle movement. Furthermore, the forecasting performance and predictive capability of the existing CLI is evaluated based on its ability to provide a signaling effect to the RGDP under the growth-cycle approach. From this perspective, per se, the performance of the existing CLI as a predictor of business cycle analysis is deemed to be fairly adequate.

Another important finding worth noting is that we observed a diminishing capability of CLI to reveal an early signal to the business cycle turning points. This finding is in line with Yap (2009), who reported that the lead times of CLI over CCI have become shorter over the years. Given that diminishing lead times of CLI to business cycle turning points weaken the fundamental function of a leading index as an early warning tool to economic vulnerability, future study is encouraged to construct a more resilient leading indicator that can contribute significantly to the reliable forecasts of the business cycle with remarkable lead times.

Notes

1. Interpolation technique proposed by Gandolfo (1981), applied to interpolate quarterly GDP series into its monthly basic.
2. The compilation of CLI utilizes eight economic series: (a) KLSE share price index, industrial (1970 = 100); (b) growth rate of CPI for services sector (inverted); (c) growth rate of industrial material price index; (d) ratio of price to unit labor cost for the manufacturing sector; (e) M1 in real term; (f) housing permits approved; (g) real total traded from eight major trading partners and (h) new companies registered.

References

Ahmad, N. (2003) *Malaysia Economic Indicators: Leading, Coincident and Lagging Indicators*. Paper presented at the Workshop on Composite Leading Indicators and Business Tendency Survey, Bangkok.

Bascos-Deveza, T. (2006) 'Early Warning System on the Macroeconomy Identification of Business Cycles in the Philippines', *Bangko Sentral Review*, January, 7–16.

Bry, G. and Boschan, C. (1971) 'Cyclical Analysis of Time Series, Selected Procedures and Computer Programs', National Bureau of Economic Research, *Technical Paper 20,* Cambridge, MA: Columbia University Press.

Burns, A.F. and Mitchell, W.C. (1946) 'Measuring Business Cycles' in National Bureau of Economic Research, *Studies in Business Cycles*, Columbia University Press: New York.

Cotrie, G., Craigwell, R.C. and Maurin, A. (2009) 'Estimating Indexes of Coincident and Leading Indicators for Barbados', *Applied Econometrics and International Development*, 9, 1–33.

Department of Statistics Malaysia. *Malaysia Economic Indicators: Leading, Coincident and Lagging Indexes*. Department of Statistics Malaysia, Kuala Lumpur (various issues).

Dickey, D. and Fuller, W. (1979) 'Distribution of the Estimators for Autoregressive Times Series with a Unit Root', *Journal of the American Statistical Association*, 74, 427–31.

Dickey, D. and Fuller, W. (1981) 'Likelihood Ratio Statistic for Autoregressive Times Series with a Unit Root', *Econometrica*, 49, 1057–72.

Engle, R. F. and Granger, C. W. J. (1987) 'Cointegration and Error Correction Representation, Estimation and Testing', *Econometrica*, 55, 251–76.

European Central Bank (2001) 'The Information Content of Composite Indicators of the Euro Area Business Cycle' in ECB *Monthly Bulletin*, 39–50 (ECB, Germany).

Everhart, S. S. and Duval-Hernandez, R. (2000) 'Leading Indicator Project: Lithuania', Policy Research Dissemination Center, *Policy Research Working Paper, Series 2365*.

Gandolfo, G. (1981) *Qualitative Analysis and Econometric Estimation of Continuous Time Dynamic Models,* Amsterdam: North-Holland Publishing Company.

Hodrick, R. J. and Prescott, E. C. (1980) 'Postwar U.S. Business Cycles: An Empirical Investigation', Carnegie Mellon University *Discussion Paper, No. 451*.

International Monetary Fund (IMF) *International Financial Statistics*, (various issues) IMF, Washington, D.C.

Johansen, S. and Juselius, K. (1990) 'The Maximum Likelihood Estimation and Inference on Cointegration with Application to Demand for Money', *Oxford Bulletin of Economics and Statistics*, 52, 169–210.

Kranendonk, H., Bonenkamp, J. and Verbruggen, J. (2005) 'A Leading Indicator for the Dutch Economy', Central Planning Bureau (CPU), *Discussion Paper, No. 32*.

Mitchell, W. C. and Burns, A. F. (1938) *Statistical Indicators of Cyclical Revivals,* National Bureau of Economic Research, New York.

Phillips, P. C. B and Perron, P. (1988) 'Testing for a Unit Root in Time Series Regression', *Biometrika*, 75, 335–46.

Polasek, W. (2010) 'Dating and Exploration of the Business Cycle in Iceland', The Rimini Centre for Economic Analysis, *Working Paper 10–13*.

Yap, M. M. C. (2009) 'Assessing Malaysia's Business Cycle Indicators', Monash University *Discussion Paper 04*.

Zalewski, K. (2009) 'Forecasting Turning Points with Composite Leading Indicators – The Case of Poland', *Ekonomia Journal*, 24, 61–93.

Zhang, W. D. and Zhuang, J. Z. (2002) 'Leading Indicators of Business Cycles in Malaysia and the Philippines', *Working Paper Series No. 32,* Asian Development Bank, Economics and Research Department.

Part III

Regional Financial Market Integration

5
Financial Integration between China and Asia Pacific

Tze-Haw Chan and Ahmad Zubaidi Baharumshah

1 Introduction

Unlike her neighboring countries in East Asia, China's economic reform programs are relatively recent, attributed to the closed-door policy and centrally planned economic system of the 1950s to the 1970s. However, the affluent human capital and economic resources have provided China the new impetus to reinvigorate the economic reforms since 1978, and the economic progress of this economy is eye-catching. Within three decades, China has transformed itself from a rigid central-planning system to an increasingly open and market-oriented economy, with the achievement of an average 9.7 per cent real GDP growth per annum. As of November 2007, China recorded a nominal GDP of US$3.42 trillion and has the fourth largest economy after the United States, Japan and Germany. China's GDP officially overtook Japan in the second quarter of 2010, although the per capita GDP ($8,394) is still significantly lower than that of Japan ($39,731) and the United States ($46,380).

China's role in global trading and finance has steadily grown, especially after accession to the World Trade Organization (WTO) in November, 2001. China is presently the world's largest exporter and second-largest importer. In 2010, China's total trade exceeded $2.8 trillion[1] and its current account surplus amounted to $0.2 trillion, which ranked at the top globally (Datastream). Despite being the major trading partner for many of the Asia-Pacific (APEC) economies,[2] China has also actively become involved with the Chiang Mai Initiative (2000), the Bali Accord (2003) and the Singapore Declaration (2007), and is devoted to closer cooperation within the ASEAN+3+2+1 framework. Additionally,

China's efforts toward regionalism in most of the countries under review (East Asian in particular), which started in the last decades, are expected to have some impact on her integration process with the APEC countries (see Yu, 2011). In line with the trade and exchange-rate liberalization,[3] China has gradually opened up financial markets by: permitting a wide variety of private enterprise in services and light manufacturing; developing a more diversified banking system and capitalized stock market; and increasing foreign investments. According to World Bank statistics, China has doubled her accumulated FDI since 1999, from $39 billion to around $574 billion in 2010, to become the largest FDI destination in East Asia. Besides the European counterparts, Hong Kong, Taiwan, Japan and the United States hold the major shares of foreign investments in China. Similarly, half of the stocks of foreign bank lending are also sourced from United States and East Asian trading partners.

Taking into account these developments mentioned above, markets convergence and future economic events anchored by China are well expected in the Asia-Pacific region. Yet, to what extent China has truly integrated with the regional economies remains a major uncertainty. The recent proposal of Trans-Pacific Partnership (TPP) negotiations on regional trade arrangements has elevated further debates among scholars (see Armstrong, 2011), since the 2011 Honolulu APEC meeting. Two unsolved, but essential, questions thus arise. First, is regional trade competition sufficient to eliminate prices arbitrage and, hence, reflecting the exchange value of the Chinese yuan when more and more trading of goods and services is promoted across borders? Second, are China's pricing and investment structures integrated with the regional standards to facilitate cross-border financial assets' substitutability or and hence allow for greater portfolio diversification? The former question relates to Purchasing Power Parity (PPP), while the latter addresses the Real Interest Rate Parity (RIP) condition.

Without answers to these questions, we are unable to draw any concrete conclusion about the extent of economic integration between China–APEC and, affect the formulation of regional monetary and exchange rate policy coordination.[4] Yet, the empirical evidence of PPP and RIP, which has hitherto been abundant, is still contentious especially among developing economies (see Rogoff, 1996; Taylor & Taylor, 2004; Cheung et al., 2005; in recent surveys). Moreover, the assessment of parity conditions based on China-denominated exchange rates and financial securities are notably lacking and inconclusive. Among the few China-based studies, Finke and Rahn (2005) and Coudert and Couharde (2007) revealed that the Chinese yuan significantly deviates from PPP, whereas Gregory and Shelley (2011) found evidence of PPP – only for the real, effective yuan, but not for the real yuan/USD rates. Cheung et al. (2003), in a separate endeavor, examined three parity conditions (PPP, UIP, RIP) consecutively and concluded that parities hold among China–Taiwan–Hong Kong. Chan et al. (2012) then conducted a structural system to assess PPP and UIP for China–Japan. They confirm that both parity conditions hold in the long run when structural breaks of the Asia crisis, subprime crisis and six over-identifying restrictions were taken into account. Meanwhile, Cavoli et al. (2004) examined the parity conditions for China, East Asia and ASEAN, but failed to find clear indication of intensified financial integration. Likewise, Laurenceson (2003) shows that China–ASEAN financial linkages remain weak, although the market integration of goods and services is relatively well-established.

This chapter aims to jointly investigate the validity of PPP and RIP conditions for China vis-à-vis her 13 trading partners in the Asia-Pacific region. Such a practice of joint investigation is not frequently applied in the literature but is supported by Cheung et al. (2003) and Cavoli et al. (2004), among others. A different but clearer insight, or perspective, may be gained from the joint assessment of China and APEC emerging economies with different regulatory regimes at different stages of development. More important, monetary and exchange rate coordination policies derived from the PPP and RIP conditions within similar time zones would enable the Asia-Pacific region to exert an important influence upon the future evolution of the global trade and financial system.

To assess PPP and RIP, a convenient strategy is to scrutinize the mean-reversion behaviors of bilateral real exchange rates (REX) and real interest differentials (RID) among China–APEC. Monthly observations and subsamples within 1986–2007 are being considered to accentuate the effects of institutional changes and financial crisis, both local and regional. Due to the deficiency in extant econometric tests, various estimation methods have been adopted to increase the likelihood of establishing well-defined results. These include the endogenous break test advocated by Saikkonen and Lütkepohl (2002), the first-generation panel tests by Levin-Lin-Chu (2002) and Im-Pesaran-Shin (2003) as well as the second-generation panel test by Pesaran (2007), which allow for cross-sectional dependency. Results of univariate and panel tests are compared in considering of the robustness within the macro-panel setting. To capture the degree of shock adjustments towards equilibrium, we also construct the half-life and confidence intervals by means of the correction factor model put forward by Rossi (2005).

The present study is organized in the following manner. Section 2 elaborates on the theoretical framework, followed by the estimation procedures and data description in Section 3. The literature arguments are presented in both sections. Estimation results are then presented and discussed in Section 4. Finally, conclusions are drawn in the closing section.

2 International parity conditions and empirical framework

PPP and RIP constitute fundamental building blocks of international macroeconomics. PPP theorem requires a constant real exchange which at least exhibits reversion towards the long run mean rate over time, and which is not driven by stochastic trends. On the other hand, RIP is verified via the real interest differential hypothesis or real interest co-movement that implies financial asset substitutability and capital mobility across borders. If we let $s_t$be the log spot exchange rate, p_t^* and p_t be the log foreign and domestic price levels, respectively, the PPP condition is defined as

$$s_t = p_t - p_t^* \tag{1}$$

Real exchange rates (REX), q_t (in logarithm) as deviation from the PPP is then given by

$$q_t = s_t + p_t^* - p_t \tag{2}$$

And, the ex ante PPP can be shown as

$$\Delta s_{t,t+k}^e = \pi_{t,t+k}^e - \pi_{,t+kt}^{e*} \tag{3}$$

which imply that PPP holds with expected depreciation ($\Delta s_{t,t+k}^e$) equals the expected inflation differential, and * denotes foreign variables. Subsequently, RIP can be obtained by combining the Fisher effect in each country, the ex ante PPP and the Uncovered Interest Parity (UIP) relationship. UIP anticipates expected depreciation as being explained by interest rate differentials so that

$$\Delta s_{t,t+k}^e = i_t^k - i_t^{k*} \tag{4}$$

Equating (3) and (4) thus yields $i_t^k - \pi_{t,t+k}^e = i_t^{k*} - \pi_{,t+kt}^{e*}$. If the Fisher equation holds so that real interest equals nominal interest minus expected inflation, the ex ante RIP condition will be

$$E_t(r_{t+k}) = E_t(r_{t+k}^*) \tag{5}$$

When rational expectations are considered, ex post RIP also implies ex ante RIP. And the Real Interest differential (x_t) as deviation from RIP is shown as

$$r_t - r_t^* = x_t \tag{6}$$

Given the respective specification of PPP and RIP in (2) and (6), both international parities hold if REX and RID are mean reverting. Suppose that q_t and x_t follow AR (1) process, then

$$q_t = \rho q_{t-1} + \varepsilon_t \tag{7}$$

and

$$x_t = \varpi x_{t-1} + \mu_t \tag{8}$$

where $0 < |\rho| < 1$ and $0 < |\varpi| < 1$ whereas ε_t and μ_t are white noise innovations. Evidence of long run PPP and RIP can be verified by a test of unit root in REX (q_t) and RID (x_t), say, the Augmented Dickey–Fuller (ADF) regression with intercept and time trend which is given by

$$\Delta g_t = \mu + \beta t + \varphi g_{t-1} + \sum_{i=1}^{k} \gamma_i \Delta g_{t-i} + \varepsilon_t \tag{9}$$

where g_t represents q_t or x_t. Δg_t is the first difference of REX or RID, k is the number of lagged g_{t-i} whilst ε_t is the error term. To be consistent with the international parities, both q_t and x_t must exhibit mean reversion behavior devoid of a unit root. The φ is to be significantly less than 0. Otherwise, deviations from PPP or RIP are permanent aftershocks.

While PPP is an elegant hypothesis, early studies have shown that it fails to hold empirically (e.g., Edison, 1985; Frankel, 1986; Meese & Rogoff, 1988; Mark, 1990; Edison & Pauls, 1993). Likewise, the empirical literature does not support entirely the mean reversion behaviour of RID (see *inter alia* Mishkin, 1984; Cumby & Obstfeld, 1984; Frankel & MacArthur, 1988). The consensus arrived at by recent literature surveys (Rogoff, 1996; Taylor & Taylor, 2004) suggests that despite the presence of excessive short-term exchange rate volatility, the deviations from the long-run equilibrium PPP rates are too persistent with the estimated half-life of real exchange shocks at about 3–5 years. For stationary REX and RID, the degree of mean reversion and extent of deviations can be further estimated by half-life, h – a concept defined as the horizon at which the percentage deviation from the long-run equilibrium of PPP or RIP is one-half. By formula, $h = \ln(1/2)/\ln(\alpha)$, where $\phi = (\alpha - 1)$. The two-sided 95 per cent confidence intervals of the half-life, which are based on normal sampling distributions, is then defined as $\hat{h} \pm 1.96\hat{\sigma}_{\hat{\alpha}}\left(\frac{\ln(0.5)}{\hat{\alpha}}[\ln(\hat{\alpha})]^{-2}\right)$, where $\hat{\sigma}_{\hat{\alpha}}$ is an estimate of the standard deviation ofα. Lately, Rossi (2005) defined half-life as $h = \ln(0.5)b(1)/\ln\alpha$ with $b(1) = (1 - \sum_{j=1}^{k} \alpha^*_{j-1})$ being the correction factor that sums the estimated AR coefficients of an AR (ρ) model fitted onto the residuals of the ADF regression. In the present study, we applied both methods on the REX and RID series, which are found to be stationary.

3 Data and methodology

3.1 Univariate unit root test in presence of level shifts

The ADF test may, however, be distorted if a potential structural break (currency crises, oil shocks, Great Crash, etc.) in the series is simply ignored (Perron, 1989). The issue was tackled in a recent assessment of both theorems using various methods (Narayan, 2006; Holmes et al., 2011; Chan et al., 2011). For instance, if real exchange rates are subjected to structural breaks, then large and permanent devaluations of the currencies during a currency crisis will bias the test toward acceptance of the unit root hypothesis. Likewise, cross-border real interest may vary for the period of monetary adjustments due to hyperinflation or currency instability. Among others, Saikkonen and Lütkepohl (2002, SL hereinafter) and Lanne et al. (2002) developed break models which add to the deterministic term shift functions of a general nonlinear form using GLS de-trending procedure. The approach is extended to estimate unknown break dates by Lanne et al. (2003). Unlike much of the literature that followed, this approach dealt with the case in which a break occurs during one period only, nonlinear break tests follow the reasoning logic that breaks occur over a number of periods and display smooth transition to a new level. Say, a level shift function, which is here denoted by a general nonlinear form $f_t(\theta)'\gamma$, is added to the deterministic term, ε_t of the data-generating process. Hence, the model of

$$g_t = \varepsilon_0 + \varepsilon_1 t + f_t(\theta)'\gamma + v_t \tag{10}$$

is shown, where θ and γ are unknown parameters or parameter vectors, whereas v_t are residual errors generated by an AR(p) process with possible unit root. In this study, we consider the shift function based on the exponential distribution function which allows for a nonlinear gradual shift to a new level, starting at time T_B,

$$f_t(\theta) = \begin{cases} 0, & t < T_B \\ 1 - \exp\{-\theta(t - T_B + 1)\}, & t \geq T_B \end{cases}. \tag{11}$$

In the shift term $f_t(\theta)'\gamma$, both θ and $\gamma$are scalar parameters; θ is to be positive real line ($\theta > 0$), whereas γ may assume any value. The asymptotic null distribution is nonstandard, and critical values are tabulated in Lanne et al. (2002). In applying this test, one has to select the AR order as well as the shift date T_B. Lanne et al. (2002) suggested that we should chose a reasonably large AR order and then pick the break date which minimized the GLS objective function used to estimate the parameters of the deterministic part.

3.2 First and second generation panel unit root tests

Recent studies have also progressed into panel tests of unit root and cointegration to uncover more evidence for PPP (e.g., Wu, 1996; Papell, 1997; O'Connell, 1998; Baharumshah et al., 2007) and RIP (e.g., Holmes, 2002; Holmes et al., 2011; Baharumshah et al., 2011). The advantages of panel tests rely on the exploitation of cross-border variations of the data and the increased sample size, which yield higher test power in the estimation.

Among the first-generation panel tests, Levin et al. (2002, LLC) proposed to modify the ADF statistics based on homogenous pooled statistics. An estimate of the coefficient α may be obtained from proxies for $\Delta g_{it}$and g_{it} which are standardized and free of autocorrelations and deterministic components, such that:

$$\Delta \tilde{g}_{it} = \alpha \tilde{g}_{it-1} + \eta_t \tag{12}$$

Where $\Delta \tilde{g}_{it} = (\Delta \overline{g}_{it}/se_i)$ and, $\tilde{g}_{it-1} = (\overline{g}_{it-1}/se_i)$, with s_i being the estimated standard error from estimating single ADF statistics of the REX and RID series. Then, LLC show that under the null, a modified t-statistics for the resulting $\hat{\alpha}$is asymptotically normally distributed:

$$t_\alpha^* = \frac{t_\alpha - (NT)S_N\hat{\alpha}^{-2}se(\hat{\alpha})\mu_{mT}^*}{\alpha_{mT}^*} \rightarrow N(0,1) \tag{13}$$

where t_α^* is the standard t-statistics for $\hat{\alpha} = 0$, $\hat{\alpha}^2$ is the estimated variance of the error term η, $se(\hat{\alpha})$ is the standard error of $\hat{\alpha}$, S_N is the mean of the ratios of the long-run standard deviation to the innovation standard deviation for each individual series, which is derived using kernel-based techniques, μ_{mT}^* and α_{mT}^* are adjustment terms for the mean and standard deviation respectively and, lastly, $T = T - (\sum_i p_i/N) - 1$.

Im et al. (2003, IPS) then proposed a popular panel test that assumed cross-sectional independence among panel units (except for common time effects), but allowed for heterogeneity in the form of individual deterministic effects (constant and/or linear time trend), and heterogeneous serial correlation structure of the error terms. The IPS testing procedure follows the mean group approach: the t-bar statistics and the group mean Lagrange Multiplier test (LM-bar). Conceptually, the IPS test is a way of combining the evidence on the unit root hypothesis from the N unit tests performed on the N cross-section units. Through Monte Carlo experiments, the average LM and the t-statistics have better finite sample properties than the homogenous panel tests. Briefly, the test statistics are given by:

$$\Gamma_{\bar{t}} = \frac{\sqrt{N}\left\{\bar{t}_{NT} - E(t_{iT}|\beta_i = 0)\right\}}{\sqrt{Var(t_{iT}|\beta_i = 0)}} \Rightarrow N(0,1) \text{ where } \bar{t}_{NT} = \frac{1}{N}\sum_{i=1}^{N} t_{iT} \tag{14}$$

and

$$\Gamma_{\overline{LM}} = \frac{\sqrt{N}\left\{\overline{LM}_{NT} - E(LM_{iT}|\beta_i = 0)\right\}}{\sqrt{Var(LM_{iT}|\beta_i = 0)}} \Rightarrow N(0,1) \text{ where } \overline{LM}_{NT} = \frac{1}{N}\sum_{i=1}^{N} LM_{iT} \tag{15}$$

such that $\bar{t}_{NT}$ is based on averaging individual ADF tests while $\overline{LM}_{NT}$ is the average across the group. Both means $E(t_{iT}|\beta_i = 0)$, $E(LM_{iT}|\beta_i = 0)$ and both variances $Var(t_{iT}|\beta_i = 0)$, $Var(LM_{iT}|\beta_i = 0)$ are obtained from the Monte Carlo simulations with i= 1,2,...,N.

The first-generation panel unit root tests (LLC, IPS) discussed earlier assume that the panel members are independent so that a Gaussian distribution can be justified by central limit arguments. In our case, this assumption can be overly restrictive because international parity conditions are expressed relative to the same benchmark as suggested in Dreger (2010) and others. In what follows, the presence of cross dependencies across panel members can lead to considerable size distortions and power loss in panel tests (Banerjee et al., 2004; Pesaran, 2007; Breitung & Pesaran, 2008). While some scholars (e.g., Bai & Ng, 2004; Moon & Perron, 2004; among others) focused on the residual factor models to capture the cross-sectional dependency, Pesaran (2006) proposed that cross-sectional means of differenced data, and cross-section mean of lagged data are good proxies for unknown factors. The idea is applied in Pesaran (2007) to proxy for unobserved factors instead of using factor estimation, which involves estimating the number of factors and then the factors themselves. Specifically, Pesaran (2007) proposed two types of estimation namely Common Correlated Effects Mean Group (CMG) and Common Correlated Effects Pooled (CEP). Individual specific regressors are filtered by taking the average across cross section to eliminate the effects of the unobserved common factors. The OLS procedure is taken to regress the dependent variable with regressor, the mean of cross-section dependent and individual specific regressor. Consider the dynamic panel model:

$$g_{it} = \alpha_i + \beta_i g_{it-1} + e_{it}, \quad i = 1,2,\ldots,N, \quad t = 1,2,\ldots,T \tag{16}$$

where α_i, β_i are parameters and differ across$i$, $g_{it-1}$is the first lagged value of REX or RID, and $e_{it}$is the random errors. In the present of cross dependency, the random errors will have the following form:

$$e_{it} = \gamma_i f_t + \omega_{it}, \quad i = 1,2,\ldots,N, \quad t = 1,2,\ldots,T \tag{17}$$

where f_t is the latent factors, γ_i are factors loadings that are probably influenced by the factors, and ω_{it} is the random errors of e_{it}. Following Pesaran (2007), two assumptions will be considered before testing for a unit root in the panel model: (a) the ω_{it} and f_t are serially uncorrelated for each i with zero mean and the variance, $0 < \sigma_i^2 < \infty$, and (b) the ω_{it}, f_t and γ_i are independently distributed for all i. Eq. (16) subtracted with g_{it-1}:

$$\Delta g_{it} = \alpha_i + b_i g_{it-1} + \gamma_i f_t + \omega_{it}, \quad i = 1,2,\ldots,N,\ t = 1,2,\ldots,T \tag{18}$$

where $\Delta g_{it} = g_{it} - g_{it-1}$ and $b_i = \beta_i - 1$. The OLS estimate for b_i is based on the regression:

$$\Delta g_{it} = \alpha_i + b_i g_{it-1} + c_i \Delta \overline{g}_t + d_i \overline{g}_{t-1} + \omega_{it}, \quad i = 1,2,\ldots,N,\ t = 1,2,\ldots,T \tag{19}$$

Under the null the model is unit root ($b_i = 0$ for all i) against stationary ($b_i < 0$ for some i), the test statistics, $t = \frac{\sqrt{TN}(\overline{b} - b)}{\sqrt{\sum_{i=1}^{N} Var(b_i)}} \xrightarrow{d} N(0,1)$ with $t = \frac{\sqrt{T}(\hat{b}_i - b)}{\sqrt{Var(b_i)}} \xrightarrow{d} N(0,1)$ where $b_i = \left(g_{i,-1}^T \overline{M} g_{i,-1}^T\right)^{-1} \left(g_{i,-1}^T \overline{M} \Delta g_i\right)$, $var(b_i) = \hat{\sigma}_i^2 \left[g_{i,-1}^T \overline{M} g_{i,-1}^T \big/ T\right]^{-1}$, $\hat{\sigma}_i^2 = \frac{(\Delta g_i - g_{i,-1}\hat{b}_i)^T \overline{M}((\Delta g_i - g_{i,-1}\hat{b}_i)}{T-4}$ and, the properties of $\overline{b} = \sum_{i=1}^{N} b_i/N$, $\frac{\sqrt{TN}(\overline{b} - b)}{\sqrt{\sum_{i=1}^{N} Var(b_i)}} \xrightarrow{d} N(0,1)$.

However, the properties of CMG is $\frac{\sqrt{N}(\hat{\beta}_{CMG} - \beta)}{\sqrt{\sum_{CMG}}} \rightarrow N(0,1)$ where $\hat{\beta}_{CMG} = \frac{\sum_{i=1}^{N} \hat{\beta}_i}{N}$ and $\hat{\sum}_{CMG} = \frac{\sum_{i=1}^{N} (\hat{\beta}_i - \hat{\beta}_{CMG})(\hat{\beta}_i - \hat{\beta}_{CMG})^T}{N-1}$. The $\hat{\beta}_i$ for $i = 1,2,\ldots,N$ are obtained by computing $\hat{\beta}_i = (X_i^T \overline{M} X_i)^{-1} X_i^T \overline{M} g_i$ and $\overline{M}$ is defined as $\overline{M} = I_t - \overline{H}(\overline{H}^T\overline{H})^{-1}\overline{H}^T$ with $\overline{H} = (D, \overline{g}_t, \overline{g}_{t-1})$. I_t is a unit matrix of order $T \times T$ and $\overline{H}$ is the combinations of dummy variables, and average of cross section of the first difference of g_{it} and its g_{it-1}. The properties of CEP are $\frac{\sqrt{N}(\hat{\beta}_{CEP} - \beta)}{\sqrt{\sum_{CEP}}} \rightarrow N(0,1)$ where $\hat{\beta}_{CEP} = (\sum_{i=1}^{N} X_i^T\overline{M}X_i)^{-1}(\sum_{i=1}^{N} X_i^T\overline{M}gX_i^T)$ and $\hat{\sum}_{CEP} = \hat{\psi}^{-1}\hat{V}\hat{\psi}^{-1}$. The $\hat{\psi} = \frac{\sum_{i=1}^{N} X_i^T\overline{M}X_i}{NT}$ and $\hat{V} = \frac{\sum_{i=1}^{N} (X_i^T\overline{M}X_i)(\hat{\beta}_i - \hat{\beta}_{CMG})(\hat{\beta}_i - \hat{\beta}_{CMG})^T(X_i^T\overline{M}X_i)^T}{(N-1)T^2}$.

3.3 Data description

Various tests outlined in the previous section are applied to a sample of monthly observations for China and her 13 major trading partners in the Asia Pacific. Except for India, all trading partners are APEC members, including the economic giants (United States, Japan), the Oceania economies (Australia, New Zealand), the developed NIE-4 (Hong Kong SAR, Singapore, South Korea, Taiwan) and the developing ASEAN-4 (Indonesia, Malaysia, Philippines, Thailand). Our joint investigation of PPP and RIP involves the bilateral real exchange rates (REX) and real interest rate differentials (RID) of China–APEC. The construction of 13 China-denominated REX is based on Equation (2), which consists of nominal yuan-based exchanges rates, individual APEC CPI as the domestic price and the China CPI as the foreign price. As for RID, China is again considered as a foreign country (numeraire) and we follow the Fisher equation to construct the real interest rate by subtracting the expected inflation from the nominal interest rate. Since ex post RIP implies ex ante RIP, actual inflation is taken as proxy for expected inflation. The nominal interest rates used in the study are generally non-control and medium-term lending rates due to the fact that long-term interest rates, such as government bond yields are incomplete or unavailable for most of these Asian countries. To uphold the consistency and reliability of the data, we cross-check with various data sources, namely Datastream, International Financial Statistics of IMF and Central Banks of the respective economies.

4 Results and discussion

4.1 Empirical discussion of endogenous breaks and unit root tests

It is widely recognized that classical unit root tests might be biased by the presence of structural breaks and non-linearities in the deterministic

Table 5.1 Univariate unit root test with endogenous break

	REX-CHINA			RID-CHINA		
	k	**Break**	**SL test**	*k*	**Break**	**SL test**
US	7	1993M6	−2.515	3	1988M8	−2.920[b]
Japan	1	1993M6	−1.764	5	1988M8	−2.951[b]
India	4	1993M6	−2.707[a]	5	1998M11	−2.998[b]
Australia	1	1993M7	−1.984	3	1990M1	−2.747[a]
New Zealand	7	1993M6	−2.614[a]	2	1989M8	−3.191[b]
Hong Kong	1	1993M6	−2.300	1	1988M8	−2.880[b]
Taiwan	2	1993M7	−2.762[a]	6	1989M9	−3.284[b]
South Korea	2	1997M12	−2.062	2	1988M10	−2.312
Singapore	5	1993M6	−1.480	2	1992M4	−2.906[b]
Indonesia	6	1998M1	−2.648[a]	4	1999M2	−2.963[b]
Malaysia	7	1993M6	−2.495	5	1988M8	−3.012[b]
Philippines	1	1993M6	−1.562	2	1991M11	−3.221[b]
Thailand	5	1993M6	−1.647	3	1989M8	−2.963[b]

Critical values

1%[c]	5%[b]	10%[a]
−3.48	−2.88	−2.58

Notes: [(a)], [(b)] and [(c)] denote for the significant level at 10%, 5% and 1% respectively. Critical values are obtained from Lanne et al. (2002).

components. An alternative approach that captures the structural breaks with a smoother functional form for the transition period could be more informative. For this purpose, we apply the SL test with the optimal lag length (k) being determined by the standard Schwarz Information Criterion (SIC). As can be seen in Table 5.1, all the exponential shift parameters appear to be highly significant to capture the endogenous shift dates. For REX, endogenous break(s) occur mainly in 1993, except for two where the break date is detected in 1997/98. The first break date is due to the major downward adjustment (appreciation) of Chinese yuan in 1993/94 against the USD and other major currencies. The second break date coincides with the Asian financial turmoil that witnessed a sharp fall of the East Asian currencies. As can be seen in the table, only four out of 13 yuan-based REX (Taiwan, Indonesia, India and New Zealand) rejected the unit root null hypothesis at the indicated significant levels. Results based on the SL tests indicate the absence of mean reversion behaviors even when graduate shifts are allowed in the model. If this is true, then for any shocks on the REX series, deviations will be too persistent to witness necessary adjustment to the equilibrium level, and the PPP puzzle remains unsolved. Such a finding is inconsistent with the recent USD- and Japanese yen-based PPP studies, but tends to support the argument that the Chinese yuan is misaligned and inconsistent with the PPP rules.

As for RIDs, most breaks occurred in 1988 when China experienced high inflation that resulted in an imbalance rate of real interest. Also, some adjustments of interest rates were found in 1998/99 among the crisis-affected nations in order to defend their currencies and to tackle stagflation (e.g., Indonesia). Unlike the results from the PPP presented above, most China-denominated RID (except South Korea) have exhibited mean reversion behavior, and they lend support for RIP. Nevertheless, the rejection of the univariate unit root alone is necessary but is neither sufficient to gauge the degree of mean reversion of the APEC–China series as a group nor to identify the potential changes in the process of integration due to market and policy reforms over time. Next, we proceed with the panel tests that utilize both cross-sectional and time series information to allow us to validate the respective PPP and RIP condition using sub-sample analysis.

Information about the endogenous break dates has been useful to construct our sub-samples in panels. Considering the frequency of break dates, we separate the study periods into 1987–93, 1994–2007, 1987–97, 1998–2007 and 1987–2007. However, we are unable to consider the 1988 break because the sample size is too short and inappropriate for econometric estimation. To improve the robustness of our findings, homogenous and heterogeneous panel tests are both conducted. For the early sub-periods of 1987–93 and 1987–97, the panel results of REX support the SL findings reported earlier, which are generally against the PPP theory. The finding indicates the inflexibility of exchange rate since deviations from equilibrium rate are permanent. This is indeed the period when the Chinese yuan practiced multiple rates and the official rates were de facto crawling band around USD (+/– 2 per cent) with the premium peaks at 124 per cent on June 1991. Even when the full sample size is considered, null hypothesis of unit root fail to be rejected and no evidence of mean reversion is captured. The results differ, and improve drastically when the sub-sample of post-liberalization (1994–2007) and post-crisis (1998–2007) are considered. Rejections of unit roots are highly significant as reported by LLC and IPS tests, implying that the deviations of the group of yuan-based REX are now temporal, and exchange rates are more responsive to changes in price ratios. These are mainly attributed to the unification of China's two main currency rates in 1994 and the deregulation on foreign invested enterprises in exchanging funds freely at selected banks without approval from the State Administration for Exchange Control (SAEC) in 1996. These market practices have driven the renminbi (RMB) a step further towards the full convertibility (see Zhang, 1999). The adjustment of undervalued renminbi since 2005 may also allow for some extent of market completeness by PPP rules. But, overall, the liberalization process is still insufficient to display full support for PPP, and further flexibility in the exchange rate regime is needed.

A somewhat comparable trend of mean reversion behavior is found when the APEC–China real interest differentials (RID) are taken as a group. For instance, LLC has failed to reject the null hypothesis of common unit root for two early sub-samples but did highly reject for two late sub-samples. Similar but not identical, the IPS heterogeneous panel test detected weak rejection of individual unit roots for the early period sub-samples, but strong rejection of unit roots for late period sub-samples. Putting them together, the supports for RIP are generally weaker during the pre-liberalization era but evidently improved for the post-liberalization period, before and after the crisis (Table 5.2). In most cases, both the univariate and panel tests of unit root seem more supportive of RIP rather than PPP for China vis-à-vis Asia-Pacific economies.

Nevertheless, a final conclusion is yet to be drawn at this stage.[5] There are still questions as to whether the sub-sample analysis bias toward unit root null or alternative hypothesis when the cross sectional dependency is present in the series. The Lagrange Multiplier of Bruesch and

Table 5.2 First generation panel unit root tests

	LLC-Homogeneous panel test		IPS-Heterogeneous panel test	
	REX-CHINA	RID-CHINA	REX-CHINA	RID-CHINA
1987M1–1993M12	2.887	−0.861	1.158	−1.595[a]
	(0.998)	(0.195)	(0.876)	(0.055)
1987M1–1997M12	1.428	−0.155	2.476	−2.465[b]
	(0.923)	(0.438)	(0.993)	(0.007)
1987M1–2007M1	−0.537	−2.065[b]	−0.376	−2.962[c]
	(0.296)	(0.020)	(0.354)	(0.002)
1994M1–2007M1	−6.616[c]	−2.727[c]	−5.056[c]	−2.367[c]
	(0.000)	(0.003)	(0.000)	(0.009)
1998M1–2007M1	−2.040[b]	−2.676[c]	−2.439[c]	−4.804[c]
	(0.021)	(0.004)	(0.007)	(0.00)

Note: (a), (b) and (c) denote for the significant level at 10%, 5% and 1% respectively.

Pagan's (1980) and Pesaran's (2007) cross-dependency tests are, by this means, deployed for additional analysis. The result is reported in Table 5.3. Columns 2 and 7 show the respective sample pair-wise correlation of the residuals ($|\hat{\rho}_{ij}|$) for REX-China and RID-China. CD_{lm} refers to the Lagrange Multiplier of Bruesch and Pagan, and PCD refers to Pesaran's cross-sectional dependence tests. Under the null of no cross dependency, both of the tests overwhelmingly reject the null in favor of at least one cross-sectional dependence at the 5 per cent significance level in all the sub-samples for REX and RID. These have prompted us to utilize the Pesaran's CMG and CEP panel unit root tests to account for cross-sectional dependence for the sub-sample panel. As shown in Columns 5 and 10 for CMG, and Columns 6 and 11 for CEP, both the RIP and PPP hold significantly in all but one case. We found the REX is nonstationary and against the PPP over the 1987M1–1997M12. Our findings are consistent with Narayan (2006) who found stationarity with breaks of India's bilateral exchange rate vis-a-vis 15 out of 16 of its major trading partners.

The empirical evidence, overall, coincides with the financial liberalization process and the gradual ruling out of restrictions on capital movements in APEC, including China. In June 1996 the ceiling rates of inter-bank loans were removed, and later then the interest rates expanded twice in China in 1998 to 1999, while state-owned financial institutions were allowed to be commercialized. By September 2000 the controls on large, fixed deposits and foreign currency loans were lifted, and the China Banking Association took over the responsibility of interest rates' decisions on small foreign currency deposits. Because China is taken as the base country, support for RIP would confirm the improved influence of China in the regional capital markets since the 1990s. Future fluctuations of APEC real interest rates possibly can be determined or forecast using the Chinese real rates as part of the information set. In addition, the results do indicate the benefits of using panel tests in exploiting the cross cross-country variations of the data, thus yielding higher test power in the sub-sample and also in the whole sample estimation over time.

4.2 Half-life estimation and confidence intervals

To obtain insight into the degree of mean reversion of REX and RID as further justification of PPP and RIP, the estimation of half-life for series that are found stationary is essential. But, since the point estimates of half-life may provide an incomplete picture of the speed of convergence

Table 5.3 Second generation panel unit root tests

	REX-CHINA					RID-CHINA				
	$\lvert\hat{\rho}_{ij}\rvert$	CD_{lm}	PCD	CMG	CEP	$\lvert\hat{\rho}_{ij}\rvert$	CD_{lm}	PCD	CMG	CEP
1987M1–1993M12	0.880	5044.471[c]	70.782[c]	−4.394[c]	−1.709[b]	0.787	4033.751[c]	62.960[c]	−6.196[c]	−4.664[c]
		(0.000)	(0.000)	(0.000)	(0.044)		(0.000)	(0.000)	(0.000)	(0.000)
1987M1–1997M12	0.789	6371.780[c]	79.403[c]	0.094	−1.011	0.782	6308.004[c]	78.722[c]	−4.165[c]	−6.165[c]
		(0.000)	(0.000)	(0.462)	(0.156)		(0.000)	(0.000)	(0.000)	(0.000)
1987M1–2007M1	0.693	9239.572[c]	94.608[c]	−6.126[c]	−3.702[c]	0.668	8974.175[c]	91.233[c]	−6.005[c]	−2.699[c]
		(0.000)	(0.000)	(0.000)	(0.000)		(0.000)	(0.000)	(0.000)	(0.003)
1994M1–2007M1	0.525	3589.059[c]	57.729[c]	−4.634[c]	−2.882[c]	0.566	4482.899[c]	62.213[c]	−6.515[c]	−3.221[c]
		(0.000)	(0.000)	(0.000)	(0.002)		(0.000)	(0.000)	(0.000)	(0.001)
1998M1–2007M1	0.541	2614.405[c]	49.426[c]	−5.150[c]	−3.770[c]	0.478	2330.419[c]	43.504[c]	−6.706[c]	−10.689[c]
		(0.000)	(0.000)	(0.000)	(0.000)		(0.000)	(0.000)	(0.000)	(0.000)

Notes:
(1) [(b)] and [(c)] denote significant at 5% and 1% significant levels, respectively.

(2) $\left|\hat{\rho}_{ij}\right|$ denotes the sample wise correlation of the residual denoted as $\hat{\rho}_{ij} = \hat{\rho}_{jj} = \sum_{t=1}^{T} \hat{e}_{it}\hat{e}_{jt} \Big/ \left(\sum_{t=1}^{T} \hat{e}_{it}^2\right)^{1/2} \left(\sum_{t=1}^{T} \hat{e}_{jtt}^2\right)^{1/2}$.

(3) Reject H_0 when $CD_{lm} = T \sum_{i=1}^{N-1} \sum_{j=i+1}^{N} \hat{\rho}_{ij} > \chi^2_{(N(N-1)/2)} = 99.62$ and $PCD = \sqrt{2T/N(N-1)} \sum_{i=1}^{N-1} \sum_{j=i+1}^{N} \hat{\rho}_{ij} > N(0,1) = 1.96$.

towards the equilibrium rates in the long run, the corresponding confidence intervals are also computed. Such practice offers better indications of the uncertainty around the estimates of half-life. For univariate series, this study estimates the half-life based on the AR (ρ) method and the correction factor model proposed by Rossi (2005). For panel series with sub-samples, only the AR (ρ) method is employed.

We first select four REX series that support PPP for estimation and 16–59 months (1.3–4.9 years) of half-life is reported by the classical method (Table 5.4). All except Taiwan have reported a slightly shorter half-life when the Rossi method is applied, and they displayed moderate speed of adjustments to the equilibrium PPP rate. In the panel analysis with

Table 5.4 Univariate half-life estimations

	REX-CHINA		RID-CHINA	
	HL-AR(ρ) [95%CI]	**Rossi (2005) [95%CI]**	**HL-AR(ρ) [95%CI]**	**Rossi (2005) [95%CI]**
US	–	–	27.33 [9.28, 45.38]	8.08 [0, 26.13]
Japan	–	–	24.85 [8.43, 41.26]	7.24 [0, 23.65]
India	15.87 [3.91, 27.84]	14.97 [3.01, 26.94]	19.16 [5.43, 32.90]	8.52 [0, 22.25]
Australia	–	–	28.05 [6.19, 49.91]	11.29 [0, 33.15]
New Zealand	26.13 [1.29, 50.96]	16.59 [0, 41.43]	25.31 [9.32, 41.31]	7.96 [0, 23.96]
Hong Kong	–	–	21.13 [5.49, 36.77]	11.27 [0, 26.91]
Taiwan	58.85 [0, 160.04]	61.18 [0, 162.38]	15.32 [5.39, 25.25]	6.20 [0, 16.14]
South Korea	–	–	–	–
Singapore	–	–	24.38 [8.23, 40.54]	8.53 [0, 24.69]
Indonesia	19.67 [2.92, 36.42]	12.89 [0, 29.64]	13.98 [7.55, 20.42]	3.06 [0, 9.50]
Malaysia	–	–	24.48 [7.98, 40.98]	7.50 [0, 24.00]
Philippines	–	–	17.37 [5.57, 29.17]	8.92 [0, 20.71]
Thailand	–	–	25.52 [7.56, 43.48]	9.26 [0, 27.22]

Note: Half-life is computed only for stationary series confirmed by SL test.

Table 5.5 Panel half-life estimations

	REX-CHINA		RID-CHINA	
	N	HL-AR(ρ) [95%CI]	N	HL-AR(ρ) [95%CI]
1987M1–1993M12	–	–	–	–
1987M1–1997M12	–	–	–	–
1987M1–2007M1	–	–	3108	30.96 [23.31, 38.61]
1994M1–2007M1	2041	18.10 [14.41, 21.80]	2041	27.41 [20.07, 34.75]
1998M1–2007M1	1417	23.98 [14.04, 33.92]	1417	7.60 [5.87, 9.33]

Notes: N represents the number of observations utilized in the panel analysis. Half-life is computed based on the AR (ρ) methodology only for stationary series confirmed by both LLC and IPS tests.

all APEC–13 countries pooled as a group, the post-liberalization and post-crisis period recorded a half-life of around 18–24 months (1.5–2 years). The standard errors are considered minimal and contribute to less-widened, but stable, confidence intervals. There are signs that deviations of REX exhibit somewhat faster adjustments back to the long-run PPP since 1994.

On the other hand, supports for RIP as indications of financial integration are somewhat greater than supports for PPP. Univariate series show, on average, 14–28 months (1.2–2.3 years) of half-life. Then again, the scale of half-life drops to about 3–11.3 months under the Rossi estimation. For panel analysis, full sample (1987–2007) half-life is approximately 31 months. As for the post-liberalization, with (1998–2007) and without the crisis (1994–2007), the half-lives are recorded at 8 and 27 months respectively. Consistent with the panel results, the shortened half-life bounded with more stable confidence intervals has provided solid evidence in support for the RIP among APEC–China. The signs of decreasing deviations from RIP are evident and are in line with the increased regional financial integration prompted by financial liberalization, technological breakthroughs and growth in the volume of trade in recent years (Baharumshah et al., 2011).

All-in-all, we find that the speed of mean reversion is high, indicating that RIDs tend to be short-lived. Allowing for the possibility of structural breaks, we find even shorter-lived deviation from equilibrium. This evidence is supportive of a high degree of market integration, which is consistent with financial liberalization and the emergence of global financial markets. The varying speed of the adjustments to long-run PPP and RIP across the countries reviewed may reflect China's position in pursuing liberalization in good and capital markets at multi-speed. The rapid growth in regional capital flows has contributed to cross-border investments and optimal allocation of resources and, in some cases, has facilitated the movement towards financial convergence and closer monetary cooperation. Conservative policies directed at increasing domestic savings to increase the rate of capital formation and, hence, productivity growth, are no longer the sole option in open economy macroeconomics. Instead, cross-border capital flows raise the chances of risk-sharing and portfolio diversification and, thus, enable countries in the Asia-Pacific-region to smooth out consumption.

5 Conclusion and policy implications

This paper conducts a joint investigation of two international parities, namely the PPP and RIP, to assess the extent of goods and capital market integration between China and her 13 trading partners in the Asia-Pacific region. Endogenous and exponential breaks are confirmed for the real exchange and real interest differential series, which mostly occur in 1988, 1993/94 and 1997/98. The break dates coincide with the major events in the region. Our major findings are threefold. First, we observe that RIP holds better than PPP, suggesting the greater financial integration than trade integration among APEC–China. Second, both parities tend to hold better as one moves to recent years. Third, China and APEC have improved the ability to absorb regional shocks, as indicated by the shortened half-life reported over time, especially when the post-Asia crisis era is included.

Putting together, the greater integration among APEC–China implies the better equalization of the marginal utility of home and foreign currency (renminbi) which, in turn, allows for better risk sharing. The integration process is attributed to not only the liberalization process among the APEC economies, but also to Chinese trade policy and the regional commitment for the ASEAN+3+2+1 cooperation. Besides, the prospect of WTO membership is, indeed, instrumental for China to move towards liberalizing its external sectors and capital accounts. This coincides with our finding of mean reversion behavior in the China-based real interest differentials, which implies the increased influence of Chinese investments in the regional capital market. Moreover, the shorter half-lives reported over time encourage us to foresee a greater feasibility towards regional financial development and regional currency arrangements that anchored by China. By taking cooperative action, China and APEC members would be in a better position to resist the adverse consequences of sudden and sizeable movements in global capital and the potentially deleterious effects that may decelerate the growth and development of domestic economies. After all, monetary and exchange-rate policy cooperation in East Asia would enable this region to exert an important influence upon the future evolution of the global trade and financial system.

It is important to note, however, that RIP holding better than PPP may also raise some concerns on the sequencing issue of economic integration. PPP does not hold fully and the yuan-denominated currencies are still not highly competent according to PPP rules. China's market's size and its role as a production hub are yet insufficient to attract full support for PPP as an indication of perfect trade integration among APEC–China. Or, in other words, regional trade competition is as yet insufficient to eliminate price arbitrage to reflect the exchange value of the Chinese yuan. While the more liberalized exchange rate regimes among APEC members may have facilitated better integration, the prolonged undervaluation of the renminbi, has also exerted some drawbacks in the PPP theorem, especially during the 1980s–90s. Further flexibility in the Chinese exchange rate regime is expected.

Notes

1. More than a hundred times the total trade figure of US$20.6 billion in 1978.
2. The trade figure of selected APEC accounted, respectively, for 61 per cent and 59 per cent of Chinese total exports and imports in 2006. These selected APEC include the United States, Australia, New Zealand, Taiwan, South Korea, Singapore, Indonesia, Malaysia, the Philippines and Thailand.
3. China has repeatedly devalued its currency as a means of trade expansion and external competitiveness gains in the 1980s and the early 1990s. In 1994, 1996 and 2005, unification of multiple rates and liberalization of exchange rates drove the RMB a step further toward the full convertibility. Likewise, the portion of foreign trade under direct administrative control has been substantially reduced while more subject to market forces.
4. Support for PPP would imply the goods market integration attributed to price convergence and apposite alignment of exchange rate, or otherwise. Similarly, acceptance of the RIP will uphold the regional financial integration among China–APEC, while rejection of RIP may imply a greater degree of monetary autonomy.
5. The outcome of the first-generation panel tests is sensitive to the selection of series included in the group, as the null hypothesis of a common unit root (homogenous) may be rejected even if only one of the series is stationary. As a result, several studies proceed with the heterogeneous panel tests (allowed for cross-sectional independence) with uncorrelated errors or the second generation panel tests that account for cross-section correlation of errors (see Breitung & Pesaran, 2008).

References

Armstrong, S. (2011) *China's participation in the Trans–Pacific Partnership*, Available at http://www.eastasiaforum.org/2011/12/11/china-participation-in-the-trans-pacific-partnership/#more-23335.

Baharumshah, A. Z., Aggarwal, R. and Chan, T. -H. (2007) 'East Asian Real Exchange Rates and PPP: New Evidence from Panel-Data Tests', *Global Economic Review*, 36(2), 103–19.

Baharumshah, A. Z., Chan, T. -H., Masih, M. and Evan L. (2011) 'Financial Integration of East Asian Economies: Evidence from Real Interest Parity', *Applied Economics*, 43(16), 1979–90.

Bai, J. and Ng, S. (2004) 'A PANIC Attack on Unit Roots and Cointegration', *Econometrica*, 72, 1127–77.

Banerjee, A. Marcellino, M. and Osbat, C. (2004) 'Some Cautious as to the Use of Panel Methods for Integrated Series in Macroeconomic Data', *Econometrica Journal*, 7, 322–40.

Breitung, J. and Pesaran, M. H. (2008) 'Chapter 9: Unit Roots and Cointegration in Panels', in L. Matyas and P. Sevestre (Eds) *The Econometrics of Panel Data: Fundamentals and Recent Developments in Theory and Practice*, 3rd edn, 279–322 (Springer-Verlag: Berlin Heidelberg).

Bruesch, T. S. and Pagan, A. R. (1980) 'The Lagrange Multiplier Test and its Applications to Model-specification in Econometrics', *Review of Economic Studies*,47(1), 239–53.

Cavoli, T., Rajan, R. S. and Siregar, R. (2004) 'A Survey of Financial Integration in East Asia: How Far? How Much Further to Go?' *CIES Discussion Paper No. 0401*, Australia: University of Adelaide.

Chan, T. -H., Hooy, C. W. and Baharumshah, A. Z. (2012) 'A Structural VARX Modelling of International Parities between China and Japan in the Liberalization Era', *Economics Bulletin*, 32(1), 730–36.

Chan, T. -H., Chong, L. L. and Hooy, C. W. (2011) 'Japan–US Real Exchange Rates Behavior: Evidence from Linear and Non-Linear Endogenous Break(S) Tests', *Asian Academy of Management Journal of Accounting and Finance*, 7(1), 95–109.

Cheung, Y. -W., Chinn, M. D. and Fujii, E. (2003) 'China, Hong Kong and Taiwan: A Quantitative Assessment of Real and Financial Integration', *China Economic Review*, 1(3), 281–303.

Cheung, Y. W., Chinn, M. D. and Fujii, E. (2005) 'Dimensions of Financial Integration in Greater China: Money Markets, Banks and Policy Effects', *International Journal of Finance and Economics*, 10, 1–16.

Coudert, V. and Couharde, C. (2007) 'Real Equilibrium Exchange Rate in China: Is the Renminbi Undervalued?' *Journal of Asian Economics*, 18(4), 568–94.

Cumby, R. E. and Obstfeld, M. (1984) 'International Interest Rate and Price Level Linkages under Flexible Exchange Rates: A Review of Recent Developments', in J. Bilson and R. Marston (Eds) *Exchange Rates: Theory and Practice* (Chicago: University of Chicago Press).

Dreger, G. (2010) 'Does the Nominal Exchange Rate Regime Affect the Real Interest Rate Parity Condition?' *The North American Journal of Economics and Finance*, 21(3), 274–85.

Edison, H. J. (1985) 'Purchasing Power Parity: A Quantitative Reassessment of the 1920s Experience', *Journal of International Money and Finance*, 4, 361–72.

Edison, H. J. and Pauls, B. D. (1993) 'A Re-assessment of the Relationship between Real Exchange Rates and Real Interest Rates: 1974–1990', *Journal of Monetary Economics*, 31, 165–87.

Finke, M. and Rahn, J. (2005) 'Just How Undervalued is the Chinese Renminbi?' *World Economy*, 28, 465–631.

Frankel, J. A. (1986) 'International Capital Mobility and Crowding Out in the US Economy: Imperfect Integration of Financial Markets or Goods Markets?' in R.W. Hafer (Ed.) *How Open is the US Economy*? 33–67 (Lexington: Lexington Books).

Frankel, J. and MacArthur, A. (1988) 'Political vs. Currency Premia in International Real Interest Differentials: A Study of Forward Rates for 24 Countries', *European Economic Review*, 32 1083–121.

Gregory, R. P. and Shelley, G. (2011) 'Purchasing Power Parity and the Chinese Yuan', *Economics Bulletin*, 31(2), 1247–55.

Holmes, M. J. (2002) 'Does Long-Run Real Interest Rate Parity Hold Among EU Countries? Some New Panel Data Evidence', *Quarterly Review of Economic and Finance*, 42, 733–46.

Holmes, M. J., Otero, J. and Panagiotidis, T. (2011) 'Real Interest Parity: A Note on Asian Countries Using Panel Stationarity Test', *Working Paper*, 1117, Kocc University-Tüsiad Economic Research Forum.

Im, K. S., Pesaran, M. H. and Shin, Y. (2003) 'Testing for Unit Roots in Heterogeneous Panels', *Journal of Econometrics*, 115, 53–74.

Lanne, M., Saikkonen, P. and Lütkepohl, H. (2002) 'Comparison of Unit Root Tests for Time Series with Level Shifts', *Journal of Time Series Analysis*, 23, 667–85.

Lanne, M., Saikkonen, P. and Lütkepohl, H. (2003) 'Test Procedures for Unit Roots in Time Series with Level Shifts at Unknown Time', *Oxford Bulletin of Economics and Statistics*, 65, 91–115.

Laurenceson, J. (2003) 'Economic Integration between China and the ASEAN–5', *ASEAN Economic Bulletin*, 20, 103–11

Levin, A., Lin, C. F. and Chu, C. (2002) 'Unit Root Tests in Panel Data: Asymptotic and Finite-Sample Properties', *Journal of Econometrics*, 108, 1–24.

Mark, N. C. (1990) 'Real and Nominal Exchange Rates in the Long Run: An Empirical Investigation', *Journal of International Economics*, 28, 115–36.

Meese, R. A. and Rogoff, K. (1988) 'Was it real? The Exchange Rate-Interest Differential Relation Over the Modern Floating-Rate Period', *Journal of Finance*, 14(4), 933–48.

Mishkin, F. S. (1984) 'Are Real Interest Rates Equal Across Countries? An Empirical Investigation of International Parity Conditions', *The Journal of Finance*, 39, 1345–57.

Moon, H. R. and Perron, B. (2004) 'Testing for a Unit Root in Panels with Dynamic Factors', *Journal of Econometrics*, 122, 81–126.

Narayan, P. K. (2006) 'Are Bilateral Real Exchange Rates Stationary? Evidence from Lagrange Multiplier Unit Root Tests for India', *Applied Economics*, 38, 63–70.

O'Connell, P. (1998) 'The Overvaluation of Purchasing Power Parity', *Journal of International Economics*, 44, 1–19.

Papell, D. H. (1997) 'Searching for Stationarity: Purchasing Power Parity under the Current Float', *Journal of International Economics*, 43, 313–32.

Perron, P. (1989) 'The Great Crash, the Oils Price Shock, and the Unit Root Hypothesis', *Econometrica*, 57, 1361–401.

Pesaran, M. H. (2006) 'Estimation and Inference in Large Heterogeneous Panels with Cross Section Dependence', *Econometrica*, 74, 967–1012.

Pesaran, M. H. (2007) 'A Simple Panel Unit Root Test in the Presence of Cross-Section Dependence', *Journal of Applied Econometrics*, 22, 265–312.

Rogoff, K. (1996) 'The Purchasing Power Parity Puzzle', *Journal of Economic Literature*, 34, 647–68.

Rossi, B. (2005) 'Confidence Intervals for Half-Life Deviations from Purchasing Power Parity', *Journal of Business and Economic Statistics*, 23, 432–42.

Saikkonen, P. and Lütkepohl, H. (2002) 'Testing for a Unit Root in a Time Series with a Level Shift at Unknown Time', *Econometric Theory*, 18, 313–48.

Taylor, A. M. and Taylor, M. P. (2004) 'The Purchasing Power Parity Debate', *NBER Working Paper No. 10607*.

Wu, Y. (1996) 'Are Real Exchange Rates Nonstationary? Evidence form a Panel-Data Test', *Journal of Money, Credit and Banking*, 28, 54–63.

Yu, W. J. (2011) 'China and East Asian Regionalism', *European Law Journal*, 17(5), 611–29.

Zhang, Z. (1999) 'Foreign Exchange Rate Reform, the Balance of Trade and Economic Growth: An Empirical Analysis For China', *Journal Of Economic Development*, 24(2), 143–62.

6
Budget Deficits and Current Account Balances

Ahmad Zubaidi Baharumshah, Siew-Voon Soon and Hamizun Ismail

1 Introduction

Over the past three decades, the twin deficits hypothesis (TDH) – that budget deficit has a direct effect on current account deficit – has been a topic of interest in the empirical literature (see, for example, Bahmani-Oskooee, 1995; Khalid & Guan, 1999; Mohammadi, 2004; Bagnai, 2006; Salvatore, 2006; Bartolini & Lahiri, 2006; Baharumshah & Lau, 2007; Ito, 2009; Daly & Siddiki, 2009). The causal link between public budget deficit and current account balance has been analyzed extensively in the recent literature, largely because of its implications for long-term economic progress. For small, open economies that depend heavily on foreign capital, an adverse change in foreign investors' behavior may trigger a series of sharp and disorderly adjustments of external imbalances that, in turn, have serious consequences on the economy (see, for example, Milesi-Ferretti & Razin, 1998; Chinn & Prasad, 2003). In an influential paper, Rodrik (1999) warned: 'Openness to capital inflows can be especially dangerous if appropriate controls, regulatory apparatus and macroeconomic frameworks are not in place.' (p. 30).[1] From a theoretical viewpoint, fiscal expansion could worsen the current account balance and the appreciation of the real exchange rate (Salvatore, 2006).[2] These imbalances may hinder economic growth and undermine a nation's wealth creation. From a policy perspective, it is important to determine whether budget deficit can influence current account in a predictable manner. If it is known that rising current account deficits indeed occur due to escalating budget deficits, then the external balance cannot be remedied unless other policies that address government budget deficits are first put into place. In other words, if TDH is valid, a government can improve the country's current account through fiscal contraction and vice versa. Therefore, policy recommendations will vary according to the type of relationship between the two variables; this is a relevant topic for emerging Asian economies.

The primary purpose of this chapter is to empirically assess the effects of budget balance and investment on current account balance in 13 Asian countries, including the fast-growing economies of China and India. Here, the focus is on data from Asian countries with a variety of environments (e.g., exchange rate regime), for which little empirical evidence exists. The analysis was conducted using cointegration analysis and the Granger non-causality test, including the method introduced by Gregory and Hansen (1996) and the panel cointegration method recently developed by Westerlund and Edgerton (2008), which is specifically designed to handle endogenous breaks in underlying relationships. Structural breaks are allowed in economic models because countries are often affected by exogenous shocks, regime changes or other economic events. Given the time span of the data being studied (1980–2009), we can expect to see some structural breaks in the relationship due to shifts in exchange rates and in underlying macroeconomic policies. This study contributes to the current literature in several ways. First, we consider a model that includes both budget balance and investment as determinants of the current account; the majority of the empirical studies to date emphasize either one of these two factors. Second, we apply time series and up-to-date panel techniques to test for cointegration to address the issue of structural breaks in analyzing the relationship between current account balance and budget balance. We also apply the panel cointegration methods, including the one recently developed by Westerlund and Edgerton (2008), which is designed to endogenously determine break dates in the cointegrating relationship. In contrast to earlier studies, we investigate the dynamic link between variables using the Granger non-causality method introduced by Toda and Yamamoto (1995) to specifically overcome some of the statistical limitations associated with standard unit roots and cointegration tests. By applying the various new tools developed in the past few years, we hope that this study will produce robust results on the fiscal imbalance of the countries under review. The inclusion of India and China in our sample that extends over the period of the global imbalances is to fill the current gaps in the literature on the host subject.

For many Asian countries, both budget balance and current account have experienced dramatic changes in direction following the financial crisis of the late 1990s. Malaysia, for instance, experienced budget surpluses averaging 1.27 per cent of gross domestic product (GDP) per year from 1993–97, which were accompanied by current account balance averaging 6.35 per cent of GDP per year. The situation, however, was reversed following the sharp depreciation of the Malaysian ringgit in late 1997, and the economy recorded an overall fiscal deficit between 1998 and 2009 (averaging 3.59 per cent per year), while its current account recorded successive surpluses (averaging 13.25 per cent per year). In Indonesia, another Association of Southern Asian Nations (ASEAN) member country, fiscal and current account balances have moved in the opposite directions since the outbreak of the 1997 crisis. The fiscal balance has swung from a small positive percentage of GDP to a generally modest deficit in recent years due to the fiscal stimulus packages that are linked with the global financial crisis. Meanwhile, the current account has shifted from a deficit of about 3 per cent of GDP in the pre-crisis 1990s to a surplus of similar (but declining) magnitude.[3] This is partly due to declines in both capital inflows and exports due to slower economic growth in the aftermath of the financial crisis and the global economic recession late in the first decade of the twenty-first century.

The budget balances and current account balances of China, Nepal, Taiwan, the Philippines and Thailand have also moved in opposite directions since the late 1990s. China, for example, has recorded a large current account surplus of about US$300 billion (6 per cent of GDP). Unlike China and most other Asian countries, India's current account position turned negative in mid-2005, reaching US$17 billion in 2007 (Reserve Bank of India, Handbook of Statistics on the Indian Economy, 2008). India has run a deficit for every year under investigation, and this deficit has reached more than 6 per cent of GDP in recent years.

Based on the full sample period, we observed a positive correlation between budget and current account balances in 9 out of 13 countries, ranging from 0.75 (Nepal) to 0.04 (China).[4] For India, the correlation between the two variables is about 0.40. Additionally, we found a decline in the correlation during the post-crisis period in most of these countries, suggesting that the relationship between the two balances may have weakened somewhat in recent decades. In the aftermath of the 1997 financial crisis, most of the countries under investigation went through several quarters of economic recession. The ASEAN countries recorded a decline in output and a worsening fiscal balance due to 'active budget' deficits resulting from expansionary fiscal policies. Visual inspection of our time series data shows significant improvements in the current account as the falling output led to a decline in domestic investment that was greater than the declines in private and national savings. In other words, as fiscal balance worsened, external balance improved and such a phenomenon is at odds with the TDH. Therefore, the pattern that has emerged over the past few years seems to suggest that the relationship between the two deficits has been decoupled. As noted by Salvatore (2006), the current account balances of the G7 countries have responded sluggishly over the last several years due to changes in exchange rates. As such, the impact of budget balance on current accounts may not be fully understood for several years until the lagging effects are clear. Initially, we may expect the current account surplus to be associated with a contemporaneous budget deficit before the direct relationship between the two deficits becomes evident – the so-called *J*-curve phenomenon (see Salvatore, 2006).[5] Alternatively, one may view the linkage between budget and current account deficits as much stronger in the long-run than in the short-run.

In the next section, we will briefly review the analytical framework of the study. Section 3 describes the methodology adopted and the data used in the empirical analysis, and Section 4 details the empirical results. Finally, Section 5 summarizes the major findings and provides some policy conclusions.

2 The analytical framework

The national accounts framework is used here to define a clear link between budget balance and current account. We begin with private savings, S^p, which is defined as disposable income (income less taxes), $Y-T$, minus private consumption, C. Public (government) savings, $S^g = T - G$, is defined as the difference between direct taxes from households and firms, T, and public expenditures, G. By adding private and public savings, we obtain[6]

$$S_t^p + S_t^g = (Y_t - C_t - T_t) + (T_t - G_t) = Y_t - (C_t + G_t) = S_t^n \tag{1}$$

where S^n is national savings. Then with the national account identity,

$$Y_t = C_t + INV_t + G_t + N_t \tag{2}$$

where INV is the investment and N is the net export, national savings can be written as

$$S_t^n = Y_t - (C_t + G_t) = C_t + INV_t + G_t + N_t - C_t - G_t = INV_t + N_t \tag{3}$$

The current account balance, CA, is defined as 'payment received from abroad in exchange for currently produced goods and services, minus the analogous payments made to foreigners by the domestic economy'. In the simplest case, the current account can be taken to be equal to net exports. Rearranging the national savings equation, the current account can be written as national savings minus investment. Further, replacing N with current account and substituting for S^n yields

$$CA_t = S_t^p - INV_t - (G_t - T_t) \tag{4}$$

Equation (4) provides a convenient framework with which to examine the relationship between the budget balance, $G - T$, and the current account. If private savings is almost equal to investment ($S^p \approx INV$), then the budget balance and current account will be directly correlated. In other words, the external account and the budget balance, labeled the twin deficits, will have to move in the same direction by the same amount (Fidrmuc, 2003).

Next, we looked for a long-term relationship between the current account and the budget balance. The current account identity states that the current account has to equal the capital and financial account, that is,

$$CA_t = B_{t+1} - B_t \tag{5}$$

where B represents the capital and financial account change of an economy's net foreign assets. It follows that accumulated current account is equal to the external debt associated with a particular period t, $\sum_{i=1}^{\tau} CA_i = \sum_{i=1}^{\tau} B_{i+1} - B_i$. As we can see from this equation, external debts generate a continuous flow of interest payments and possibly repayment or debt rescheduling at some point in the future (Fidrmuc, 2003). A country has to meet all of these liabilities by generating current account surplus (i.e., export surplus). Therefore, the current account has to be sustainable at a particular point in time and the entire trajectory of the current account has to be considered. In addition to illustrating the current account as a long-run phenomenon, this argument also highlights the importance of distinguishing between investment-induced and consumption-induced current accounts because only the former raises productivity and export capacity over the long-term.

Recent studies have shown that the public sector may meet its financing needs through domestic and international financial markets (Fidrmuc, 2003; Bagnai, 2006).[7] Considering the significant role of private investment in the intertemporal approach to the balance of payments, as discussed above, the long-run relationship between current account (CA), budget balance (BD), and investment (INV) (all expressed as percentage of GDP) can be written as

$$CA_t = \beta_0 + \beta_1 BD_t + \beta_2 INV_t + \varepsilon_t \tag{6}$$

The above equation provides a useful framework for investigating the link between current account, budget balance, and investment. In Equation (6), we expect the coefficients for budget balance and investment to be positive and negative, respectively; that is, a budget deficit and high investment worsen the current account. Corresponding to this equation, the existence of large and highly sophisticated capital markets in developed countries makes it possible for these countries to finance public and private domestic needs through capital markets. Therefore, we expect a high correspondence between current account and budget balance in the long-term. It should be noted that in the absence of capital mobility the two deficits cannot be 'twins'. Finally, it is reasonable also to expect that a high correspondence between current account and investment is more likely to occur in developing countries than in more-developed countries.

TDH is concerned with the source of financial external deficits, and there is a clear connection between the hypothesis and the Feldstein–Horioka puzzle. It should be noted that if savings and investments are not highly correlated, reflecting the high capital mobility, then the BD and the CA are expected to move together; see Marinheiro (2008) for a recent discussion on the link. The model given by Equation (6) provides a convenient framework to endorse TDH and Feldstein-Horioka puzzle. The coefficients for budget balance and investment in Equation (6) should equal to unity if a country is perfectly integrated into the world economy and budgetary and investment expenditures are financed on the world financial market. Accordingly, if this restriction holds then it validates a high degree of financial integration and perfect international capital mobility amongst the markets under investigation. On the other hand, if the coefficient for investment in the current account equation is not a significant difference from zero (or near zero), this means that domestic investment is financed by domestic savings, dubbed the Feldstein–Horioka puzzle. According to Feldstein–Horioka (1980), a high portion of the investment is still reliant on domestic sources of financing. If the coefficient for investment is insignificant difference from zero, this implies that the financial market is perfectly decoupled from the world capital markets (no capital mobility). Investment is completely financed from domestic sources rather than the global financial market, and this impedes current account balances.

3 Data and statistical strategy

This empirical analysis used annual data for the period from 1980 to 2009 in 13 Asian countries: China (CHN), Hong Kong SAR (HKG), India (IND), Indonesia (INDO), South Korea (KOR), Malaysia (MYS), Nepal (NEP), Pakistan (PAK), the Philippines (PHL), Singapore (SGP), Sri Lanka (LKA), Taiwan (TWN) and Thailand (THA). The annual series of current account balance/GDP (CA/GDP) (surplus = +, deficit = −) from World Economic Outlook, budget balance/GDP (BD/GDP) (surplus = +, deficit = −) was collected from the Asian Development Bank, and investment/GDP (INV/GDP) was drawn from World Development Indicators (WDI).[8] All series were constructed as GDP ratio by division of GDP series. The time period analyzed here is particularly interesting because there were significant changes in Asian currencies vis-à-vis their major trading partners. It is expected that these sharp declines in currency values could affect relationships among the variables in the empirical model.

We start by investigating the integration properties of BD, CA and INV for all 13 Asian countries in the analysis. To accomplish this task, we applied the method developed by Hadri (2000) that was constructed based on the null hypotheses of stationarity. Because this procedure is widely used in the literature, we do not review it in this chapter. However, it is worth mentioning that, in the present context, the order of integration has important implications for the TDH and for estimating the long-run cointegration relationship. Bagnai (2006), for instance, argued that if CA is generated by the $I(0)$ process while the two regressors in Equation (6) are $I(1)$, then CA cannot be explained by BD and INV. This outcome would rule out the existence of twin deficits behavior. Similarly, if BD is an $I(0)$ variable while both CA and INV are $I(1)$, then the current account movement may be associated with a decline (or increase) in investment ratios. Hence, such a characterization could rule out this hypothesis.

The Johansen and Juselius (1990) cointegration test (referred to hereinafter as Johansen–Juselius), which applies maximum likelihood to a vector autoregression (VAR) model, is commonly used to determine whether there is a long-term relationship between the variables of interest (here CA, BD and INV). Gregory and Hansen (1996, Gregory–Hansen hereinafter) demonstrate that the standard Johansen–Juselius test for cointegration fails because no allowance is made for structural shifts in the relationships between nonstationary series. To overcome this problem, Gregory–Hansen developed a residual-based test that allows an endogenously determined structural break in the cointegration relationship. Briefly, the Gregory–Hansen test modifies the Engle and Granger (1987) approach to testing for the existence of a single cointegrating relationship by allowing the coefficient of this equation to undergo a structural break.

Specifically, the Gregory–Hansen test allows a structural change to be reflected in the intercept μ and/or changes to the slope of α and is usually modeled as below:

Model 1: level shift (C)

$$CA_t = \mu_1 + \mu_2\phi_{t\tau} + \beta_1 BD_t + \beta_2 INV_t + \varepsilon_t, \quad t = 1, 2, \ldots, n \tag{7}$$

where μ_1 represents the intercept before the shift, and μ_2 represents the change in intercept at the time of the shift. The dummy variable $\phi_{t\tau}$ is defined as

$$\phi_{t\tau} = \begin{cases} 0, & if\ t \leq [\mu\tau] \\ 1, & if\ t > [\mu\tau] \end{cases} \tag{8}$$

where the unknown parameter $\tau \in (0, 1)$ denotes the (relative) timing of the change point, and $[\mu\text{T}]$ denotes the integer part.

Model 2: level shift with trend (C/T)

$$CA_t = \mu_1 + \mu_2\phi_{t\tau} + \lambda t + \beta_1 BD_t + \beta_2 INV_t + \varepsilon_t, \quad t = 1, 2, \ldots, n \tag{9}$$

where t represents a time trend.

Model 3: Regime shift (C/S)

$$\begin{aligned} CA_t = {} & \mu_1 + \mu_2\phi_{t\tau} + \lambda t + \beta_1 BD_t + \mu_3 BD_t\phi_{t\tau} + \beta_2 INV_t \\ & + \mu_4 INV_t\phi_{t\tau} + \varepsilon_t, \quad t = 1, 2, \ldots, n \end{aligned} \tag{10}$$

where β_1 and β_2 denote the cointegrating slope coefficients prior to the regime shift, and μ_3 and μ_4 denote the change in the slope coefficients.

To investigate the causal relationship(s) between CA, BD and INV, we used the procedure first described by Toda and Yamamoto (1995, TY). To briefly demonstrate the application of the TY Granger causality test, consider the following autoregressive model with k lags:

$$\begin{bmatrix} x_{1,it} \\ x_{2,it} \\ x_{3,it} \end{bmatrix} = \begin{bmatrix} \beta_{10} \\ \beta_{20} \\ \beta_{30} \end{bmatrix} + \sum_{j=1}^{k} \begin{bmatrix} \alpha_{11,j} & \alpha_{12,j} & \alpha_{13,j} \\ \alpha_{21,j} & \alpha_{22,j} & \alpha_{23,j} \\ \alpha_{31,j} & \alpha_{32,j} & \alpha_{33,j} \end{bmatrix} \begin{bmatrix} x_{1,it-j} \\ x_{2,it-j} \\ x_{3,it-j} \end{bmatrix} + \begin{bmatrix} v_{1,it} \\ v_{2,it} \\ v_{3,it} \end{bmatrix}, \tag{11}$$

where x_1, x_2 and x_3 represent the CA, BD and INV, respectively. We also consider a dummy shifter as an exogenous variable in the relationship to accommodate regional or country specific events. For example, to test whether x_1(CA) Granger causes x_2 (BD), one may simply test the joint restriction where all $\alpha_{11,j} = 0$ (1,...k). Unlike the ordinary differential vector autoregression (VAR), the above formulation involves variables appearing in their level. As shown by the authors, the advantage of this method is that it does not require any prior knowledge of the cointegration properties of the system. It has a normal limiting chi-squared distribution, and the standard lag selection procedure can be applied even if there is no cointegration and (or) the stability and rank conditions are not satisfied, 'so long as the order of integration of the process does not exceed the true lag length [of] the model' (TY, 1995, p. 225). The test is performed in two steps. First, the appropriate (optimum) lag structure of the VAR is determined using AIC (or SIC) information criteria.[9] Second, a VAR of the order $k^* = k + d_{\max}$ is estimated, where $d_{\max}$ is the maximal anticipated order of integration. The MWALD statistic is valid whether the series is $I(1)$, $I(0)$ or $I(2)$, non-cointegrated or cointegrated in an arbitrary order (Rambaldi & Doran, 1996). In effect, the procedure circumvents some pre-testing biases that researchers may encounter with the standard unit root and cointegration tests.

4 Empirical results

To determine the order of integration, we pre-tested all the variables in Equation (6) using the Hadri (2000) test at each level and then on their first differences. The optimal lag length for the test was chosen based on the Modified Schwarz information criterion (MSIC). The result of the panel stationarity test is displayed in Table 6.1. The Hadri tests rejected the null hypothesis of a stationarity at first difference for CA, BD and INV, all at the 1 per cent significance level. Based on Hadri tests and additional panel unit root tests to check for robustness (not shown), we concluded that BD is $I(1)$ and not $I(0)$. Every variable (including CA) was stationary after its first difference, suggesting that the order of integration for our panel series does not exceed one. For the countries in our sample, CA appears to be an $I(1)$ variable.

The above outcome confirms the hysteresis of the current account in all countries studied. In Gundlach and Sinn (1992), the authors demonstrate that the degree of capital mobility can be verified by assessing the order of the integration of the CA series. Specifically, they claim that the null hypothesis of capital mobility can be verified by simply performing a unit root test (see also Bagnai, 2006)[10]. Based on the panel stationarity test alone, we may conclude that the Asian countries are closely linked

Table 6.1 Panel stationarity test

Test/Variable	CA	ΔCA	BD	ΔBD	INV	ΔINV
Constant						
Hadri*Z*-stat	8.547[a]	−0.092	2.715[a]	1.142	5.081[a]	−0.724
	[0.0000]	[0.5367]	[0.0033]	[0.1267]	[0.0000]	[0.7655]
Heteroscedastic	5.682[a]	0.089	2.510[a]	1.436	3.810[a]	−0.172
consistent *Z*-stat	[0.0000]	[0.4645]	[0.0060]	[0.7550]	[0.0001]	[0.5684]

Notes: [(a)] denotes rejection of the null hypothesis of stationarity for Hadri. (Δ) refers to first difference operator. The values in [ ] denote associate *p*-value. Newey-West automatic bandwidth selection and Bartlett Kernel were used. The lag length selection was based on the modified Schwarz information criterion.

to the international markets, that is, they exhibit strong degree of capital mobility. This finding appears to support recent work by Baharumshah et al. (2008) and others that show high capital mobility in five ASEAN countries based on real interest rate parity (RIP).[11] The left- and right-hand sides are of the same order of integration and, hence, constitute a balanced regression model (Maddala & Kim, 1998). Analysis based on the order of integration provides no prior information, and we must conduct additional tests to reach a conclusion about TDH. In the section that follows, we present evidence based on pure time series and panel cointegration techniques.

4.1 Single equation test with break

Having verified that we cannot reject the hypothesis that all variables are $I(1)$ and there is no evidence to suggest that all the variable are $I(2)$, the next step is to perform cointegration tests to determine whether there have stable long-term relationships between CA, BD and INV. Our purpose was to find out whether fiscal and external accounts developed along a joint path. However, the sampling period (1980–2009) was marked by significant regime shifts and a sharp fall in currencies in most of the countries under review. Cointegration tests that ignore breaks may be problematic as they assume that the cointegration vector is *time-invariant*. A recent study by Daly and Siddiki (2009), who looked at the 23 OECD (Organization for Economic Co-operation and Development) countries, showed that ignoring regime shifts in the cointegration between CA and BD could be biased towards a non-cointegrating relationship (that is, rejecting TDH). To this end, we applied the Gregory–Hansen procedure to date the timing of the break

Table 6.2 Gregory and Hansen results

Country/Model	C		C/T		C/S	
INDO	−4.438	[1990]	−5.106^{c}	[2003]	−4.161	[1998]
PHL	−3.775	[1985]	−5.091^{c}	[1987]	−4.377	[1987]
KOR	−4.432	[1985]	−5.177^{c}	[1985]	−4.931	[1994]
THA	−4.397	[1987]	−6.318^{a}	[2001]	−4.666	[1992]
CHN	−4.424	[2004]	−4.355	[2004]	−5.281^{c}	[1997]
IND	−3.776	[2000]	−6.216^{a}	[2002]	−4.599	[2002]
MYS	−3.703	[1997]	−5.034^{c}	[2001]	−3.618	[1997]
PAK	−3.815	[2005]	−3.955	[2005]	−4.272	[1997]
LKA	−4.870^{c}	[1997]	−4.984	[2005]	−5.690^{b}	[2001]
HKG	−4.049	[1991]	−5.890^{a}	[1997]	−6.550^{a}	[1997]
SGP	−5.521^{a}	[1996]	−5.696^{b}	[1984]	−5.523^{b}	[1996]
TWN	−2.255	[1995]	−5.159^{c}	[1995]	−2.826	[1984]
NEP	−4.759	[1995]	−5.040^{c}	[1995]	−3.397	[1995]

Notes: $^{(a)}$, $^{(b)}$ and $^{(c)}$ denote statistical significance at the 1%, 5% and 10% significance levels, respectively. Critical values are obtained from Gregory and Hansen (1996, Table 1, p.109) for $m = 2$. Figures in [ ] refers to the break date.

for consideration in the cointegration test. The results from Model C (level shift), Model C/T (level shift with trend) and Model C/S (regime shift) are summarized in Table 6.2.

As shown in Table 6.2, the test statistic from Model C is significant only for Sri Lanka and Singapore at the usual significance levels. In contrast, the test statistic from Model C/T reveals that the null hypothesis of non-cointegration is rejected in all but three cases – China, Pakistan and Sri Lanka. The test statistic from Model C/T is significant at the 10 per cent level for Indonesia, the Philippines, South Korea, Malaysia, Taiwan and Nepal, and at the 5 per cent significance level or better for Thailand, India, Hong Kong SAR and Singapore. The evidence supports the twin deficit view in China only when a regime shift (C/S) is allowed in the model (10 per cent significance level). Overall, the results from the time series method show strong evidence of cointegration between the three variables in all countries but one – Pakistan.[12]

All in all, the empirical outcomes from the Gregory–Hansen tests appear to support cointegration with a break for the Asian countries, including China and India. It is worth noting here that the timing of the break appears to coincide with major historical events in the region, such as the commodity crisis in the mid-1980s, financial deregulation and the recession it initiated, the 1997 Asian crisis that started in Thailand, and the bursting of the dot-com bubble in 2000.[13] The dates detected are around 1984–87 (e.g., PHL, KOR and SGP), 1995–97 (e.g., CHN, HKG, TWN and LKA) and 2000–05. In India, the break date coincides with oil price shocks in the early 2000s and a significant growth in the import of capital goods, which added to India's production capacity and the performance of the export sectors. India's current account position turned positive in 2001 before reversing sharply in 2005; it has remained in a deficit position since then. Overall, our results justify the increasing use of cointegration analysis with breaks in recent years.[14]

4.2 Panel cointegration tests with break

It is possible that our small sample size might have affected the above results. To extend the analysis and to provide additional insight into the TDH in Asian countries, we repeated the exercise with the same data using Pedroni's (2001) fully modified ordinary least squared (FMOLS) estimator. The main motivation for considering testing cointegration in a panel framework is that the power of the tests increases with the number of cross-sections in the panel. Additionally, the panel data techniques advocated by Pedroni (2001) provide reliable estimates of the long-run parameters and facilitates tests of restrictions on individual countries, which will be shown later. Before estimating long-run relationships in panel context, we applied the Lagrange Multiplier (LM) used by Breusch and Pagan (1980) and Pesaran (2004) to test the possibility of cross-sectional dependency. In Table 6.3, CD_{lm} refers to the LM used by Breusch and Pagan while PCD refers to Pesaran's cross-sectional dependence tests. Columns 2 and 3 show the pair-wise correlations of the residuals for CD_{lm} and PCD, respectively[15]. As shown in Table 6.3, the CD_{lm} test clearly rejects the null hypothesis of no cross-sectional dependency in favor of the alternative hypothesis, implying that there is evidence of cross-sectional dependence (1 per cent significance level). However, the outcome from the PCD test indicates that we cannot reject the null hypothesis of no cross-sectional dependency. Pesaran (2004) demonstrates that the PCD test has correct size under the structural break(s), and it is reasonable in small properties that do not depend on a particular spatial weight matrix. Given that the CD_{lm} test is likely to exhibit substantial size distortions for small properties and is not robust for structural break(s), we conclude that there is no evidence for cross-sectional dependency based on the PCD test. Having determined that the sample countries are immune from cross-sectional dependency, we then proceeded to the Pedroni panel analysis.

Table 6.3 Cross dependency tests

	CD_{lm}	PCD
$\left\|\hat{\rho}_{ij}\right\|$	|5.0851|	|4.5891|
Test-statistics	152.5518[a]	1.2051
$\chi^2_{(N(N-1)/2)}$	[0.000]	
Critical value – 10%	96.578	1.697
– 5%	101.879	2.042
– 1%	112.329	2.750

Notes: [(a)] denote statistical significance at the 1% significance level. Values in [ ] indicate the p-value. $\hat{\rho}_{ij}$ denotes the sample-wise correlation of the residual denoted as $\hat{\rho}_{ij} = \hat{\rho}_{ji} = \sum_{t=1}^{T} \hat{e}_{it}\hat{e}_{jt} / \left(\sum_{t=1}^{T} \hat{e}_{it}^2\right)^{1/2} \left(\sum_{t=1}^{T} \hat{e}_{jt}^2\right)^{1/2}$. H_0 is rejected when the test statistic $CD_{lm} = T\sum_{i=1}^{N-1}\sum_{j=i+1}^{N}\hat{\rho}_{ij}^2 > \chi^2_{(N(N-1)/2)}$ and $PCD = \sqrt{2T/N(N-1)}\left(\sum_{i=1}^{N-1}\sum_{j=i+1}^{N}\hat{\rho}_{ij}\right) > N(0,1) = 2.04$.

Pedroni (1999, 2004) developed two sets of statistics to test the null hypothesis of no cointegration for heterogeneous panels. Pedroni's first four statistics are based on pooling the residuals along the 'within' dimension of the panel while the remaining three statistics are based on pooling the residuals along the 'between' dimension of the panel. We estimate the long-run relationship as given in Equation (6) with the addition of a dummy variable to account for the break. The results from the panel cointegration method are given in Table 6.4. Panels A, B and C refer to the analysis with dummy variables to accommodate the break as identified in Model C, Model C/T and Model C/S, respectively. The results provide strong evidence of a cointegration relationship between the variables under investigation for all the panels.

Recently, Westerlund and Edgerton (2008) expanded the panel cointegration test to accommodate cross-sectional dependence among panel units and multiple breaks in the deterministic component of the model.[16] The latter issue is of importance here because our data span an extended period of time, which obviously increases the probability of structural breaks. For completeness and to complement the Pedroni (1999, 2004) test statistics, we conducted the test introduced by Westerlund and Edgerton (2008). The results are reported in Table 6.4. The maximum lag was selected based on int$\{4 * (t/100)\wedge(2/9)\}$ and the number of lags was determined by a sequential procedure based on the significance of the lag parameters, as proposed by Campbell and Perron

Table 6.4 Panel cointegration with structural break tests

	Panel A		Panel B		Panel C	
Pedroni (2004): H_0: no cointegration						
Panel ADF-stat	−8.621[a]	(0.000)	−3.699[a]	(0.000)	−6.334[a]	(0.000)
	[−8.001[a]]	(0.000)	[−10.493[a]]	(0.000)	[−5.405[a]]	(0.000)
Group ADF-stat	−9.357[a]	(0.000)	−5.084[a]	(0.000)	−6.723[a]	(0.000)
	[−8.546[a]]	(0.000)	[−11.399[a]]	(0.000)	[−7.567[a]]	(0.000)

Westerlund and Edgerton (2008): H_0:no cointegration

Test/Model	Regime shift		Level shift	
$Z_\tau(N)$	−2.1000[b]	(0.0180)	−3.2960[a]	(0.0000)
$Z_\varphi(N)$	−1.8450[b]	(0.0330)	−5.8330[a]	(0.0000)

Notes: (a) and (b) indicate statistical significance at the 1% and 5% significance levels, respectively. For panel statistics and Group-ADF statistics, Newey-West bandwidth selection using the Bartlett kernel was used; lag selection was based on SIC with max lag of 5. Dummies relied on break dates advocated by Gregory and Hansen (1996) for Pedroni (2004). Panels A, B and C refer to analysis with break dummies from dates detected by models C, C/T and C/S, respectively. The values in [ ] and ( ) denote test statistics for model with intercept and trend, and associate *p*-value, respectively. The break dates for Westerlund and Edgerton (2008) were selected using a grid search procedure (see Westerlund & Edgerton, 2008).

(1991). By allowing structural breaks in both the level and the slope of the relationship amongst CA, BD and INV, the cointegration results suggest that the null hypothesis of no cointegration should be rejected for both of the models. Accordingly, the tests detect a single break in all of the countries tested; the dates of these breaks are mostly in the mid-1990s and early 2000s. Therefore, the results from the Westerlund and Edgerton (2008) analysis confirm the findings based on the Gregory–Hansen and Pedroni tests: a long-run relationship amongst CA, BD and INV exists for the 13 Asian countries when structural breaks are accounted properly. The evidence appears to be robust with regard to the cointegration tests used in the analysis.

Next, we applied the Pedroni FMOLS procedure to obtain the individual slope coefficients of the BD, CA and INV variables. Unlike previous works, we formally tested the null hypothesis that the individual coefficients of BD and INV are significantly different from unity using the Wald test as suggested by Pedroni. The major findings as reported in Appendix A1 may be summarized as follows: When breaks in the cointegrating relationship are not allowed (appendix A.1), the null hypothesis H_0: $\beta_1 = 1$ cannot be rejected for eight countries (the Philippines, South Korea, Thailand, Malaysia, Pakistan, Sri Lanka, Singapore, and Nepal).

Appendix A.1 FMOLS for CA = f(BD, INV)

Country/ Model	without time dummy				with time dummy			
	$\hat{\beta}_{1i}$	$H_0: t_{\hat{\beta}_{1i}} = 1$	$\hat{\beta}_{2i}$	$H_0: t_{\hat{\beta}_{2i}} = 1$	$\hat{\beta}_{1i}$	$H_0: t_{\hat{\beta}_{1i}} = 1$	$\hat{\beta}_{2i}$	$H_0: t_{\hat{\beta}_{2i}} = 1$
INDO	0.93[a]♠	−1.07♠	−0.49[c]	−5.64[a]	0.08	3.47[a]	−0.60[a]	−10.16[a]
PHL	0.36[a]♠	−5.25[a]♠	−0.66[a]	−15.87[a]	1.54[a]	1.39	−0.17	−7.39[a]
KOR	1.48[b]	0.88	−0.42[b]♠	−8.79[a]♠	0.63	−0.53	−0.78[a]♠	−6.50[a]♠
THA	1.31[b]	0.51	−1.03[a]	−1.33	−0.74[b]♠	−6.10[a]♠	−0.44[b]	−7.22[a]
CHN	−0.59[c]♠	−4.30[a]♠	0.59[a]	−3.12[a]	0.77[b]♠	−5.14[a]♠	−0.18[c]♠	−11.55[a]♠
IND	0.45[b]	−2.97[a]	−0.19[a]♠	−21.62[a]♠	0.44[c]	−2.49[b]	−0.51[a]	−24.27[a]
MYS	1.00[a]	−0.02	−1.02[a]♠	−1.06♠	0.73[a]	−1.57	−1.14[a]	−21.42[a]
PAK	1.08[a]♠	0.33♠	−1.04[a]#	−1.55#	0.82[b]	−0.52	−1.08[a]♣	1.00♣
LKA	1.09[a]	0.28	−0.59[b]	−6.18[a]	0.76[b]	−0.70	−0.74[a]	−8.14[a]
HKG	0.13	−7.25[a]	−1.49[a]	−25.03[a]	0.20[c]	−2.86[a]	−1.48[a]	−8.78[a]
SGP	0.95[a]	−0.32	−1.03[a]	−1.04	0.88[a]	−0.81	−0.91[a]	−1.10
TWN	0.30[a]♠	−11.72[a]♠	−1.00[a]	−1.58	0.49[b]♠	−2.60[b]♠	−2.09[a]♣	−7.18[a]♣
NEP	1.72[a]	1.89[c]	0.20	−1.71[c]	0.67[b]	−1.20	−0.25[c]♣	−9.42[a]♣
	$\hat{\beta}_1$	$H_0: t_{\hat{\beta}_1} = 1$	$\hat{\beta}_2$	$H_0: t_{\hat{\beta}_2} = 1$	$\hat{\beta}_1$	$H_0: t_{\hat{\beta}_1} = 1$	$\hat{\beta}_2$	$H_0: t_{\hat{\beta}_2} = 1$
Group	0.71[a]	−5.40[a]	−0.62[a]	−40.29[a]	0.53[a]	−5.42[a]	−0.71[a]	−37.49[a]
Group ♠	0.20[a]	−16.26[a]	−0.66[a]	−61.61[a]	0.32[a]	−9.32[a]	−0.74[a]	−44.05[a]
Group ♣	0.48[a]	−10.68[a]	−0.70[a]	−48.46[a]	0.43[a]	−8.81[a]	−0.76[a]	−46.94[a]
Group #	0.57[a]	−8.86[a]	−0.62[a]	−46.19[a]	0.58[a]	−6.03[a]	−0.70[a]	−43.27[a]

Notes: (a), (b) and (c) indicate statistical significance at 1%, 5% and 10% significance levels, respectively. FMOLS panel data estimates using dummies generated by models C, C/T and C/S from Gregory and Hansen (1996). ♠ refers to results from model C, ♣ indicates results from Model C/T and # indicates results from Model C/S.

Meanwhile, the hypothesis H_0: $\beta_2 = 1$ cannot be rejected for only three countries (Thailand, Singapore and Taiwan). When a single break in the cointegrating relationship is allowed, additional cases can be added to the list. For the unity investment coefficient, we have two additional countries – Malaysia and Pakistan. For BD, Indonesia and Pakistan are not different from unity at the usual significance levels (see appendix A.1).

Summing up, we found that the coefficient for BD is unity in 9 countries, and the coefficient for INV is in 5 out of 13 countries. Interestingly, in 4 (Thailand, Malaysia, Pakistan and Singapore) of the 13 countries tested, we found that both the coefficient of the BD and investment are not statistically different from unity. This means that these countries are perfectly integrated into the world economy and that both BD and INV are globally financed (Marinheiro, 2008). We then turned to the Feldstein–Horioka test (H_0: $\beta_2 = 1$). We found that the puzzle seems to hold in eight countries.[17] For Malaysia, Singapore, Thailand and Pakistan, the puzzle is not valid, indicating that the integration processes in these countries, which started as early as the late 1970s (Singapore), have been completed. We note that the case of Pakistan should be interpreted with caution as it appears to be sensitive to alternative model specifications. Pakistan is a low-income country with a weak capital market and is highly dependent on national savings for domestic investment.

One important question that is often raised in the literature is whether there is a causal relationship between CA and BD (Kalou & Paleologou, 2012) and, if so, whether the nexus runs from BD to CA or the other way around. The design of any policy to manage external (or internal) balances must consider the causal relationship between these two balances. Failure to do so may lead to erroneous policy prescriptions based on incorrect inferences. A unidirectional positive causality that runs from BD to CA would be consistent with the Keynesian view. Bahmani-Oskooee (1995), Salvatore (2006) and Baharmshah and Lau (2007), among others, find that BD will either create CA or widen the external imbalance. In this case, the appropriate policy tool would be to reduce aggregate demand in order to promote a corresponding decrease in demand. The reverse causality, running from CA to BD, is referred to by Summers (1988) as current account targeting and would require the use of the budget as an instrument to correct large external balances (Khalid & Guan, 1999; Kalou & Paleologou, 2012).

Table 6.5 displays the results of the application of the TY Granger noncausality test. To implement this procedure, we determined the optimum lag in the VAR model based on the SIC. The selection procedures led to the choice of two lags for all of the countries under investigation. We

Table 6.5 Granger non-causality results

H_0	N = 13 Panel A	N = 13 Panel B	N = 13 Panel C	N = 11 Panel A	N = 11 Panel B	N = 11 Panel C
MWALD (χ^2-statistics) ($k = 2$ $d = 1$)						
	[+]	[+]	[+]	[+]	[+]	[+]
$BD/\to CA$	**15.8736**[a]	**15.8737**[a]	**15.8737**[a]	**18.8123**[a]	**18.8123**[a]	**18.8124**[a]
	(0.0004)	(0.0004)	(0.0004)	(0.0001)	(0.0001)	(0.0001)
	[−]	[−]	[−]	[−]	[−]	[−]
$INV/\to CA$	**39.6491**[a]	**39.6491**[a]	**39.6491**[a]	**37.9777**[a]	**37.9778**[a]	**37.9778**[a]
	(0.0000)	(0.0000)	(0.0000)	(0.0000)	(0.0000)	(0.0000)
	[+]	[+]	[+]	[+]	[+]	[+]
$CA/\to BD$	0.8610	0.8610	0.8610	0.2485	0.2485	0.2485
	(0.6502)	(0.6502)	(0.6502)	(0.8832)	(0.8832)	(0.8832)
	[+]	[+]	[+]	[+]	[+]	[+]
$INV/\to BD$	0.0302	0.0302	0.0302	0.0118	0.0118	0.0118
	(0.9850)	(0.9850)	(0.9850)	(0.9941)	(0.9941)	(0.9941)
	[−]	[−]	[−]	[−]	[−]	[−]
$CA/\to INV$	**24.9075**[a]	**28.5485**[a]	**29.5822**[a]	**17.9453**[a]	**20.7611**[a]	**23.9252**[a]
	(0.0000)	(0.0000)	(0.0000)	(0.0001)	(0.0000)	(0.0000)
	[+]	[+]	[+]	[+]	[+]	[+]
$BD/\to INV$	**3.5240**[c]	**4.1756**[b]	**3.4540**[c]	**5.0124**[b]	**6.5550**[b]	**3.7747**[c]
	(0.0605)	(0.0410)	(0.0631)	(0.0252)	(0.0105)	(0.0520)

Notes: [(a)] and [(b)] indicate statistical significance at the 1 and 5% significance levels, respectively. The null hypothesis $H_0 : BD/\to CA$states that budget balance does not Granger-cause current account. Figures in ( ) are p-values for the MWALD. k = optimum lag and d = maximum order of integration. The optimum lag is based on model selection criteria. Panels A, B, and C refer to analyses with break dates detected by model C, model C/T, and model C/S, respectively. The analysis reported in last three columns (N = 11) in the table exclude China and India from the panel.

then re-ran the test with dummy breaks and the breaks predicted by Model C, Model C/T and Model C/S, and reported as panels A, B and C, respectively. As shown in the table, the MWALD test statistics for BD and INV in the CA equation were all significant at the 1 per cent level. This means that it is BD that Granger causes the external balances. However, there was no reverse causality from CA to BD and, importantly, this finding appears to hold for all of the countries under review. Therefore, these findings imply that there is one-way (positive) causality between the CA and BD, and are consistent with the Keynesian view. As expected, we discovered that the INV negatively Granger-caused CA. The BD however is positively Granger-caused INV at least 10 per cent or better. It should be noted that the above outcomes appear to be robust across the three specifications (Model C, Model C/T and Model C/S).

Next, as shown in columns 5–7, we excluded China and India from the full panel (sub-panel) and found that their exclusion does not significantly change the results of these analyses. It bears noting that the problem in the 1990s and early 2000s was not one of large deficits, but rather one of large surpluses (except for IND and LKA).[18] Finally, apart from the direct channel as discussed above, we also find indirect channels between the two balances through investment (INV) channel: BD→INV→CA. These and other causal links are displayed in Table 6.5.

5 Summary and conclusion

Overall, after examining the relationship between current account, budget balance and investment in the 13 Asian countries, our data results reveal strong support for the TDH for all of the countries investigated. Importantly, our analysis on the issue allows for the presence of a break in the cointegration analysis. In all of these countries, we find strong support for the Keynesian (conventional) view when formally taking a single break in the relationship into account. This finding appears to support the view that the TDH is not unique to the United States or other OECD countries (Daly & Siddiki, 2009; Bartolini & Lahiri, 2006); the problem exists in the emerging Asian countries as well (Mohammadi, 2004; Baharumshah & Lau, 2007; Ito, 2009). Hence, the recent fiscal stimulus packages introduced in response to the 2007–12 global financial crises are expected to shrink or even widen (worsen) the external balance in some countries (e.g., Sri Lanka, Pakistan and India). We also observed that the impact of the budget deficit in general is much larger than that of investment. This is in sharp contrast to the results of several studies that have shown that only a small fraction of public deficit is reflected in the current account, especially in developed economies (see Chinn & Prasad, 2003; Papadogonas & Stournaras, 2006).

Another important result of our empirical work is that it endorses the notion that government spending crowds out private investment. As such, the governments of these countries should be cautious not to crowd out domestic private investment by adopting expansionary fiscal policies. Nonetheless, the magnitude of the impact of the budget deficit on external balances tends to vary among the countries reviewed. As expected, we also found that investment has played an important role in the current account in the past decades. Asian countries have relied on foreign capital – particularly foreign direct investment (FDI) – as a source of financing for domestic investment. This finding highlights a degree of commonality in the twin deficits nexus for the group of countries under study.

We also examined the Feldstein–Horioka puzzle in order to reach conclusions regarding integration with the global financial markets. Our analyses have shown that the investment coefficient is less than one for China, India, Indonesia, Korea and many other countries, despite the opening up of Asian capital markets in recent years. This result confirms that the Feldstein–Horioka puzzle holds in these economies. Both China and India introduced drastic financial reforms in the late 1990s. These reforms were launched with the aim of enhancing the role of market forces in capital allocation. Our results (in line with past studies) reveal that these reforms are far from sufficient to enable these countries to develop a significant link to the global capital markets. There is, however, ample evidence to show that the puzzle has weakened (or been eliminated) in three countries – Thailand, Singapore and Malaysia. Thus, we may conclude that these three countries have higher capital mobility and financial integration then the other ten Asian countries, after accounting for breaks. For the ten countries, their financial markets have partially decoupled from the world capital markets, implying that these countries are less integrated with the world. They are more reliant on domestic sources of financing than on the world financial market. The weak financial integration also highlighted the role of independent monetary policy. Any movement of the foreign or domestic interest rate will drive massive capital inflow or outflow in the economy, which lead to an unstable financial market.

Although our focus has been on Asian countries, we were also interested in comparisons with other countries, especially OECD members. Using data sets from the 13 OECD countries, Roa et al. (2010) also found that the long-term relationship between savings and investment has disappeared (or weakened) in these countries. Guzel and Ozdemir (2011) examined the puzzle in Japan and the United States, both of which are capital-importing countries, and showed that the puzzle disappears in both of these countries when structural breaks are accounted for. An article by Kim et al. (2007) is also worth mentioning here; these authors compared the difference in capital mobility between the OECD countries and ten Asian countries, including those reviewed here. Their results reveal that the savings–investment correlation in Asian countries has declined steadily over the years but is still higher than that in the OECD countries, indicating that the degree of capital mobility in Asia is lower than that in OECD countries.

From a policy perspective, the empirical findings appear to support the argument that government spending in the post-crisis era and the large fiscal stimulus packages introduced following the recent global recession will eventually affect the Asian countries' external imbalances, but the extent of these effects may vary from one country to another. The overall macroeconomic effects of fiscal policy in the Asian countries have not weakened, at least not in the last few decades. Therefore, in our view, budget deficits are a valid concern for policymakers in crisis-impacted countries with large fiscal deficits.

As a final remark, we did not account for movements in exchange rate and/or interest rate in the model. Many observers have pointed out that achieving orderly global trade imbalances would require more rapid adjustments of key Asian currencies. The global financial market is distorted, with the value of the dollar being artificially high. They warned that a gradual decline of the U.S. dollar is necessary to minimize any disruption of the global economy. The literature has also highlighted the significance of interest rates as one of the important financial variables in the budget–current account deficits. The interest rate is important in determining capital inflows and, hence, current account balances. All of these issues could be interesting areas for future research.

Notes

1. These two papers discuss the role of current account deficits and currency crises in emerging markets. A persistent deficit in external accounts is usually attributed to poor macroeconomic management of the country's external sector. Some studies have provided evidence for a direct link between persistent large current account and the probability of financial crisis (Kaminsky et al., 1998).
2. Salvatore provides the empirical evidence for the G7 countries over the past three decades. The author finds a direct relationship between budget deficit and current account deficit in the major industrialized countries. In explaining the relationship between the two variables, Salvatore emphasizes that budget deficit leads current account by one or more years.
3. Notably, Singapore has experienced a fiscal surplus over most the sample period and improvement in its current account as it moves to the present.
4. A negative correlation was found in the remaining four Asian countries studied – the Philippines, Thailand, Hong Kong SAR and Indonesia. The casual observation that the relationship between the two balances has diverged (or declined) in many of the Asian countries during the past decade is not a definitive demonstration that TDH has weakened in Asian countries. We demonstrate this here through a thorough econometric investigation.
5. Salvatore also discussed two popular approaches to testing the relationship between budget deficit and the current account deficit. The first test examines

the relationship directly, without examining the details of any intermediate links (e.g., Abell, 1990; Khalid & Guan, 1999; Baharumshah & Lau, 2007). The second is an indirect approach that focuses on the links between budget balance and domestic interest rates, between interest rates and exchange rates, and finally between exchange rates and current account deficit (Bagnai, 2006; Fidrmuc, 2003).

6. A major portion of this section was taken from the work of Fidrmuc (2003).
7. The inclusion of gross capital information as a share of GDP (investment) in the long-run relationship between current account and budget balance is suggested by the intertemporal approach to balance of payments popularized by Obstfeld and Rogoff (1995, 1996).
8. The data for Taiwan are sourced from *DataStream*.
9. Yamada and Toda (1998) emphasized that the lag selection procedure is a crucial step in the augmented Granger causality test. To choose the optimum lag (k), the Schwarz selection criterion was implemented. A series of diagnostic tests were also conducted to ensure that the standard properties of the tests were satisfied. For another application of the TY Granger causality test, see Kim and Kim (2006).
10. For more discussion of this issue, the reader may refer to Gundlach and Sinn (1992) and Bagnai (2006).
11. In the paper, authors show that RIP holds for most of the countries under investigation based on nonlinear unit root tests. This suggests that both the material and asset markets are integrated in a non-linear fashion.
12. Examining data from several Asian countries, Khalid and Guan (1999) found that the CA caused BD for Pakistan (and Indonesia), rejecting the Keynesian view in favor of the so-called current account targeting hypothesis (Summers, 1988).
13. Gruber and Kamin (2007) and others have noted that the large current surpluses of 1997–2003 were closely associated with the ongoing effects of the financial crisis that started in 1997.
14. Break dates that are close to the beginning or end of the sampling period are excluded from consideration in the Gregory–Hansen tests.
15. Pesaran (2004) modified the Bruesch–Pagan LM test and uses a simple average of all pair-wise correlations of individual regression residuals from the panel. The PCD test is applicable for any values of N and T and it is correctly centered. The test is also robust for multiple breaks and/or error variance as long as the unconditional means of the variables in the panel remain constant over time.
16. Westerlund and Edgerton (2008) have proposed two versions of test statistics that allow for heteroscedastic and serially correlated errors, unit-specific time trends, cross-sectional dependence and unknown structural breaks in both the intercept and slope of the cointegrated regression. Westerlund (2006) suggests a related test procedure that relaxes the assumption of a stable cointegrating relationship and allows for breaks in the deterministic component. However, like its predecessors, the test ignores the possibility of strong inter-economy linkages among the countries in the panel. We conducted this test and the results (not reported) reveal no evidence of a cointegrating relationship among the three variables.
17. The strong correlation between domestic savings and INV is well documented in the literature and is referred to as the Feldstein–Horioka puzzle. The

evidence indicates that the long-run relationship between savings and INV disappeared when structural breaks are taken into account. One such example is given in Ozmen and Parmaksiz (2003). Specifically, they found that the puzzle disappears once the break due to capital control (1984–98) is accounted for UK data. More recently, Ketenci (2012) highlights similar results but in the context of European Union member countries.

18. According to the current account targeting hypothesis, the government may resort to adjusting fiscal policies, to adjust its external position. In the context of the Asian countries, we find no empirical support of this view; rather, we fail to establish a unidirectional causality running from CA to BD (see Table 6.5).

References

Abell, J. D. (1990) 'Twin Deficits during the 1980s: An Empirical Investigation', *Journal of Macroeconomics*, 12(1), 81–96.

Bagnai, A. (2006) 'Structural Breaks and the Twin Deficits Hypothesis', *International Economics and Economic Policy*, 3(2), 137–55.

Baharumshah, A. Z. and Lau, E. (2007) 'Dynamics of Fiscal and Current Account Deficits in Thailand: An Empirical Investigation', *Journal of Economic Studies*, 34(6), 454–75.

Baharumshah, A. Z., Liew, V. K. S. and Hamzah, N. A. (2008) 'Real Interest Rate Parity in the ASEAN-5 Countries: A Nonlinear Perspective', *Applied Economics Letters*, 15, 955–58.

Bahmani-Oskooee, M. (1995) 'The Long-Run Determinants of the U.S. Trade Balance Revisited', *Journal of Post Keynesian Economics*, 17(3), 457–65.

Bartolini, L. and Lahiri, A. (2006) 'Twin Deficits, Twenty Years Later', *Current Issues in Economics and Finance: Federal Reserve Bank of New York*, 12(7), 1–7.

Breusch, T. S. and Pagan, A. R. (1980) 'The Lagrange Multiplier Test and Its Applications to Model Specification in Econometrics', *Review of Economic Studies*, 47(1), 239–53.

Campbell, J. Y. and Perron, P. (1991) 'Pitfalls and Opportunities: What Macroeconomists Should Know about Unit Roots' in Blanchard, O. and S. Fischer (Eds) *NBER Macroeconomics Annual*, 141–201 (MIT Press, Cambridge, MA).

Chinn, M. D. and Prasad, E. S. (2003) 'Medium-Term Determinants of Current Accounts in Industrial and Developing Countries: An Empirical Exploration', *Journal of International Economics*, 59(1), 47–76.

Daly, V. and Siddiki, J. U. (2009) 'The Twin Deficits in OECD Countries: Cointegration Analysis with Regime Shifts', *Applied Economics Letters*, 16(8), 1155–64.

Engle, R. F. and Granger, C. W. J. (1987) 'Co-integration and Error Correction: Representation, Estimation, and Testing', *Econometrica*, 55(2), 251–76.

Feldstein, M. and Horioko, C. (1980) 'Domestic Saving and International Capital Flows', *The Economic Journal*, 90(358), 314–29.

Fidrmuc, J. (2003) 'The Feldstein–Horioka Puzzle and the Twin Deficits in Selected Countries', *Economics of Planning*, 36(2), 135–52.

Gregory, A. W. and Hansen, B. E. (1996) 'Residual-Based Tests for Cointegration in Models with Regime Shifts', *Journal of Econometrics*, 70(1), 99–126.

Gruber, J. W. and Kamin, S. B. (2007) 'Explaining the Global Pattern of Current Account Imbalances', *Journal of International Money and Finance*, 26(4), 500–22.

Gundlach, E. and Sinn, S. (1992) 'Unit Root Tests of the Current Account Balance Account: Implications for International Capital Mobility', *Applied Economics*, 24(6), 617–25.

Guzel, A. and Ozdemir, Z. A. (2011) 'The Feldstein–Horioka Puzzle in the Presence of Structural Shifts: The Case of Japan versus the USA', *Research in International Business and Finance*, 25(2), 195–202.

Hadri, K. (2000) 'Testing for Stationarity in Heterogeneous Panel Data', *The Econometrics Journal*, 3(2), 148–61.

Ito, H. (2009) 'U.S. Current Account Debate with Japan then, with China Now', *Journal of Asian Economics*, 20(3), 294–313.

Johansen, S. and Juselius, K. (1990) 'Maximum Likelihood Estimation and Inference on Cointegration with Applications to the Demand for Money', *Oxford Bulletin of Economics and Statistics*, 52(2), 169–210.

Kalou, S. and Paleologou, S. -M. (2012) 'The Twin Deficit Hypothesis: Revisiting an EMU Country', *Journal of Policy Modeling*, 34(2), 230–41.

Kaminsky, G., Lizondo, S. and Reinhart, C. M. (1998) 'Leading Indicators of Currency Crises', *IMF Staff Papers*, 45(1), 1–48.

Ketenci, N. (2012) 'The Feldstein–Horioka Puzzle and Structural Breaks: Evidence from EU Members', *Economic Modelling*, 29(2), 262–272.

Khalid, A. M. and Guan, T. W. (1999) 'Causality Tests of Budget and Current Account Deficits: Cross-Country Comparisons', *Empirical Economics*, 24(3), 389–402.

Kim, C.-H. and Kim, D. (2006) 'Does Korea have Twin Deficits?' *Applied Economics Letters*, 13(10), 675–80.

Kim, S., Kim, S. H. and Wang, Y. (2007) 'Saving, Investment and International Capital Mobility in East Asia', *Japan and the World Economy*, 19(2), 279–91.

Maddala, G. S. and Kim, I. -M. (1998) *Unit Roots, Cointegration and Structural Change*, Cambridge: Cambridge University Press.

Marinheiro, C. F. (2008) 'Ricardian Equivalence, Twin Deficits, and the Feldstein–Horioka Puzzle in Egypt', *Journal of Policy Modeling*, 30(6), 1041–56.

Milesi-Ferretti, G. M. and Razin, A. (1998) 'Current Account Reversals and Currency Crises: Empirical Regularities', *NBER Working Papers No. 6620*, National Bureau of Economic Research, Inc.

Mohammadi, H. (2004) 'Budget Deficits and the Current Account Balance: New Evidence from Panel Data', *Journal of Economics and Finance*, 28(1), 39–45.

Obstfeld, M. and Rogoff, K. (1995) 'The Intertemporal Approach to Current Account' in Grossman, G. M. and K. Rogoff (Eds) *Handbook of International Economics*, 1731–99 (Amsterdam: Elsevier).

Obstfeld, M. and Rogoff, K. (1996) 'The Intertemporal Approach to the Current Account', *NBER Working Papers No. 4893*, National Bureau of Economic Research, Inc.

Ozmen, E. and Parmaksiz, K. (2003) 'Policy Regime Change and the Feldstein–Horioko Puzzle: The UK Evidence', *Journal of Policy Modeling*, 25(2), 137–49.

Papadogonas, T. and Stournaras, Y. (2006) 'Twin Deficits and Financial Integration in EU Member-States', *Journal of Policy Modeling*, 28(5), 595–602.

Pedroni, P. (1999) 'Critical Values for Cointegration Tests in Heterogeneous Panels with Multiple Regressors', *Oxford Bulletin of Economics and Statistics*, 61(Special Issue, Nov.), 653–70.

Pedroni, P. (2001) 'Purchasing Power Parity Tests in Cointegrated Panels', *The Review of Economics and Statistics*, 83(4), 727–31.

Pedroni, P. (2004) 'Panel Cointegration: Asymptotic and Finite Sample Properties of Pooled Time Series Tests with an Application to the PPP Hypothesis', *Econometric Theory*, 20(3), 597–625.

Pesaran, M. H. (2004) 'General Diagnostic Tests for Cross Section Dependence in Panels', *Cambridge Working Papers in Economics No. 0435*, University of Cambridge.

Rambaldi, A. N. and Doran, H. E. (1996) 'Testing for Granger Non-Causality in Cointegrated Systems Made Easy', *Working Paper in Econometrics and Applied Statistics No.88*, University of New England: Department of Econometrics.

Rodrik, D. (1999) 'The New Global Economy and Developing Countries: Making Openness Work', *Overseas Development Council*, Policy Essay No. 24, Washington, D.C. (distributed by the Johns Hopkins University Press, Baltimore).

Roa, B. B., Tamazian, A. and Kumar, S. (2010) 'Systems GMM Estimates of the Feldstein–Horioka Puzzle for the OECD Countries and Tests for Structural Breaks', *Economic Modelling*, 27(5), 1269–73.

Salvatore, D. (2006) 'Twin Deficits in the G-7 Countries and Global Structure Imbalances', *Journal of Policy Modeling*, 28(6), 701–12.

Summers, L. H. (1988) 'Tax Policy and International Competitiveness', in Frenkel J. A. (Ed.) *International Aspect of Fiscal Policies* (Chicago University Press: Chicago).

Toda, H. Y. and Yamamoto, T. (1995) 'Statistical Inference in Vector Autoregressions with Possibly Integrated Processes', *Journal of Econometrics*, 66(1–2), 225–50.

Westerlund, J. (2006) 'Testing for Panel Cointegration with Multiple Structural Breaks', *Oxford Bulletin of Economics and Statistics*, 68(1), 101–32.

Westerlund, J. and Edgerton, D. (2008) 'A Simple Test for Cointegration in Dependent Panels with Structural Breaks', *Oxford Bulletin of Economics and Statistics*, 70(5), 665–704.

Yamada, H. and Toda, H. Y. (1998) 'Inference in Possible Integrated Vector Autoregressive Models: Some Finite Sample Evidence', *Journal of Econometrics*, 86(1), 55–95.

7
Asia-Pacific Currency Excess Returns

Yuen-Meng Wong

1 Introduction

In a rational and risk-neutral setting, the forward exchange rate should be an unbiased predictor of the future spot exchange rate. However, there is a wide body of literature indicating the failure of the forward exchange rates to provide an unbiased prediction to the future spot exchange rate. According to Froot and Thaler (1990), the forward rates are not only biased but also systematically wrong as evidenced by the widespread finding of negative beta coefficient in the regression of changes in spot exchange rates on the lagged forward premium. The average value of the negative beta coefficient among 75 published papers is –0.88 (Froot & Thaler, 1990). This phenomenon has come to be known as the *forward bias puzzle*[1] (Obstfeld & Rogoff, 2000; Sarno, 2005). The forward bias puzzle has now become one of the classic issues in the field of international finance which remains unresolved. The failure of the forward exchange rate to provide unbiased prediction for future spot exchange rate proves to be a persistent phenomenon among the developed countries' currency. The failure of the unbiasedness hypothesis indicates the existence of currency excess returns (CER) from trading the forward exchange rates (Villanueva, 2007). As compared to the developed country currencies, the Asia-Pacific currencies are under-researched. This study attempts to fill the gap regarding the characteristics of the CER for the Asia-Pacific currencies.

There are four objectives to this study. First, we would like to investigate the extent of the forward bias puzzle in the Asia-Pacific currency market. Secondly, we would like to test for the predictability of the CER from the lagged forward premium. Our third objective is to identify some of the possible risk factors which could explain the CER. Finally, we are also interested to find out whether there exists any calendar effect in determining the CER. Our results show that the forward bias puzzle is present in the Asia-Pacific foreign exchange market even though it is not as pronounced as in the developed currency markets reported in the extant literature. There are four currency excess returns (i.e., Indonesian rupiah, Thai baht, Chinese yuan & Indian rupee) which show the evidence of predictability from the lagged forward premium. We also find that the individual equity market excess return, forward premium and individual inflation rate are significant factors in explaining the currency excess returns. Finally, there is generally an absence of calendar effect in determining the CER. Only some weak evidence of calendar effect is present in selected currencies' excess returns.

Our report is organized as follows: Section 2 reviews some related literature followed by the methodology and some econometric models in Section 3. Section 4 describes the data while Section 5 presents the empirical analysis. Section 6 concludes.

2 Literature review

The efficiency of the foreign exchange market remains inconclusive up to these days. Many studies have pointed out that the forward exchange rates are biased predictors of the future spot exchange rates (e.g., Lothian & Wu, 2011; Bansal & Dahlquist, 2000). This finding implies that there exists a profit opportunity by trading against the forward premium in the foreign exchange market. Hansen and Hodrick (1980) and Fama (1984) are among the early studies which show that the efficient market hypothesis (EMH) is violated in the foreign exchange market. Fama (1984) has provided an exemplary explanation to the widespread finding of the negative beta coefficient and, hence, the regression is now popularly known as the *Fama regression*. The popular belief at that time is that this condition would be traded away and the market would return to the state of efficiency. However, this problem has persisted. Some recent studies (e.g., Ahmad et al., 2012; Frankel & Poonawala, 2010; Hochradl & Wagner, 2010) show that the forward exchange rates are still biased predictors of future spot exchange rates. The Fama regression is portrayed as follows:

$$\Delta s_{t+1} = \alpha + \beta(f_t - s_t) + \varepsilon_{t+1} \tag{1}$$

s and f are logarithm spot and forward exchange rates quoted in terms of the U.S. dollar (USD) per foreign currency while Δ denotes first differencing operator and ε is a white noise error. The difference between the forward and spot exchange rates is also called the forward premium. According to the uncovered interest-rate parity (UIP), the value of α and β should be insignificantly different from zero and unity respectively. The EMH is violated when the regression estimates of α and β do not conform to the theoretical values. As already mentioned, most of the empirical results show that this condition is often violated. Moreover, the slope coefficient is not only significantly different from one but for most time shows a negative value. This finding has come to be known as the forward bias puzzle. Sarno (2005). has provided a commendable review on the current status of this puzzle.

The mystery is: Why is this phenomenon so persistent? Researchers have proposed a few explanations to this question. In the late 1980s and early 1990s, the most popular of all the proposed explanations was the distortion in the Fama regression caused by the existence of risk premium. Most of the researchers in this direction have found it hard to reconcile the risk premium with the high risk-aversion parameter usually reported in the test of the UIP (Engel, 1996). This puzzle is often considered the equivalence of the equity premium puzzle. Wu (2007), who utilizes the term *structure of interest rate* to extract the possible currency risk premium, shows that even after adjusting for the risk premium, the findings of the forward bias puzzle are still reported. Engel (1996) provides a lengthy but exemplary survey on the extent of success by using the risk premium explanation for the pervasive findings of the forward bias puzzle. He concludes that the risk premium explanation fails in this purpose. Chinn (2006) has provided a review of some of the promising explanations of the forward bias puzzle. He shows evidence that the UIP usually holds true when long-horizon data are employed or when alternative expectations theories are adopted. Chinn also reports that there is less rejection of UIP among the emerging market currencies. Some of the recent papers which emerged after Chinn (2006) provide vindications to his claims (e.g., Lothian & Wu, 2011; Frankel & Poonawala, 2010; Chakraborty & Evans, 2008).

Villanueva (2007) argues that the forward bias puzzle provides directional predictability to the currency excess returns. He finds that the larger the forward premium, the stronger is the signal of expected excess returns. Villanueva (2007) also reports that the returns on the forward bias trading strategies are not compensation for market risk. Taking the MSCI index returns for the four countries (i.e., United States, United

Kingdom, Germany & Japan) over their respective one-month euro rates, a world market risk premium is calculated as the capitalization-weighted average of the four individual market premiums. After regressing the currency excess returns on the world market risk premium, Villanueva finds no clear evidence of any systematic risk for the trading returns. On the other hand, Bansal and Dahlquist (2000) have pooled a set of currencies and run Fama regression to estimate the beta coefficient. They have reported that the forward bias puzzle is less severe (i.e., less negative or slightly positive but still significantly less than the hypothesized value of one) when the currencies are pooled than the individual currency regression. They have further divided their sample of currencies based on the country's income level and found that the forward bias puzzle is only restricted to the currencies of high-income economies and only to states when the U.S. interest rate is higher than its foreign counterparts. The lower-income countries are mainly the developing or emerging economies and, hence, the claim that the situation of the forward bias puzzle is less biased among these group of currencies. These results are generally supported by subsequent studies. Frankel and Poonawala (2010) and Ahmad et al. (2012) have also reported that the forward bias puzzle is less evident among the emerging market currencies. We have drawn on some of the methodological approach used in Villanueva (2007) and Bansal and Dahlquist (2000) in this study. We have also proposed a few more intuitive factors to be tested as possible determinants of the currency excess returns.

3 Methodology and econometric model

To determine the extent of the forward bias puzzle in the Asia-Pacific foreign exchange markets, we run the regression of one-month changes in the spot exchange rate on the lagged one-month forward premium as shown in Equation (1). The null hypothesis of H_0: $(\alpha,\beta) = (0,1)$ against the alternative of H_1: $(\alpha,\beta) \neq (0,1)$ is tested using the Wald F-test. The rejection of the null hypothesis implies that the forward exchange rate fails to provide an unbiased prediction to the future spot exchange rate and, thus, the violation of foreign exchange market efficiency. Besides the hypothesis testing, we are also interested in observing the sign of the slope coefficient. If the sign is less than zero, it indicates a serious violation of the uncovered interest-rate parity (UIP) and the existence of the forward bias puzzle.

As mentioned, Villanueva (2007) claims that the existence of the forward bias puzzle suggests that the currency excess returns (the difference between the changes in the spot exchange rate and the forward premium) are predictable by the forward premium. The currency excess returns (CER) can be understood as taking a long position in the forward contract of a foreign currency from the perspective of a U.S. investor. The summary statistics for each currency excess returns (CER) against the USD are provided in the empirical analysis section. The relationship of the CER is presented under Equations (2) and (3).

$$cer_{t+1} = (s_{t+1} - s_t) - (f_t - s_t) \tag{2}$$

$$cer_{t+1} = s_{t+1} - f_t \tag{3}$$

To investigate the predictability of the currency excess returns from the forward premium, we have run a regression of currency excess returns (CER) on the lagged forward premium. This regression is drawn on Villanueva (2007). The CER regression is equivalent to the Fama regression with a little rearrangement as shown in Equation (4).

$$cer_{t+1} = \gamma + \theta(f_t - s_t) + \varepsilon_{t+1} \tag{4}$$

The γ and θ in the CER regression are equivalent to α and (β-1) in the Fama regression. Under strict UIP, the γ and θ in the CER regression should be both equal to zero. However, in a relaxed UIP condition, a constant risk premium is introduced in the regression and it is represented by the γ. Therefore, in line with Villanueva (2007), we would only test for the significance of the slope coefficient in the CER regression to determine the predictability of the CER.

Finally, in order to determine the variables which could explain the CER as well as to study the month-of-the-year effect for the CER, we propose to test the following model:

$$cer_t^i = a + \sum_{j=1}^{11} b_j^i D_j + b_{12}^i fp_{t-1} + b_{13}^i RE_t^i + b_{14}^i RE_t^{US} + +b_{15}^i \lambda_t^i + b_{16}^i \lambda_t^{US} + \varepsilon_t \tag{5}$$

In the above equation (5), *cer* is the currency excess returns, D_1 to D_{11} are the dummy variables for months January to November, *fp* is the forward premium, *RE* is the one-month stock market excess returns, λ is the inflation rate and ε is a white noise error term. The superscript *i* is to denote the currency while *t* is to denote the time series.

In order to ensure proper inferences in the structural analysis for the above model, we conduct some diagnostic tests on the data as well as the whole regression model. These diagnostic tests are the multicollinearity, heteroscedasticity, autocorrelation, regression stability tests and unit root test. We compute a pair-wise correlation between the explanatory variables to detect for multicollinearity. While, the heteroscedasticity is tested with the White's test. If there is evidence of heteroscedasticity, the problem is corrected with the White's heteroscedasticity consistent coefficient covariance. Meanwhile the Durbin–Watson statistics are used to detect for autocorrelation in the error term. The stability of the regression is tested with Ramsey's RESET test in which two additional fitted terms are included into the regression equation. Finally, we adopt the augmented Dickey–Fuller (ADF) test to identify the stationarity property of the returns variables.

4 Data description

We have selected 12 currencies from the Asia Pacific for the purpose of this study. They are the Indonesian rupiah (IDR), Malaysian ringgit (MYR), Philippines peso (PHP), Singapore dollar (SGD), Thai baht (THB), Taiwanese dollar (TWD), South Korean won (KRW), Japanese yen (JPY), Australian dollar (AUD), New Zealand dollar (NZD), Chinese yuan (CNY) and Indian rupee (INR). Our main data are the spot and one-month forward exchange rates. The exchange rates are quoted in USD per unit of the Asia-Pacific currency. The exchange rates data are all stated in natural logarithm. We have also collected the stock market benchmark indices, one-month interest rate and national consumer price index (CPI) for each individual country. To avoid overlapping of data, we use observations at one-month frequencies. Our sample period is from January 1997 to June 2010 which translates to 162 observations for each variable.

Data related to the Korean won (KRW) starts from March 2002 due to data availability issues. There was a period of time in which the Malaysian ringgit (MYR) and Chinese yuan (CNY) were under the fixed exchange rate regime. This period is intentionally omitted for these two currencies from our analysis in order to obtain more accurate inferences. All of these data are obtained from various databases available through the Datastream. Appendix A.2 provides a list of the shorthand of the data and their respective sources.

5 Empirical results and analyses

First of all, the returns variables adopted in this study are mostly found to be stationary and can be appropriately used in the regression analysis.[2] Table 7.1 shows the results of the Fama regression for all 12 Asia-Pacific currency markets. The rejection of the null hypothesis implies that the

Table 7.1 Conventional Fama regression results

	AUD	CNY	IDR	INR	JPY	KRW	MYR	NZD	PHP	SGD	THB	TWD
Beta	0.7700	0.4771	0.1270	−1.0651	0.3371	−0.4883	1.3276	0.6711	0.5156	1.1125	0.3041	0.6380
s.e.	0.8367	0.1031	0.2101	0.5556	0.8398	1.0511	1.1358	0.8109	0.6512	0.7237	0.1381	0.3825
t-stat	−0.2749	−5.0715	−4.1546	−3.7169	−0.7894	−1.4160	0.2884	−0.4056	−0.7439	0.1554	−5.0374	−0.9464
Intercept	0.0014	0.0018	−0.0079	−0.0056	0.0005	0.0004	−0.003	0.0014	−0.0012	−0.0012	0.0011	−0.0015
s.e.	0.0033	0.0006	0.0069	0.0025	0.0037	0.0040	0.004	0.0038	0.0036	0.0016	0.0032	0.0014
t-stat	0.4262	2.8288	−1.1472	−2.2272	0.1269	0.0986	−0.7548	0.3572	−0.3351	−0.7205	0.3542	−1.0723
R-sq	0.0053	0.2696	0.0023	0.0241	0.0010	0.0022	0.0172	0.0043	0.0039	0.0146	0.0296	0.0172
Wald-F	0.199	12.951*	8.826*	7.775*	0.487	1.094	0.3895	0.303	0.372	0.277	15.592*	1.273
p-value	0.8200	0.0000	0.0002	0.0006	0.6152	0.3389	0.0000	0.7388	0.6899	0.7587	0.0000	0.2829

Notes: Fama regression, $\Delta s_{t+1} = \alpha + \beta(f_t - s_t) + \varepsilon_{t+1}$ is estimated with ordinary least squares (OLS). The period covered is from January 1997 to June 2010 for most of the currency markets except for Malaysian ringgit (MYR) and Chinese yuan (CNY) markets in which the 'fixed-regime' period is excluded. The Wald statistic F-value is computed to test for the null hypothesis of H_0: $(\alpha, \beta) = (0, 1)$ against the alternative hypothesis of H_1: $(\alpha, \beta) \neq (0, 1)$. The rejection of null hypothesis implies that the forward premiums fail to provide unbiased prediction for future changes in the spot exchange rates and thus the foreign exchange market is not efficient.

* indicates that the foreign exchange market is not efficient at all reasonable levels of significance.

forward premiums fail to provide an unbiased prediction for the future changes in the spot exchange rate and, in turn, implies the failure of market efficiency. From the results, most of the foreign exchange markets cannot reject the null hypothesis and, thus, are considered as efficient. The foreign exchange markets which are not efficient from this analysis are the Indonesian rupiah (IDR), Thai baht (THB), Chinese yuan (CNY) and Indian rupee (INR) markets.

From the results of Fama regression, there is some evidence of forward bias puzzle in the Asia-Pacific foreign exchange markets. Next we move on to present the results regarding the predictability of currency excess returns (CER) from the lagged forward premium. The summary statistics for each CER against the USD are provided first in Table 7.2 followed by the results of the slope coefficient from the CER regression in Table 7.3. There are four currency excess returns which are predictable by the forward premium as shown in Table 7.3. These are Indonesian rupiah (IDR), Thai baht (THB), Chinese yuan (CNY) and Indian rupee (INR). These results are consistent with the Fama regression's results. Even though the slope coefficients of these four CER regressions are significant, it must be noted that their corresponding R^2 are relatively low, ranging from 0.10 for IDR to 0.31 for CNY.

Another interesting result to note from Table 7.3 is the sign of the slope coefficient of the CER regressions. Most are negative except for the CERs of the Malaysian ringgit (MYR) and Singapore dollar (SGD). Let us take the perspective of a U.S. investor to interpret this finding. Holding covered interest rate parity, the forward premium is a measure of the interest rate differential between the United States and the respective foreign country. A positive forward premium indicates that the U.S. interest rate is higher than the foreign interest rate. From the CER regression, it is clear that the CERs move inversely with the forward premium. When the U.S. interest rate is higher than the foreign interest rate (i.e., positive forward premium), the currency excess returns tend to be smaller. On the contrary, when the foreign interest rate is higher than the U.S. interest rate (i.e., negative forward premium), the currency excess returns are expected to be higher. In addition, the higher the foreign interest rate (i.e., the larger the negative forward premium), the higher the currency excess returns.

Finally, we move on to look at some of the possible factors which could explain the currency excess returns and whether there is any calendar effect in the relationship. Before we discuss the results from the regression of the full model, it is helpful for us to look at the diagnostic test results. The results of the diagnostic tests are presented in Table 7.4. The pair-wise correlations between the independent variables

Table 7.2 Summary statistics for currency excess returns (CER)

CER	IDR	MYR	PHP	SGD	THB	TWD	KRW	JPY	AUD	NZD	CNY	INR
Mean	−5.14	−3.94	1.13	−1.26	8.53	−2.05	2.01	−1.88	2.08	2.59	0.28	2.36
Median	2.50	0.44	4.50	−1.22	5.08	−1.19	4.89	−4.09	2.89	5.65	0.10	4.05
Std. dev.	31.62	12.12	9.49	6.35	13.92	5.84	13.55	11.62	13.36	14.25	1.77	6.63
Sharpe ratio	−0.16	−0.32	0.12	−0.20	0.61	−0.35	0.15	−0.16	0.16	0.18	0.16	0.36
Observations	161	80	161	161	161	161	99	161	161	161	60	151

Notes: Summary statistics of currency excess returns (CER). The mean, median and standard deviation are stated in term of annualized percentage. The initial estimates of the summary statistics are generated in monthly percentage. Both the monthly mean and median CER are annualized by multiplying the monthly figure with 12 while the monthly standard deviation is multiplied by $\sqrt{12}$. The Sharpe ratio is calculated by taking the annualized mean CER to divide by the annualized standard deviation. The period covered is from Jan-1997 to Jun-2010 for most currency markets except for Malaysian ringgit (MYR) and Chinese yuan (CNY) markets in which the 'fixed-regime' period is excluded.

Table 7.3 CER regression results

CER's slope	AUD	CNY	IDR	INR	JPY	KRW	MYR	NZD	PHP	SGD	THB	TWD
Slope	−0.2300	−0.5229*	−0.8730*	−2.0651*	−0.6629	−1.4883	0.3276	−0.3289	−0.4844	0.1125	−0.6959*	−0.3620
s.e.	0.8367	0.1031	0.2101	0.5556	0.8398	1.0511	1.1358	0.8109	0.6512	0.7237	0.1381	0.3825
t-stat	−0.2749	−5.0715	−4.1546	−3.7169	−0.7894	−1.4160	0.2884	−0.4056	−0.7439	0.1554	−5.0374	−0.9464
R-sq	0.0005	0.3072	0.0979	0.0849	0.0039	0.0203	0.0011	0.0010	0.0035	0.0002	0.1376	0.0056

Notes: Beta estimates from the CER regression, $cer_{t+1} = \gamma + \theta(f_t - s_t) + \varepsilon_{t+1}$. The period covered is from Jan-1997 to Jun-2010 for most currency markets except for Malaysian ringgit (MYR) and Chinese yuan (CNY) markets in which the 'fixed-regime' period is excluded. The significance of the slope coefficient implies that the currency excess returns are predictable from the forward premium.

* indicates significance at the 0.05 level.

Table 7.4 Diagnostic test results on the regression variables

Panel A: Pairwise correlation

IDR	FPIDR	REIDR	REUSD	INFID	INFUS	KRW	FPKRW	REKRW	REUSD	INFKR	INFUS
FPIDR	1.000					FPKRW	1.000				
REIDR	0.115	1.000				REKRW	−0.147	1.000			
REUSD	0.132	0.012	1.000			REUSD	−0.456	0.098	1.000		
INFID	−0.028	0.055	−0.037	1.000		INFKR	−0.081	0.038	−0.007	1.000	
INFUS	−0.020	0.148	−0.013	−0.046	1.000	INFUS	−0.166	0.316	0.080	0.381	1.000
MYR	FPMYR	REMYR	REUSD	INFMY	INFUS	JPY	FPJPY	REJPY	REUSD	INFJP	INFUS
FPMYR	1.000					FPJPY	1.000				
REMYR	0.162	1.000				REJPY	0.017	1.000			
REUSD	0.127	0.105	1.000			REUSD	−0.004	0.155	1.000		
INFMY	−0.021	0.041	−0.094	1.000		INFJP	−0.018	0.031	0.181	1.000	
INFUS	0.029	0.192	0.042	0.444	1.000	INFUS	0.070	0.297	−0.013	0.207	1.000
PHP	FPPHP	REPHP	REUSD	INFPH	INFUS	AUD	FPAUD	REAUD	REUSD	INFAU	INFUS
FPPHP	1.000					FPAUD	1.000				
REPHP	−0.034	1.000				REAUD	0.040	1.000			
REUSD	−0.018	0.183	1.000			REUSD	0.036	0.112	1.000		
INFPH	0.096	−0.081	0.005	1.000		INFAU	−0.149	−0.155	−0.185	1.000	
INFUS	0.073	0.228	0.079	0.507	1.000	INFUS	−0.003	0.291	−0.013	0.062	1.000
SGD	FPSGD	RESGD	REUSD	INFSG	INFUS	NZD	FPNZD	RENZD	REUSD	INFNZ	INFUS
FPSGD	1.000					FPNZD	1.000				
RESGD	0.121	1.000				RENZD	0.043	1.000			
REUSD	0.001	0.680	1.000			REUSD	0.027	0.038	1.000		
INFSG	0.043	−0.057	−0.002	1.000		INFNZ	−0.289	−0.189	−0.234	1.000	
INFUS	0.088	0.031	−0.013	0.128	1.000	INFUS	−0.031	0.140	−0.030	−0.025	1.000

Continued

Table 7.4 Continued

THB	FPTHB	RETHB	REUSD	INFTH	INFUS	CNY	FPCNY	RECNY	REUSD	INFCN	INFUS
FPTHB	1.000					FPCNY	1.000				
RETHB	0.090	1.000				RECNY	0.043	1.000			
REUSD	−0.033	−0.018	1.000			REUSD	0.150	0.281	1.000		
INFTH	−0.104	0.101	−0.018	1.000		INFCN	0.130	−0.031	0.311	1.000	
INFUS	−0.047	0.200	−0.013	0.428	1.000	INFUS	0.560	0.220	0.082	0.168	1.000
TWD	FPTWD	RETWD	REUSD	INFTW	INFUS	INR	FPINR	REINR	REUSD	INFIN	INFUS
FPTWD	1.000					FPINR	1.000				
RETWD	0.124	1.000				REINR	0.073	1.000			
REUSD	−0.043	0.079	1.000			REUSD	−0.079	0.033	1.000		
INFTW	0.122	−0.093	0.027	1.000		INFIN	−0.327	−0.113	0.042	1.000	
INFUS	0.018	0.181	−0.013	0.113	1.000	INFUS	0.156	0.260	−0.006	−0.201	1.000

Panel B: Hetreroscedasticity white's test

	IDR	MYR	PHP	SGD	THB	TWD	KRW	JPY	AUD	NZD	CNY	INR
F-stat	8.1220	2.3073	1.0968	1.0533	3.5964	1.8880	1.8154	0.7718	1.4595	1.3668	2.6371	0.9681
p-value	0.0000	0.0097	0.3861	0.4055	0.0000	0.0259	0.0530	0.7150	0.1229	0.1662	0.0058	0.4949

Panel C: Ramsey's RESET test

	IDR	MYR	PHP	SGD	THB	TWD	KRW	JPY	AUD	NZD	CNY	INR
F-stat	17.7101	3.7746	1.6623	3.3001	0.2186	0.1024	0.8778	0.1216	1.5194	0.5975	11.5809	5.3892
p-value	0.0000	0.0285	0.2017	0.0397	0.8040	0.9027	0.4218	0.8856	0.2224	0.5516	0.0001	0.0056

Table 7.5 Full model regression results

	IDR	MYR	PHP	SGD	THB	TWD	KRW	JPY	AUD	NZD	CNY	INR
Jan	−0.004	0.002	0.012	0.006	0.003	−0.003	0.036	0.000	−0.006	0.000	0.004*	0.011*
Feb	−0.034	0.005	0.004	−0.007	0.003	−0.003	0.020	−0.003	−0.005	−0.019	0.002	0.018***
Mar	0.022	0.021	−0.013	0.006	0.017	−0.001	0.006	−0.006	0.003	−0.003	0.002	0.000
Apr	0.011	0.019	−0.005	−0.002	0.020	−0.006	0.013	−0.015	−0.012	−0.018	0.002	0.022***
May	0.023	0.019	−0.007	0.013*	0.010	0.000	0.015	−0.004	0.007	−0.001	0.000	0.011
Jun	−0.026	0.004	−0.022*	−0.005	−0.006	−0.010	−0.013	0.007	−0.012	−0.013	0.000	0.000
Jul	0.012	−0.001	−0.022*	−0.003	0.005	−0.003	−0.004	0.002	0.001	−0.012	0.001	0.006
Aug	0.020	0.005	−0.007	0.002	−0.017	−0.010	0.018	−0.009	−0.010	−0.026	0.001	0.010*
Sep	0.013	0.006	−0.022*	−0.002	−0.007	−0.008	−0.015	0.018	−0.023	−0.010	−0.003	−0.001
Oct	0.013	−0.005	0.005	0.004	−0.002	0.000	−0.002	−0.001	0.005	0.004	0.003	0.012*
Nov	0.045	0.029	−0.001	0.008	0.001	−0.007	0.004	0.020	0.001	−0.009	0.001	0.014**
fp_{t-1}	−0.896***	−2.067*	−0.365	−0.592	−0.810***	−0.355	1.339	−0.936	−0.711	−1.227	−0.508***	−1.625***
RE	0.106	0.203***	0.099**	0.077***	0.045	0.089***	0.310***	−0.051	0.306***	0.286***	−0.016***	0.092***
RE-US	−0.217	0.023	0.029	−0.090**	−0.019	−0.022	0.234*	−0.005	0.069	0.056	−0.006	0.041
Λ	−2.388***	−0.920	−0.109	0.532	−2.378***	0.348*	−4.072**	0.811	−0.579	−1.123	0.143*	−0.067
λ−US	2.679	0.885	0.698	1.214**	1.941*	0.292	2.064*	−0.193	3.339***	2.601**	0.061	0.647
Intercept	0.002	−0.010	0.010	−0.005	0.000	0.002	−0.005	0.001	0.000	0.007	0.001	−0.015***
R^2	0.386	0.320	0.421	0.176	0.270	0.243	0.483	0.091	0.272	0.176	0.571	0.427
Adj. R^2	0.317	0.147	0.215	0.084	0.189	0.158	0.330	−0.010	0.192	0.085	0.412	0.358
F-stat	5.646	1.854	2.041	1.917	3.332	2.883	3.155	0.903	3.369	1.927	3.580	6.231
p-value	0.000	0.043	0.031	0.023	0.000	0.000	0.001	0.567	0.000	0.022	0.000	0.000
D-W Stat	1.650	1.745	1.481	2.211	1.635	1.734	2.366	2.192	1.970	2.160	1.336	1.758

Notes: The slope coefficients for the full model, $cer_t^i = a + \sum_{j=1}^{11} b_j^i D_j + b_{12}^i fp_{t-1} + b_{13}^i RE_t^i + b_{14}^i RE_t^{US} + + b_{15}^i \lambda_t^i + b_{16}^i \lambda_t^{US} + \varepsilon_t$, are estimated with OLS. The rows from Jan to Nov are coefficients for dummy variables of January to November, fp_{t-1} is the coefficient for lagged forward premium while RE & RE-US are coefficients for stock index excess returns for the Asia-Pacific countries and the USA and λ & λ-US are coefficients for inflation rate for the respective Asia-Pacific countries and the USA. The period covered is from Jan-1997 to Jun-2010 for most currency markets except for Malaysian ringgit (MYR) and Chinese yuan (CNY) markets in which the 'fixed-regime' period is excluded. * indicates significance at the 0.10 level, ** significance at the 0.05 level and *** significance at the 0.01 level.

show no evidence of multicollinearity. About half of the regressions of the full model show rejection of the null hypothesis of no heteroscedasticity in the error term at the 0.05 level. The models which reject the null hypothesis are IDR, MYR, THB, TWD and CNY excess returns. In order to ensure correct inferences of the regression results, we corrected this problem with the White's heteroscedasticity consistent coefficient covariance. The Durbin–Watson (D–W) statistics shown in the results indicate the existence of weak autocorrelation in some of the regression models. We choose to maintain our models because the autocorrelation problem as indicated by the D–W statistics is relatively mild. From the Ramsey's RESET test results, about half of the CER models reject the null hypothesis of no misspecification. These are IDR, MYR, SGD, CNY and INR excess returns. Thus, we must interpret the regression results with caution.

Table 7.5 shows the results from running the regression of Equation (5). The F-statistics as reported in Table 7.5 show that these models are generally significant in explaining the currency excess returns (CER) for the Asia-Pacific foreign exchange markets, with the exception of Japanese yen market. The R^2 of the models ranges from 0.09 (JPY) to 0.57 (CNY). The calendar effect is not significant in most of the foreign markets. The lagged forward premium is significant in explaining the CER in five of the foreign exchange markets. Most of the foreign exchange markets' CER (9 out of 12) are significantly explained by the individual country equity market excess returns. However, the U.S. equity market excess return is not significant in most of the foreign exchange markets. Finally, the individual country inflation factor is significant only in the IDR, THB, TWD, KRW and CNY foreign exchange markets. While the U.S. inflation factor is significant in the SGD, THB, KRW, AUD and NZD foreign exchange markets. These results have highlighted the individual equity market excess returns as the most important factor in explaining the CER. There is also some evidence to show that the lagged forward premium and the individual country inflation rate are significant factors in explaining the CER. This finding also implies that the CER are not explainable by common factors, such as the U.S. equity market excess returns and the U.S. inflation rate.

6 Conclusion

This study has shed further light in the foreign exchange markets of the Asia-Pacific region. Our results highlight the key risk factors which are important in explaining the currency excess returns. Market participants would find these results useful in strategizing their investment strategies. We have documented the existence of the forward bias puzzle in the Asia-Pacific foreign exchange markets. The sign of the slope coefficients of the Fama regression are mostly positive, and this implies that the forward bias puzzle in the Asia-Pacific foreign exchange markets are not as severe as the advanced markets in which the slope coefficients are usually negative. Our findings in this respect are consistent with Frankel and Poonawala (2010) and Bansal and Dahlquist (2000).

We have also found that the currency excess returns, defined as the difference between the one-month realized spot exchange rate, s_{t+1}, and the one-month forward rate, f_t, are predictable for some of the foreign exchange markets in the Asia-Pacific region. Most of the currency excess returns move inversely with the forward premium. This relationship implies that when the U.S. interest rate is higher than the foreign interest rate (i.e., positive forward premium), the currency excess returns tend to be smaller, and vice versa. This finding is consistent with Lustig et al. (2008). who prove that the currency excess returns are dependent on the size of the forward premium (or, equivalently, the interest differential).

Finally, we have conducted multiple linear regressions to identify the possible factors which could explain the currency excess returns. We have found that most of the CER are significantly explained by the individual country equity market excess returns, lagged forward premium and the

Appendix A.2 Data

Constructed series	
Currency excess returns	$s_{t+1} - f_t$
Forward premium	$f_t - s_t$
Inflation rate	$(CPI_t - CPI_{t-1}/CPI_{t-1}$
Stock market excess returns	$[SI_t - SI_{it-1}/SI_{t-1}] - i_{im}$
Symbol (in-text)	
Log spot exchange rate	s
Log forward exchange rate	f
Log forward premium	fp
Log currency excess returns	cer
Inflation rate	λ
Consumer price index	CPI
Stock market excess returns	RE
Stock index	SI
Interest rate (1m)	i_{1m}

Appendix A.3 Data

Variables	Source code	
	Spot	1m forward
Exchange rate data (against USD)		
Indonesian rupiah (IDR)	TDIDRSP	USIDR1F
Malaysian ringgit (MYR)	TDMYRSP	USMYR1F
Philippines peso (PHP)	TDPHPSP	USPHP1F
Singapore dollar (SGD)	TDSGDSP	USSGD1F
Thai baht (THB)	TDTHBSP	USTHB1F
Taiwanese dollar (TWD)	TDTWDSP	USTWD1F
Korean won (KRW)	TDKRWSP	USKRW1F
Japanese yen (JPY)	TDJPYSP	USJPY1F
Australian dollar (AUD)	TDAUDSP	USAUD1F
New Zealand dollar (NZD)	TDNZDSP	USNZD1F
Chinese yuan (CNY)	TDCNYSP	USCNY1F
Indian rupee (INR)	TDINRSP	USINR1F
Sock market indices		
JAKARTA SE COMPOSITE	JAKCOMP(PI)	
FTSE BURSA MALAYSIA KLCI	FBMKLCI(PI)	
PHILIPPINE SE index (PSEi)	PSECOMP(PI)	
STRAITS TIMES INDEX	STI	
BANGKOK S.E.T.	BNGKSET(PI)	
TAIWAN SE	TAIWGHT(PI)	
KOREA SE COMPOSITE (KOSPI)	KORCOMP(PI)	
TOPIX	TOKYOSE(PI)	
ASX ALL ORDINARIES	ASXAORD(PI)	
NZX ALL	NZSEALL(PI)	
SHANGHAI SE COMPOSITE	CHSCOMP(PI)	
INDIA BSE (100) NATIONAL	IBOMBSE(PI)	
US DOW JONES INDUSTRIALS	USSHRPRCF	
Interest rate (1month)		
INDONESIAN INTERBANK	IDIBK1M	
MALAYSIA INTERBANK	MYIBD1M	
MANILA INTERBANK	PHIBK1M	
SINGAPORE INTERBANK	SNGIB1M	
THAILAND INTERBANK	THBBIB1	
TAIWAN DEPOSIT	TADEP1M	
SEOUL INTERBANK	KRIBK1M	
TOKYO INTERBANK JP YEN	JPIBK1M	
AUSTRALIAN $ DEPO	GSAUD1M	
NEW ZEALAND $ DEPO	GSNZD1M	
CHINA INTERBANK	CHIB1MO	
INDIA BANK DEPOSIT	INFD46D	
US EURO$ DEP.	FREDD1M	

Appendix A.3 Continued

Variables	**Source code**	
	Spot	**1m forward**
Exchange rate data (against USD)		
Consumer price index/Inflation rate*		
Indonesia	IDCONPRCF	
Malaysia	MYCONPRCF	
Philippines	PHCONPRCF	
Singapore	SPCONPRCF	
Thailand	THCONPRCF	
Taiwan	TWCONPRCF	
South Korea	KOCONPRCF	
Japan	JPCONPRCF	
Australia	AUCPANNL	
New Zealand	NZCPANNL	
China	CHCONPRCF	
India	INCPANNL	
US CPI	USCONPRCE	

Source: All data are from Datastream, except exchange rates are also from Thomson Reuters & WM-Reuters, STI stock index is from Yahoo Finance.
Note: * annual inflation rate for Australia and New Zealand are converted to monthly rate by dividing them by 12.

individual country inflation rate. The common factors are usually not significant in the relationship. The calendar effects are also absent from the relationship.

Notes

1. The forward bias puzzle is also known as the forward premium puzzle and forward discount puzzle (Sarno, 2005). We use only the term forward bias puzzle for the sake of consistency.
2. Mild non-stationarity is identified for only inflation series for the following three countries: Australia, India and New Zealand.

References

Ahmad, R., Rhee, S. G. and Wong, Y. M. (2012) 'Foreign Exchange Market Efficiency Under Recent Crises: Asia-Pacific Focus', *Journal of International Money and Finance*, 31(6), 1574–92.

Bansal, R. and Dahlquist, M. (2000) 'The Forward Premium Puzzle: Different Tales from Developed and Emerging Economies', *Journal of International Economics*, 51(1), 115–14.

Chakraborty, A. and Evans, G. W. (2008) 'Can Perpetual Learning Explain the Forward-Premium Puzzle?' *Journal of Monetary Economics*, 55(3), 477–90.
Chinn, M. D. (2006) 'The (Partial) Rehabilitation of Interest Rate Parity in the Floating Rate Era: Longer Horizons, Alternative Expectations, and Emerging Markets', *Journal of International Money and Finance*, 25(1), 7–21.
Engel, C. (1996) 'The Forward Discount Anomaly and the Risk Premium: A Survey of Recent Evidence', *Journal of Empirical Finance*, 3(2), 123–92.
Fama, E. F. (1984) 'Forward and Spot Exchange Rates', *Journal of Monetary Economics*, 14(3), 319–38.
Frankel, J. and Poonawala, J. (2010) 'The Forward Market in Emerging Currencies: Less Biased than in Major Currencies', *Journal of International Money and Finance*, 29(3), 585–98.
Froot, K. A. and Thaler, R. H. (1990) 'Anomalies: Foreign Exchange', *The Journal of Economic Perspectives*, 4(3), 179–92.
Hansen, L. P. and Hodrick, R. J. (1980) 'Forward Exchange Rates as Optimal Predictors of Future Spot Rates: An Econometric Analysis', *The Journal of Political Economy*, 88(5), 829–53.
Hochradl, M. and Wagner, C. (2010) 'Trading the Forward Bias: Are There Limits to Speculation?' *Journal of International Money and Finance*, 29(3), 423–41.
Lothian, J. R. and Wu, L. (2011) 'Uncovered Interest-Rate Parity Over the Past Two Centuries', *Journal of International Money and Finance*, 30(3), 448–73.
Lustig, H., Roussanov, N. and Verdelhan, A. (2008) 'Common Risk Factors in Currency Markets', *NBER WP 14082*.
Obstfeld, M. and Rogoff, K. (2000) 'The Six Major Puzzles in International Macroeconomics: Is There a Common Cause?' *NBER Macroeconomics Annual*, 15, 339–90.
Sarno, L. (2005) 'Viewpoint: Towards a Solution to the Puzzles in Exchange Rate Economics: Where Do We Stand?', *Canadian Journal of Economics–Revue Canadienne D Economique*, 38(3), 673–708.
Villanueva, O. M. (2007) 'Forecasting Currency Excess Returns: Can the Forward Bias be Exploited?' *Journal of Financial and Quantitative Analysis*, 42(4), 963–90.
Wu, S. (2007) 'Interest Rate Risk and the Forward Premium Anomaly in Foreign Exchange Markets', *Journal of Money Credit and Banking*, 39(2–3), 423–42.

Part IV

Foreign Direct Investments and Equity Investments

8

Openness, Market Size and Foreign Direct Investments

Catherine Soke-Fun Ho, Khairunnisa Amir, Linda Sia Nasaruddin and Nurain Farahana Zainal Abidin

1 Introduction

Foreign direct investment (FDI) has come to play a major role in the internationalization of business in the past decades. Reacting to changes in technology coupled with growing liberalization of the national regulatory framework governing investment in enterprises and changes in capital markets, profound changes have occurred in the size, scope and methods of FDI. Productive FDI usually brings along lasting and stable capital flows as investments in long-term assets. These funds are introduced into a country's economy, contributing to the aggregate demand of the economy and, therefore, eventual growth. Companies within the country experience competitive pressure brought about by FDI and tend to be more productive to effectively counter the threat of the competitor from abroad, which contributes to the growth of a country's income. Employment generation is also another positive effect of FDI when a country becomes more productive. With increased productivity and competitiveness, employment is created and introduction to the world economy is more feasible. New informational technological systems and the decline in global communication costs have made management of foreign investments far more effective than in the past.

The sea of change in trade and investment policies and in the regulatory environment – including trade policy and tariff liberalization, easing of restrictions on foreign investment and acquisition in many nations plus the deregulation and privatization of many industries – has probably been the most significant catalyst for expansion of FDI across the globe. Since the recent global financial crisis and the previous financial crises in Asia and Latin America, developing and newly industrializing countries have to rely on FDI in order to supplement national savings and promote economic development. Most of the emerging and transition economies in Central and Eastern Europe have built their economies largely on period infrastructure, and it is widely recognized that much this infrastructure should be replaced if these economies plan to accelerate economic growth and participate successfully within the broader European Union economic zone. Emerging economies derive benefits from foreign investments to improve their balance of payments, increase exports to earn more hard currency, reduce imports to save more of their own hard currency, increase employment to improve their fiscal positions and enhance their access to newer technologies.

According to Vijayakumar and Sridharan (2010), in the face of the U.S. credit turmoil and growth slowdown, the emerging economies of Brazil, Russia, India, China and South Africa (BRICS) are found to exhibit economic strength by their strong domestic demand growth. The demographic trends, labour supply dynamics and low urbanization ratios seem to remain favourable for Brazil, India and South Africa. These countries find their working age population will continue to expand until the middle of the current century, while in China its population may decline after 2015 and Russia is at risk of a steep decline. A low urbanization ratio in China can help to neutralize the projected decline in the working age of the population by allowing the transfer of labour from the countryside to the more productive urban economy. Brazil is already very highly urbanized relative to many of the developed countries in the world. The BRICS countries are expected to face prosperity in economic and social development in the coming decades. The economic growth of these countries should be tremendous and should exert competition with, and challenges to, developed countries. The current flow of FDI into BRICS is extremely complex and subject to the competitive environment in the home and host countries. In this context, this study intends to examine whether openness to trade, market size and other major determinants are significant in affecting FDI flows into Malaysia and BRICS countries.

The world economy has seen vast changes in foreign investments, and investors are currently looking into new markets. Countries such as Brazil, Russia, China, India and South Africa are currently the new and hot FDI destinations. These countries offer not only an enormous untapped market, but also much lower production costs. China, India and Malaysia are countries in the Asian region. The availability of human capital, infrastructure and education are factors that attract investors to these countries. Recent development in Malaysia shows a decline in FDI inflows (Figure 8.1). This country has lost some of its appeal in attracting those foreign investors who are instead looking to neighbouring countries like China and India due to Malaysia's shortage of human capital and upward pressure on wages. It is believed that Malaysia still has the ability to improve economically by enhancing and stimulating its domestic economy.

Other parts of the world, including Brazil, Russia and South Africa, are attracting vast amounts of FDI (Figures 8.1 and 8.2). Many factors may have influenced increasing FDI to these countries, amongst them

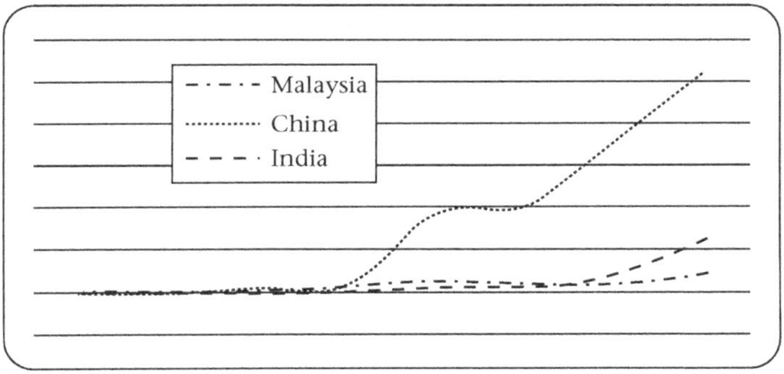

Figure 8.1 Total FDI inflow for the past 30 years in Malaysia, China and India
Source: Data collected from International Financial Statistics, IMF.

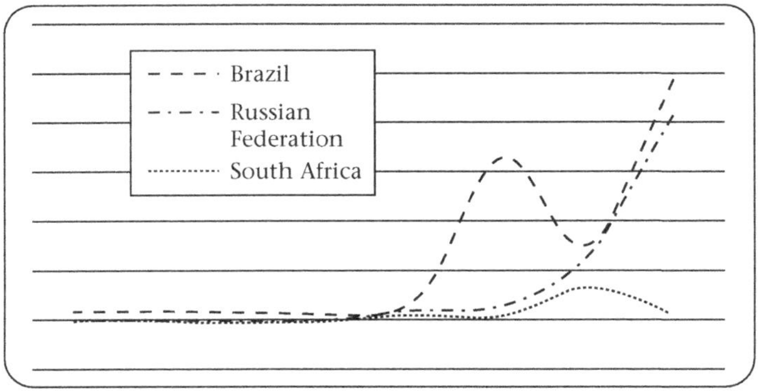

Figure 8.2 Total FDI inflow for the past 30 years in Brazil, Russia and South Africa
Source: Data collected from International Financial Statistics, IMF.

the availability of human capital, low labour costs, education and the opportunity to develop these countries. Brazil, China and Russia have attracted more FDI relative to South Africa.

China has the highest amount of FDI inflows among fast-emerging countries, and the fluctuation in FDI inflows has become a major concern for researchers and policymakers. This is because FDI is still one of the main factors that drive the economic growth of a host country. The importance of FDI has resulted in local governments implementing policies to attract FDI to their respective countries. The results from this research would enlighten policymakers and authorities in understanding the factors that encourage foreign investments for appropriate strategies and recommendations befitting the cause.

This study aims to investigate the significant relations between trade openness, market size and other fundamentals on FDI in fast-emerging countries. Understanding the drivers of foreign investment would provide authorities in respective fast-emerging countries with vital information on policy decisions that would enable them to accelerate growth and eliminate poverty. The set of fast-emerging countries included in the study are Brazil, Russia, India, China, South Africa and Malaysia. Independent variables are divided into two sets of macroeconomic fundamentals and country-specific factors. These determinants are market size, trade openness, financial depth, exchange rate, government consumption, inflation rate, interest rate, economic freedom, employment, literacy rate and infrastructure quality.

2 Literature

Most previous studies have identified a variety of variables as key factors that drive the flows of FDI. The next section details the literature, and this study specifically included some other variables which are very relevant to emerging countries but not commonly researched, including economic freedom, financial development and trade openness.

2.1 Macroeconomic fundamentals

Market size is considered one of the most important determinants for horizontal market-seeking FDI. Market size directly affects investment return and profits, and larger market growth indicates potential for a larger market and more promising prospects for products. Duanmu and Guney (2009) found that China's and India's FDI are positively related to the host country's market size, and they concluded that both countries' FDIs are attracted to locations with large market size. Zhang (2001) found similar results and confirmed that market size and infrastructure are key factors in attracting foreign investments.

Torrisi et al. (2008) applied generalized least squares regression to identify the determinants of FDI in Central Europe and found that market size was a critical factor for FDI inflows during the economic transition period from 1989 to 2006. A dynamic economy and appropriate economic growth policies are also crucial in order to attract FDI to Central Europe. In addition, according to Quazi (2007), greater market size (measured by per capita real GDP) is found to attract more FDI in East Asia. On the other hand, Kimino et al. (2007) found contradicting results in their research where there exists a negative relationship between the market size of source countries and FDI flows into Japan. Their results confirmed that market size does not exert a statistically significant influence on FDI into Japan, a developed country. Hailu (2010) conducted an empirical analysis of the demand side determinants of FDI into African nations and found that the host country's market has a statistically significant positive effect on FDI inflow. This clearly shows that investors target local markets besides the export market when undertaking FDI decisions.

Another study, by Janicki and Wunnava (2004), found that the size of the market accurately reflects their theoretical expectations and confirmed that market size is a significant determinant of FDI among members of the European Union. Based on their result, FDI flows are greater in larger economies with well-built markets. Kim and Rhe (2009) also explored the trends as well as the determinants of South Korean FDI and found that South Korean investors prefer larger markets and strategic assets. In addition, Bakir and Alfawwaz (2009) conducted a study to identify the determinants of foreign direct investment (FDI) in Jordan for the period 1996 to 2007 and confirmed that GDP was positively related to FDI. The important role of market size in terms of GDP is found to significantly affect the volume of FDI flow to Jordan.

Agosin and Machado (2007) developed an ordinal index in order to measure the openness of FDI policy regimes in developing countries and found that openness is a factor that permits FDI. A later study by Vogiatzoglou (2007), who investigated the location determinants of inward FDI in South and East Asia, found that if the degree of integration of the host country to the international economy rises, inward FDI also increases in the long run. Trade openness, therefore, has a significantly positive effect on FDI. Moreover, Oladipo (2010) found that trade openness has significant positive effect on trade and investments. Results suggested that liberalization in Nigeria has significant impact on the economy with higher levels of exports due to a more flexible trade policy.

Sekkat and Veganzones-Varoudakis (2007) assessed the importance of openness in developing countries and found that increased openness as well as improvement of the other aspects of the investment climate had contributed greatly in attracting FDI. The result indicated that efforts towards openness should be initiated or further strengthened in order to make economies attractive to foreign investors. Rehman and Raza (2011) applied export of goods and services as a percentage of GDP as a proxy to measure trade openness in Pakistan and found that trade openness has negative significant impact on FDI flow in Pakistan. On the other hand, Vijayakumar and Sridharan (2010) did not find a significant effect of trade openness on FDI inflows in BRICS countries. They suggested that trade openness may not be a crucial factor in attracting FDI inflows to these fast-emerging countries. Similarly, Mateev's (2009) analysis to identify several key determinants of FDI flows into transition economies of Central and Southeast Europe indicated that trade openness is statistically insignificant.

Oladipo (2010) identified the determinants of foreign direct investment flow in a small open economy and found that the level of financial development has negative implication on the growth of FDI. It is surprising to note that in smaller economies financial development may not necessarily be induced by FDI. Moreover, Borensztein et al. (1998) tested the relations of foreign direct investment and economic growth in 69 developing countries and showed that financial development has insignificant effect on FDI. On the contrary, Kim and Lee (2008) investigated the effect of FDI on Total Factor Productivity (TFP) growth in a large sample of countries from 1970 to 2000 and confirmed that financial development is positively associated with FDI. In addition, Wang and Wong (2009) found a complementary relation between financial depth and FDI, and when financial depth increases, FDI growth increases but at a decreasing rate.

Studies have shown that the stability of a host country's currency value is able to attract more foreign investment into that host country (Rogoff & Reinhart, 2003; Brzozowski, 2006). MacDermott (2008) determined the relationship between the volatility in the exchange rate and FDI and indicated that devaluation of the home currency would lead to a fall in FDI. Furthermore, volatility in the exchange rate discouraged foreign investors from investing in a host country. Ogunleye (2009) also found that exchange rate volatility had detrimental effects on FDI inflows to Nigeria and South Africa. Alba et al. (2009) also examined the impact of exchange rates in the United States and found mixed results. Furthermore, a favourable FDI environment resulted from a positive and significant relationship between exchange rates and FDI inflows (Russ, 2007).

Researchers have long identified that there is a significant relationship between FDI and government consumption. However, results differ depending on the proxy used by the researcher (Garrett & Mitchell, 2001). Wijeweera et al. (2010) suggested that when a government increases its spending towards education, the quality of human capital improves resulting in increasing FDI inflows. Hailu (2010) found that inflation has a negative relation with FDI. When the inflation rate increases, FDI decreases. Al-Nasser (2007) also found that inflation is an important determinant of FDI, with a statistically significant negative relationship. A panel data analysis by Duanmu and Guney (2009) on location determinants of Chinese and Indian foreign direct investment found that inflation has a insignificant relationship towards FDI. In addition, Gast and Herrmann (2008) identified the determinants of foreign direct investment for the Organization of Economic Cooperation and Development (OECD) countries from 1991 to 2001 and found that inflation is negatively related to FDI. Kyrkilis and Pantelidis (2003) concluded that the interest rate is statistically significant in affecting FDI in Italy, The Netherlands and Korea.

Most literature examined the relationships between FDI, wages and productivity of a host country (Wignaraja, 2008; Lipsey & Sjoholm, 2010; Hayakawa et al., 2010), and empirical evidence indicated that the host country with a better environment for FDI in terms of fixed entry cost and lower wages tends to attract more foreign investors. Blanton and Blanton (2007) found that foreign investors prefer countries with well-trained and skilled labour with a low cost of wages, while Jensen and Rosas (2007) conducted research in Mexico and found that FDI and wages are positively significant. Mexico is among the fast-emerging countries where labour rate is still very low relative to other emerging countries and therefore it could still attract foreign investments into the country with increasing wage rates.

2.2 Country-specific

According to The Heritage Foundation,[1] economic freedom is defined as the fundamental right of every human being to control his or her own labour and property. Researchers have used an economic freedom index as a determinant, and empirical evidence indicated that there is a positive significant relationship between economic growth and economic freedom (Ayal & Karras, 1998; Heckelman, 2000). In relation to the significant relationship between economic growth and economic freedom, many researchers applied economic freedom as a variable in FDI. According to Caetano and Caleiro (2009), the risk perceived by investors is crucial in their decision to invest, especially when it concerns a particular foreign country. Results indicated that economic freedom and FDI are positively related. Quazi (2007) indicated that a host country should formulate its FDI strategies by focusing on economic freedom components in order to attract more FDI inflow into the country.

Similar to Gast and Herrman (2008) on OECD countries, Hailu (2010) also found that human capital has an insignificant effect on FDI in Africa. On the other hand, Kyrkilis and Pantelidis (2003) and Blanton and Blanton (2007) indicated that human capital has a positive effect on FDI inflows of the non-OECD countries. According to Suh and Boggs (2011), ICT infrastructure had a positive significant relationship with investments in developed markets but the results for recent years were insignificant. Hailu (2010) also found that infrastructure is positively related to FDI flows in African countries. Al-Nasser (2007) confirmed that infrastructure is one of the important factors in attracting foreign investment in Latin America and Asia. On the contrary, Quazi (2007) found an insignificant relationship between infrastructure and FDI in East Asia. Similar to Vijayakumar et al. (2010) and Rehman and Raza (2011) also found a positively significant relationship between infrastructure and FDI for Pakistan.

3 Data and method

This study collected annual data from 1977 to 2010 for Brazil, Russia, China, India, South Africa and Malaysia from International Financial Statistics (IFS) of the IMF, the department of statistics and central bank for each country. The Economic Freedom Index is collected from the Heritage Foundation. Eleven variables that consist of macroeconomic fundamentals and country-specific variables were listed as independent variables. Macroeconomic fundamentals include market size, trade openness, financial development, exchange rate, interest rate, government consumption and inflation rate, as in Model 1. While the country-specific variables are economic freedom, wages, human capital and infrastructure quality as in Model 2. The list of variables and their proxies is in Table 8.1.

3.1 Macroeconomic fundamentals (Model 1)

$$FDI_{it} = \alpha_0 + \beta_1 GDP_{it} + \beta_2 OPEN_{it} + \beta_3 FinDepth_{it} + \beta_4 ER_{it} \beta_5 IR_{it} + \beta_6 IFR_{it} + \beta_7 GOV_{it} + \varepsilon \quad (1)$$

Table 8.1 Proxy of each variable and expected relationship with FDI inflow

Variables	Proxy	Expected relationship
Total foreign direct investment (FDI)	Annual FDI	
Market size (GDP)	Annual GDP	Positive
Trade openness (OPEN)	(x + m) / GDP	Positive
Financial development (FIN DEPTH)	M2/GDP	Positive
Exchange rate (ER)	Exchange rate/US dollar	Negative
Interest rate (IR)	Annual interest rate	Negative
Government consumption (GOV)	Government consumption	Negative
Inflation rate (IFR)	Consumer price index	Positive
Wages (W)	% of total employed	Negative
Human capital (LR)	Literacy rate	Positive
Economic freedom (FREE)	Index economic freedom	Positive
Infrastructure quality (INQ)	Log per capita electricity	Positive

3.2 Country-specific factors (Model 2)

$$FDI_{it} = a_0 + \lambda_1 W_{it} + \lambda_2 FREE_{it} + \lambda_3 LR_{it} + \lambda_4 INQ_{it} + \delta \qquad (2)$$

Both Augmented Dickey–Fuller (ADF) and Kwiatkowski–Phillips–Schmidt–Shin (KPSS) unit-root tests for individual countries are applied in order to check for robustness, and all the time series are transformed to ensure there is no unit-root problem and that all the time series used in the tests are stationary as shown in Tables 8.2 and 8.3.

4 Findings

The results for both models on fundamental and country-specific factors are in Tables 8.4 and 8.5. Findings for Brazil show that there is a marginally significant positive relation between interest rate and FDI. An increase in the country's interest rates would result in an increase in the country's FDI. Besides that, positive relationship is found between FDI and economic growth, trade openness, financial depth, exchange rate and government consumption, but the results are not significant. Inflation, on the other hand, seems to exert a negative influence on FDI. The model, however, can only explain close to 4 per cent of changes in FDI. For country-specific variables in Model 2, results show that infrastructure quality (INQ) and economic freedom have statistically a significant positive relation with FDI. Improvement in domestic infrastructure and policies to allow more freedom to make decisions would improve the

Table 8.2 ADF and KPSS unit root tests for Brazil, Russia and India

	Brazil			Russia			India		
	ADF		KPSS test	ADF		KPSS test	ADF		KPSS test
Variables	**t-stats**	**t-stats (lag)**	**KPSS Statistic**	**t-stats**	**t-stats (lag)**	**KPSS Statistic**	**t-stats**	**t-stats (lag)**	**KPSS Statistic**
FDI	−5.059***	C(0)	0.080	−5.049***	C(0)	0.080	−8.338***	C(0)	0.500**
GDP	−3.467**	C(0)	0.149	−4.340***	C(3)	0.210	−5.323***	C(1)	0.273
OPEN	−5.194***	C(0)	0.154	−3.188**	C(3)	0.230	−6.085***	C(1)	0.223
FIN DEPTH	−4.925***	C(0)	0.500	−3.309*	C(0)	0.500**	−4.691***	C(1)	0.431*
ER	−3.467**	C(0)	0.149	−13.717***	C(1)	0.442*	−9.289***	C(0)	0.358*
GOV	−3.545**	C(0)	0.069	−3.087**	C(0)	0.366*	−8.210***	C(0)	0.249
IFR	−4.201***	C(0)	0.269	−12.430*	C(0)	0.255	−7.392***	C(0)	0.212
IR	−2.753*	C(0)	0.210	−3.219**	C(2)	0.159	−5.517***	C(0)	0.369*
W	−4.242***	C(1)	0.214	−3.530*	CT(2)	0.160	−6.171***	CT(0)	0.141*
LR	−10.207***	C(0)	0.584**	−4.587***	CT(0)	0.175**	−4.382***	C(1)	0.444*
FREE	−4.437***	C(0)	0.260	−3.794**	CT(0)	0.500**	−4.454***	CT(0)	0.191
INQ	−3.403**	C(0)	0.445*	−4.704***	C(0)	0.274	−6.161***	CT(0)	0.108

Note: *10% significant level, **5% significant level and ***1% significant level.

Table 8.3 ADF and KPSS unit root tests for China, South Africa and Malaysia

	China			South Africa			Malaysia		
	ADF		KPSS test	ADF		KPSS test	ADF		KPSS test
Variables	**t-stats**	**t-stats (lag)**	**KPSS Statistic**	**t-stats**	**t-stats (lag)**	**KPSS Statistic**	**t-stats**	**t-stats (lag)**	**KPSS Statistic**
FDI	−2.891*	C(1)	0.333	−6.229***	C(0)	0.194	−6.403***	C(0)	0.243
GDP	−4.281***	C(0)	0.633**	−3.949***	C(0)	0.202	−4.863***	C(0)	0.077
OPEN	−5.222***	C(0)	0.157	−5.154***	C(0)	0.213	−3.059**	C(0)	0.279
FIN DEPTH	−4.708**	CT(3)	0.203	−4.231***	C(0)	0.105	−4.779***	C(0)	0.137
ER	−4.320***	C(0)	0.341	−4.058***	C(0)	0.176	−4.581***	C(0)	0.113
GOV	−3.629**	C(0)	0.412*	−4.366***	C(0)	0.082	−4.809***	C(0)	0.108
IFR	−3.186**	C(0)	0.239	−2.716	CT(1)	0.122*	−4.795***	C(0)	0.215
IR	−5.050***	C(0)	0.500**	−3.990***	C(0)	0.172	−7.656***	C(0)	0.099
W	−3.844***	C0)	0.356*	−3.522*	C(0)	0.084	−3.347**	C(0)	0.117
LR	−3.283*	CT(0)	0.143	−4.452***	CT(4)	0.500**	−4.376***	C(2)	0.377*
FREE	−3.573**	C(0)	0.364*	−3.814**	C(0)	0.344	−3.499**	C(0)	0.279
INQ	−6.019***	C(0)	0.285	−6.893***	C(0)	0.333	−3.088**	C(0)	0.359*

Note: *10% significant level, **5% significant level and ***1% significant level.

Table 8.4 Model 1 Macroeconomic factors and FDI inflow for BRICS

Variables	Brazil	Russia	India	China	South Africa	Malaysia
C	0.088	0.328	−0.126	−0.296	4.058	−1.438
	(0.738)	(0.169)	(0.678)	(0.417)	(0.675)	(0.034)**
GDP	0.057	4.156	3.524	5.217	27.211	15.42485
	(0.981)	(0.016)**	(0.409)	(0.095)*	(0.667)	(0.0215)**
OPEN	2.246	0.961	2.235	0.0735	−9.718	6.867826
	(0.287)	(0.595)	(0.118)	(0.931)	(0.788)	(0.087)*
FIN DEPTH	0.205	–	−0.582	0.313	0.090	3.641
	(0.774)		(0.366)	(0.315)	(0.997)	(0.432)
IFR	−0.020	−0.425	0.203	−1.771	−90.133	7.252
	(0.939)	(0.162)	(0.964)	(0.595)	(0.367)	(0.712)
GOV	1.431	−4.521	−0.545	−2.438	−34.447	−6.756
	(0.505)	(0.021)**	(0.873)	(0.109)	(0.578)	(0.163)
IR	0.984	0.259	1.158	−0.477	−8.862	−0.837
	(0.085)*	(0.568)	(0.376)	(0.060)*	(0.659)**	(0.784)
ER	−0.011	−0.239	4.493	4.387	–	–
	(0.692)	(0.616)	(0.004)***	(0.163)		
Adjusted R2	0.035	0.435	0.001	0.527	0.001	0.460
F-significance	0.383	0.089	0.500	0.041	0.95	0.008

Note: *10% significant level, **5% significant level and ***1% significant level.

Table 8.5 Model 2 Country specific factors and FDI inflow for BRICS

Variables	Brazil	Russia	India	China	South Africa	Malaysia
Constant	−0.209	0.364	0.157	−0.086	−6.955	1.811
	(0.383)	(0.046)**	(0.725)	(0.477)	(0.136)	(0.162)
W	5.957	0.401	0.433	−0.796	31.373	−14.956
	(0.113)	(0.409)	(0.166)	(0.015)**	(0.500)	(0.140)
LR	−10.128	−652.1	−1.233	−1.4137	474.640	347.944
	(0.771)	(0.028)**	(0.942)	(0.760)	(0.005)***	(0.301)
INQ	7.083	2.335	1.342	2.384	12.024	19.923
	(0.015)**	(0.007)***	(0.879)	(0.023)**	(0.072)**	(0.028)**
FREE	2.673	3.470	−4.194	−1.520	−72.735	34.763
	(0.066)*	(0.111)	(0.316)	(0.012)**	(0.144)	(0.065)*
Adjusted R2	0.359	0.214	0.001	0.405	0.001	0.326
F-significance	0.074	0.218	0.787	0.053	0.506	0.092

Note: *10% significant level, **5% significant level and ***1% significant level.

potential for foreign investments to the host country. These country-specific variables can explain 36 per cent of changes in the country's FDI, and the model is marginally significant.

Findings for Russia confirm that market size (GDP) is significant in affecting FDI flows where the potential of a large market for goods and services is a vital factor in attracting investments. In addition, government consumption has a negative effect on FDI when expansionary fiscal policy is inversely related to foreign investments and foreigners perceive higher government consumption as detrimental to investments. Financial depth is not included in Russia's Model 1 due to multicollinearity with GDP ,and robustness tests performed confirm that it is not significant in affecting FDI. Model 1 for Russia is statistically significant and can account for 44 per cent of changes in FDI. In addition, results for Model 2 also verify that infrastructure and literacy rates are important considerations in the decisions of foreign investors. It is generally believed that improvement in accessibility to markets and export destinations would encourage investors locating themselves in certain geographically challenged areas.

Exchange rate is the only factor which is significant in affecting FDI decisions in India. Findings assert that a fall in the currency value of the host country would encourage foreign investors into India, which is in line with theoretical understanding. A similar result, however, is not found for the other fast-emerging countries. On the other hand, the results from country-specific factors are not significant or conclusive. There exist positive relation for wages and infrastructure but negative relation for literacy rate and economic freedom with FDI for India.

Model 1 results in Table 8.4 also affirming that market size is significant in affecting FDI flows in China. Larger market size would attract foreign investors seeking new markets in China, and the host country has attracted a substantial amount of FDI in recent years. In addition, the interest rate is another macroeconomic fundamental that possess a significant relation with FDI. However, increase in interest rates in China discourages foreign investments. The model can explain 53 per cent of changes in FDI, and it is one of the most significant models for this group of fast-emerging countries. For the country-specific factors in Model 2, significant findings are found for employment, infrastructure and economic freedom. Higher employment and indirectly higher cost are found to discourage foreign investments in China. It is interesting to note that the Economic Freedom Index is found to be negatively related to FDI where freedom in decisions would probably reduce the power of foreign firms in dictating the market. Similar to other fast-emerging countries, infrastructure improvements would enable foreign organizations to get their goods out to the market efficiently, and this would encourage FDI across all countries.

Results for South Africa show that the interest rate is the only macroeconomic fundamental that significantly affects FDI. Fast-emerging countries, including China and those in Africa, find that increasing interest rates which increase the cost of doing business would discourage not only domestic investments but also foreign investments. International finance theory supports the notion of matching assets with liabilities in the same market, so this confirms that investment in any domestic market is sensitive to the domestic cost of capital and funds. Country-specific factors are also significant in affecting FDI in South Africa. Education is a significant driver of investments when a skilled and knowledgeable workforce supports productivity and reduces costs. In addition, infrastructure improvements also enable countries to accelerate growth and productivity through attracting foreign investments.

Lastly, market size is also a significant factor in attracting FDI into the country. Similar results are also found for Russia and China. Openness to trade which indicates increasing export and import activities in Malaysia enable foreign investors to distribute their goods, not only in the domestic economy, but also to neighbouring markets which may not be attractive for location. Trade openness is only found to be significant to Malaysia and not the other fast-emerging countries. The set of country-specific factors which are significant for Malaysia include infrastructure and economic freedom. Similar to Brazil, Russia, China and South Africa, Malaysia also found positive significant effects to FDI from improvement in infrastructure. This authenticates the findings for fast-emerging countries and justifies additional government expenditure on infrastructure to improve not only domestic logistics but also to hasten the development of the domestic economy through foreign investments.

5 Conclusion

This study investigates the determinants of FDI in fast-emerging BRICS countries and Malaysia using data for six countries from 1977–2010. Results indicated that most of the findings are supported by the literature, and economic freedom is a new addition that has been included in the research model. The findings of this research add to existing literature on FDI flows. Empirical evidence would provide policymakers with suggestions on attracting foreign investments into fast-emerging countries. A summary of the findings in this research is presented in Table 8.6.

Table 8.6 Summary of analysis

Variables	Brazil	Russia	India	China	South Africa	Malaysia
GDP		√		√		√
GOV		√				
OPEN						√
FIN DEPTH						
IR	√			√	√	
ER			√			
IFR						
W				√		
LR		√			√	
FREE	√			√		√
INQ	√	√		√	√	√

It can be concluded that market size, interest rate, literacy rate, economic freedom and infrastructure quality are critical factors that determine FDI in the majority of BRICS countries and Malaysia. Market size is significant in driving FDI in Russia, China and Malaysia but not significant in the other countries. An essential macroeconomic fundamental – interest rates, which directly affect the cost of doing business – is found to be imperative in affecting FDI in Brazil, China and South Africa, which is consistent with mainstream finance literature. Government consumption is also found to be critical for FDI inflow in Russia. Trade openness for Malaysia is necessary for FDI but not for the others. Surprisingly, the exchange rate is found to be significant for India. This is also due to the high collinearity between exchange rate and GDP, and both variables cannot be included in the model at the same time. It is interesting to note that this study did not find any significant relationship between financial development and FDI. Future studies that apply a different proxy for financial development might find a more significant result.

In this study, consistent with Ayal and Karras (1998) and Heckelman (2000), economic freedom is found to have a significant relationship with FDI flows for Brazil, China and Malaysia. The element of human capital development is crucial for Russia and South Africa in positioning themselves as attractive venues for investments. Employment is only found to significantly affect FDI in China, not the other countries. It is fundamental to note that infrastructure quality is an important factor for FDI in all the countries studied except India. This may be due to the shorter time series available for this country relative to others. This study, therefore, confirms that infrastructure availability and accessibility to logistics are extremely necessary in order to promote investments and stimulate domestic economies.

Notes

* Corresponding author: E-mail: catherine@salm.uitm.edu.my Tel: 603–55444792

1. The Heritage Foundation provides information on world economic freedom. The organization works with the *Wall Street Journal* team to track the movements of economic freedom around the world and produces the Economic Freedom Index.

References

Agosin, M. and Machado, R. (2007) 'Openness and the International Allocation of Foreign Direct Investment', *Journal of Development Studies*, 43(7), 1234–47.

Al-Nasser, O. (2007) 'The Determinants of the US Foreign Direct Investment: Does the Region Matter?' *Global Economic Review*, 36(1), 37–51.

Alba, J. D., Park, D. and Wang, P. (2009) 'The Impact of Exchange Rate on FDI and the Interdependence of FDI Over Time', *ADB Asian Development Bank (ADB) Economics Working Paper Series No. 164*.

Ayal, B. E. and Karras, G. (1998) 'Components of Economic Freedom and Growth: An Empirical Study', *Journal of Developing Areas* , 32(3), 327–38.

Bakir, A. and Alfawwaz, T. (2009) 'Determinants of Foreign Direct Investment in Jordan', *International Management Review*, 5(2), 66–73.

Blanton, S. L. and Blanton, R. G. (2007) 'What Attracts Foreign Investors? An Examination of Human Rights and Foreign Direct Investment', *The Journal of Politics*, 69(1), 143–55.

Borensztein, E., Gregorio, J. and Lee, J. (1998) 'How Does Foreign Direct Investment Affect Economic Growth', *Journal of International Economics*, 45, 115–35.

Brzozowski, M. (2006) 'Exchange Rate Variability and Foreign Direct Investment: Consequences of EMU Enlargement', *Eastern European Economics*, 44(1), 5–24.

Caetano, J. and Caleiro, A. (2009) 'Economic Freedom and Foreign Direct Investment: How Different are the MENA Countries from EU', *iBusiness*, 1(2), 65–74.

Duanmu, J. and Guney, Y. (2009) 'A Panel Data Analysis of Locational Determinants of Chinese and Indian Outward Foreign Direct Investment', *Journal of Asia Business Studies*, 3(2) 1–15.

Garrett, G. and Mitchell, D. (2001) 'Globalization, Government Spending and Taxation in the OECD', *European Journal of Political Research*, 39, 145–77.

Gast, M. and Herrmann, R. (2008) 'Determinants of Foreign Direct Investment of OECD Countries 1991–2001', *International Economic Journal*, 22(4), 509–24.

Hailu, Z. (2010) 'Demand Side Factors Affecting the Inflow of Foreign Direct Investment to African Countries : Does Capital Market Matter?' *International Journal of Business and Management*, 5(5), 104–16.

Hayakawa, K., Lee, H. H. and Park, D. (2010) 'The Role of Home and Host Country Characteristics in FDI: Firm-level Evidence from Japan, Korea and Taiwan', *Institute of Developing Economies (IDE) Discussion Paper 267*.

Heckelman, J. C. (2000) 'Economic Freedom and Economic Growth: A Short-run Causal Investigation', *Journal of Applied Economics*, 3(1), 71–91.

Janicki, H. and Wunnava, P. (2004) 'Determinants of Foreign Direct Investment: Empirical Evidence from EU Accession Candidates', *Applied Economies*, 36(5), 505–09.

Jensen, N. M. and Rosas, G. (2007) 'Foreign Direct Investment and Income Inequality in Mexico 1990–2000', *International Organization*, 61, 467–87.

Kim, Y. and Lee, J. (2008) 'Productivity Growth and Technological Diffusion through Foreign Direct Investment', *Economic Inquiry*, 47(2), 226–48.

Kim, J. and Rhe, D. (2009) 'Trends and Determinants of South Korean Outward Foreign Direct Investment', *The Copenhagen Journal of Asian Studies*, 27(1), 126–54.

Kimono, S., Saas, D. and Driffield, N. (2007) 'Macro Determinants of FDI Inflows to Japan: An Analysis of Source Country Characteristics', *The World Economy*, 30(3), 446–69.

Kyrkilis, D. and Pantelidis, P. (2003) 'Macroeconomic Determinants of Outward Foreign Direct Investment', *International Journal of Social Economics*, 30(7), 827–36.

Lipsey, R. E. and Sjoholm, F. (2010) 'FDI and Growth in East Asia: Lessons for Indonesia', *IFN Working Paper 852*, 1–49 (Sweden: Research Institute of Industrial Economics).

MacDermott, R. (2008) 'Linking Exchange Rates to Foreign Direct Investment', *The International Trade Journal*, 22(1), 3–16.

Mateev, M. (2009) 'Determinants of Foreign Direct Investment in Central and Southeastern Europe: New Empirical Tests', *Oxford Journal*, 8(1), 133–49.

Ogunleye, E. K. (2009) 'Exchange Rate Volatility and Foreign Direct Investment in Sub-Saharan Africa: Evidence from Nigeria and South Africa', in Adenikiju, A., A. Busari and S.Olofin (Eds) *Applied Econometrics and Macroeconometric Modelling in Nigeria* (Ibadan: Ibadan UniversityPress).

Oladipo, O. (2010) 'Foreign Direct Investment: Determinants and Growth Effects in a Small Open Economy', *The International Journal of Business and Finance Research*, 4(4), 75–88.

Quazi, R. (2007) 'Economic Freedom and Foreign Direct Investment in East Asia', *Journal of the Asia Pacific Economy*, 12(3), 329–44.

Rehman, A. and Raza, A. (2011) 'Determinants of Foreign Direct Investment and Its Impact on GDP Growth in Pakistan', *Interdisciplinary Journal of Contemporary Research in Business*, 2(9), 198–205.

Rogoff, K. and Reinhart, C. (2003) 'FDI to Africa: The Role of Price Stability and Currency Instability', *IMF Working Paper 03/10*, International Monetary Fund, 4–39.

Russ, K. N. (2007) 'The Endogeneity of the Exchange Rate as a Determinant of FDI: A Model of Entry and Multinational Firms', *Journal of International Economics*, 71(2), 344–72.

Sekkat, K. and Veganzones-Varoudakis, M. (2007) 'Openness, Investment Climate and FDI in Developing Countries', *Review of Development Economics*, 11(4), 607–20.

Suh, T. and Boggs, D. J. (2011) 'Communications Infrastructure and Traditional Determinants of Inward Foreign Investment: A Comparison of Developed and Emerging Markets', *Competitiveness Review: An International Business Journal*, 21(2), 205–23.

Torrisi, C., Delaunay, C. J., Kocia, A. and Lubiencka, M. (2008) 'FDI in Central Europe: Determinants and Policy Implication', *Journal of International Finance and Economics*, 8(4), 136–47.

Vijayakumar, N. and Sridharan, P. (2010) 'Determinants of FDI in BRICS Countries: A Panel Analysis', *International Journal of Business Science and Applied Management*, 5(3), 1–13.

Vogiatzoglou, K. (2007) 'Vertical Specialization and New Determinants of FDI: Evidence from South and East Asia', *Global Economic Review*, 36(3), 245–66.

Wang, M. and Wong, M. (2009). 'Foreign Direct Investment and Economic Growth: The Growth Accounting Perspective', *Economic Inquiry*, 47(4), 701–10.

Wignaraja, G. (2008) 'Ownership, Technology and Buyers: Explaining Exporting in China and Sri Lanka', *Transportational Corporations*, 7(2), 1–15.

Wijeweera, A., Villano, R. and Dollery, B. (2010) 'Economic Growth and FDI Inflows: A Stochastic Frontier Analysis', *The Journal of Developing Areas*, 23(2), 143–58.

Zhang, K. H. (2001) 'What Attracts Foreign Multinational Corporations to China?' *Contemporary Economic Policy*, 19(3), 336–46.

9
Momentum and Contrarian Strategies on ASEAN Markets

Shangkari V. Anusakumar, Ruhani Ali and Chee-Wooi Hooy

1 Introduction

Momentum strategy entails buying stocks with a recent history of good performance and selling stocks with bad performance (Jegadeesh & Titman, 1993). On the contrary, contrarian strategy proposes a trading strategy of buying poorly performing stocks and selling better-performing stocks (De Bondt & Thaler, 1985). Underlying the contrarian strategy is the belief that prices will reverse, whereas proponents of momentum strategy contend that return continuation will occur. Both strategies are successful at different time horizons: intermediate term for momentum and long term for contrarian.

In this chapter we investigate momentum and contrarian strategies within the context of emerging ASEAN stock markets: Malaysia, Philippines, Thailand and Indonesia. We investigate momentum strategy for the intermediate period of 3 to 12 months and contrarian strategy for the long term (24 to 60 months) for the sample period of 2000 to 2011. The effect of survivorship bias on returns of momentum and contrarian strategies is explored because some prior studies conducted on Asian markets, especially Malaysia, have a tendency to use only active stocks. Because our sample period incorporates the recent global crisis, we also examine effects the crisis might have had on the results of this study. Last, but not least, we investigate the link between January seasonality and the two strategies: momentum and contrarian.

Emerging markets provide a unique avenue within which to examine momentum and contrarian strategies. Despite the vast literature on momentum and contrarian, the number of studies conducted on emerging markets is limited. The same holds true for Asian markets. Thus, our sample of emerging Asian countries ideally covers an intersection of both areas of interest. Our specific choice of ASEAN stock markets is motivated by several factors. As a part of the Association of Southeast Asian Nations (ASEAN), these Asian markets are growing at a similar rate. Other Asian markets, such as India and China, have different growth rates as well as drastically different stock market characteristics in terms of the number of stock listings, trading volume and liquidity. As noted by Sharma and Wongbangpo (2002), ASEAN markets have experienced massive growth in GDP and market capitalization and have attracted the attention of foreign investors with their lucrative investment opportunities. Moreover, studies have shown that ASEAN markets are cointegrated in the post–1997 Asian financial crisis period. Click and Plummer (2005) argue that 'an integrated regional stock exchange will be more appealing to investors from outside the region who would find investment in the region easier or more justifiable' (p. 7).

Needless to say, there are multiple country studies that incorporate emerging Asian markets as a part of their larger sample of countries. Often, these studies tend to group stock markets together and perform analysis as a whole. In contrast, we take a focused look at individual emerging ASEAN stock markets. More often than not, prior literature adopts the perspective of U.S. investors. The currency is denominated in U.S. dollars. Our chapter differs in this aspect as we take on the viewpoint of local investors by adopting local currency throughout the study. An additional advantage is that we are able to avoid any potential influence of exchange-rate movements on the results.

The remainder of the chapter is organized as follows: The relevant literature is discussed in Section 2. We describe the data source, screening and methodology in Section 3. In Section 4, we provide the results and discussion of the findings. Finally, Section 5 provides the conclusion.

2 Literature review

2.1 Intermediate momentum strategy

Jegadeesh and Titman (1993) were the first to document the profitability of momentum strategy. They find that a trading strategy of buying past winner stocks and selling past loser stocks could generate returns of approximately 1 per cent per month. Following this discovery, a slew of studies further confirmed the existence of momentum in the United States as well as other markets around the world. For Asia, the research has been rather limited. Among the studies conducted in Asia, Hameed and Kusnadi (2002) could not find any momentum. The sample period of 1979 to 1994 was tested using a sample of six countries, including Malaysia and Thailand. However, it should be noted that sample size was small, with 244 firms for Malaysia and only 59 firms for Thailand.

Also examining the Asian market, Chui et al. (2003) generally report positive returns to the momentum portfolio. However, only Hong Kong exhibited statistically significant momentum. Monthly momentum returns for Indonesia (0.027 per cent), Malaysia (0.216 per cent) and Thailand (0.413 per cent) were insignificant. The sample employs a larger number of firms than Hameed and Kusnadi (2002). Brown et al. (2008) examined four Asian markets – Hong Kong, Korea, Singapore and Taiwan – and found significant momentum only for Hong Kong.

Apart from direct studies of the Asian markets, several studies incorporate a number of Asian stock markets in their sample. Griffin et al. (2003, 2005) undertook an international study on momentum, finding that Asia exhibits weak momentum compared to other regions. In a recent study, Chui et al. (2010) find momentum for three Asian markets: Bangladesh, Hong Kong and India. Rouwenhorst (1999) focuses on examining momentum in emerging markets. There were several Asian markets in the sample, but none of the markets had any significant momentum returns. Of the few studies that focus on emerging market, Naranjo and Porter (2007) find that momentum exists in developed, as well as emerging markets.

2.2 Long-term contrarian strategy

De Bondt and Thaler (1985) find that there is a notable reversal in the performance of winner and loser stocks in the long term. The results indicate that a contrarian strategy would be profitable for a ranking period of two to five years. The returns are especially prominent for the 60-months ranking and holding period. The authors attributed the return reversals to the tendency for investors to overreact to unexpected news. However, Zarowin (1990) contends that contrarian returns are not due to the overreaction of investors. This author finds that significant returns are present only for January after the firm size is taken into account. Consequently, Zarowin argued that contrarian returns are merely a product of the size and/or seasonality effect. Nevertheless, De Bondt and Thaler (1987) further demonstrate that the contrarian returns cannot be attributed to the size effect and reassert that the reversal is indeed caused by overreaction. Subsequent studies confirm the profitability of contrarian strategy in international markets, including in Canada (Mun et al., 2000), Australia (Gaunt, 2000), France and Germany (Mun et al., 1999).

Fung (1999) is among the first to study contrarian strategy in the Asian market. This author presents evidence of strong contrarian profitability in Hong Kong. Furthermore, the contrarian returns are considerably higher than the returns reported in the United States. Ahmad and Hussain (2001) examine whether a contrarian strategy would be profitable in the Malaysia stock market for the period of 1986 to 1996, using a sample of 166 stocks. They find that the strategy is indeed profitable but the returns are significant for only three out of six test periods. Further evidence of contrarian profitability in the Malaysian market was provided by Lai et al. (2003) for the sample period of January 1987 to December 1999. The returns are profitable primarily for the intermediate period of less than 12 months. For the long term, only the return for the holding period of 15 months is significant. For the Japanese stock market, Chiao and Hueng (2005) document significant contrarian returns. Moreover, the returns persist after controlling for the size effect. Ramiah et al. (2011) investigate the profitability of contrarian strategies in Hong Kong. They find that the strategy performs better for dual-listed stocks than for stocks listed only on the Hong Kong stock market.

2.3 Methodology

The sample countries consist of four emerging ASEAN stock markets: Indonesia, Malaysia, Philippines and Thailand. Stock return data is obtained from Datastream for the sample period of January 2000 to December 2011. Local currency is used for the analysis. We exclude cross-listed stocks to isolate country specific effects (Naranjo & Porter, 2007). De-listed stocks are included in the sample to avoid survivorship bias. The monthly stock return is computed as follows:

$$R_{it} = \frac{RI_{it}}{RI_{it-1}} - 1 \tag{1}$$

where R_{it} is the stock i return for month t, RI_{it} is the return index for stock i at month$t$ and RI_{it-1} is the return index for stock $i$at month $t-1$.

We generally adopt Jegadeesh and Titman (1993) methodology for portfolio construction and performance evaluation. Stocks are sorted according to past performance over the ranking period. The top 10 per cent and bottom 10 per cent of the stocks are segregated into the winner and loser portfolios respectively. As per convention, one month is skipped between the ranking and holding periods to mitigate microstructure biases. For the momentum strategy, ranking (J) and holding (K) period are 3, 6, 9 and 12 months (J = K = 3, 6, 9, 12). Momentum returns are computed as the difference between the winner portfolio returns and loser portfolio returns. The portfolios are equally weighted. Momentum strategy is implemented independently for each of the four countries.

We form similar portfolios to implement the contrarian strategy. The ranking period (J) and holding period (K) are set as 24, 36, 48 and 60 months (J = K = 24, 36, 48, 60). Winner and loser portfolios are formed based on the returns in the ranking period and held over K months. Contrarian strategy takes a short position in the winner portfolio and a long position in the loser portfolio. Thus, the monthly returns to the contrarian portfolio can be computed as the difference between the loser and winner portfolios.

3 Findings

3.1 Returns for momentum and contrarian strategies

The average monthly returns (per cent) for the winner, loser and momentum portfolio are reported in Table 9.1. The associated t-statistics are provided in parentheses. The momentum strategy is implemented for ranking and holding periods of 3, 6, 9 and 12 months. Consistent with prior literature, we find no significant momentum in Malaysia. Winner and loser portfolio returns are positive but insignificant. The momentum portfolio yields returns ranging from 0.02 per cent to −0.85 per cent but, again, the portfolio returns are not significant. This indicates that investors implementing a momentum strategy in Malaysia may not be able to generate any significant profits.

As with Malaysia, we find no significant returns to the momentum portfolio in Thailand. However, the winner portfolio does earn highly significant returns for all periods. The highest return of 2.04 per cent per month (significant at the 1 per cent level) is generated for the ranking and holding period of 3 months. There appears to be an inverse association between holding period and winner portfolio return; the returns tend to decrease as the portfolio ranking and holding period (J = K) are increased. In contrast, loser portfolio returns and level of significance tend to increase as the ranking and holding periods are increased. Loser portfolio return is the highest at 12 months (J = K = 12) with a monthly return of 2.46 per cent (significant at the 1 per cent level). In general, the loser portfolio outperforms the winner portfolio. Although the momentum portfolio does not earn any abnormal returns, the winner and loser portfolios generate economically and statistically significant returns.

Table 9.1 Average monthly returns (%) for momentum strategy

Country	Portfolio	J = K = 3	J = K = 6	J = K = 9	J = K = 12
Malaysia	Winner	0.25	0.20	0.25	0.33
		(0.63)	(0.39)	(0.47)	(0.62)
	Loser	0.23	0.56	0.85	1.18
		(0.41)	(0.73)	(1.11)	(1.41)
	Momentum	0.02	−0.36	−0.61	−0.85
		(0.06)	(−0.76)	(−1.24)	(−1.46)
Philippines	Winner	1.76**	2.08***	2.17***	1.90**
		(2.25)	(2.69)	(2.98)	(2.55)
	Loser	6.89**	7.52**	6.41***	5.60***
		(2.20)	(2.34)	(3.23)	(3.65)
	Momentum	−5.12*	−5.44*	−4.24**	−3.70***
		(−1.68)	(−1.76)	(−2.35)	(−2.76)
Thailand	Winner	2.04***	1.90***	1.82***	1.69**
		(3.23)	(2.88)	(2.72)	(2.47)
	Loser	1.49*	2.31***	2.41***	2.46***
		(1.90)	(2.80)	(3.00)	(3.28)
	Momentum	0.55	−0.41	−0.58	−0.77
		(1.13)	(−0.68)	(−1.03)	(−1.53)
Indonesia	Winner	1.82**	1.52**	1.76***	1.64***
		(2.59)	(2.43)	(2.91)	(2.73)
	Loser	2.57***	2.93***	3.12***	3.17***
		(3.27)	(3.41)	(3.80)	(3.80)
	Momentum	−0.74	−1.41**	−1.37**	−1.53***
		(−1.43)	(−2.27)	(−2.43)	(−2.73)

Note: *, ** and *** represent statistical significance at 10%, 5% and 1% level respectively.

Interestingly, we find negative momentum returns for the Philippines for all holding and ranking periods. Momentum portfolio returns for the Philippines are significant at 5 per cent and 1 per cent for 9 and 12 months, respectively. Returns are marginally significant at the 10 per cent level for 3 and 6 months ranking and holding periods. The returns range from −3.70 per cent to −5.44 per cent. There is a clear pattern of increase in significance and magnitude of negative returns as the J and K increase. The winner portfolio earns significant positive returns for all periods. Similarly, the loser portfolio returns are all positive and highly significant throughout various ranking and holding periods. However, the loser portfolio performs drastically better than the winner portfolio, thus causing the negative returns to the momentum portfolio.

Negative momentum is also evident for Indonesia, where momentum returns are negative and are significant for all periods except 3 months

(J = K = 3). As in the Philippines, we find an upward trend in the negative portfolio returns. Both winner and loser portfolios generate highly significant returns for all periods. The magnitude of returns for the loser portfolio is markedly higher than that of the winner portfolio. As a result, the momentum portfolio returns are negative.

Hameed and Kusnadi (2002) generally report positive, though insignificant, returns to the momentum portfolio. In contrast, our returns are largely negative. A possible explanation could be the time period of the analysis. Chui et al. (2003) find positive momentum returns for Indonesia, Malaysia and Thailand in the pre-1997 period, but these positive returns turn negative after July 1997. Thus, it is hardly surprisingly to find negative returns for our sample period of 2000 to 2011. In any case, the presence of similar 'negative momentum' have been reported in South Korea (Chae & Eom, 2009). The negative returns imply that a contrarian strategy would be profitable rather than a momentum strategy. As the loser portfolio significantly outperforms the winner portfolio, it is only natural that a strategy of buying losers and selling winners would be capable of generating profits. The fortunes of stocks in the loser portfolio change in the intermediate term as the stocks now tend to earn greater return than those in the winner portfolios.

Table 9.2 reports the average monthly returns (per cent) for contrarian strategy implemented for varying ranking and holding periods from 24 months to 60 months. The returns are reported for the winner, loser and contrarian portfolio with the associated t-statistics presented in parentheses. Notably, returns are all positive across countries, portfolios, ranking and holding periods. However, not all returns are statistically significant.

For Malaysia, only returns for 24 months (J = K = 24) are significant (at the 10 per cent level). Winner portfolio returns are positive but not significant, whereas loser portfolio returns are significant for 24 and 36 months. The loser portfolio clearly earns greater returns than the winner portfolio for all periods. For instance, returns for the loser portfolio are 1.7 times higher than the winner portfolio for the holding period of 60 months. However, as evidenced by the returns for the contrarian portfolio, the difference in returns between the portfolios is not statistically significant. Moreover, not all returns for winner and loser portfolios are significant. The viability of contrarian strategy in Malaysia is limited.

In the case of the Philippines, winner and loser portfolio returns are all economically and statistically significant. Again, the loser portfolio has superior performance. Contrarian strategy works best for 24, 36 and 48 months with statistical significance at the 10 per cent, 1 per cent

Table 9.2 Average monthly returns (%) for long-term contrarian strategy

Country	Portfolio	J = K = 24	J = K = 36	J = K = 48	J = K = 60
Malaysia	Winner	0.50	0.74	0.49	0.80
		(0.90)	(1.24)	(0.77)	(1.23)
	Loser	1.39*	1.77**	1.02	1.37
		(1.83)	(2.10)	(1.45)	(1.56)
	Contrarian	0.89*	1.04	0.53	0.56
		(1.68)	(1.56)	(1.30)	(1.15)
Philippines	Winner	3.19***	2.93***	3.12***	3.64***
		(3.22)	(3.13)	(2.75)	(2.76)
	Loser	5.11***	6.68***	6.86***	5.17***
		(4.43)	(4.97)	(4.57)	(4.09)
	Contrarian	1.92*	3.74***	3.75**	1.52
		(1.69)	(2.95)	(2.42)	(1.21)
Thailand	Winner	1.27*	1.17	0.58	1.17
		(1.89)	(1.62)	(0.74)	(1.30)
	Loser	2.94***	3.91***	4.46***	4.81***
		(3.67)	(3.89)	(3.13)	(2.91)
	Contrarian	1.67***	2.74***	3.88***	3.63**
		(2.77)	(3.25)	(2.96)	(2.33)
Indonesia	Winner	1.95***	2.35***	1.97**	2.00**
		(2.98)	(3.36)	(2.36)	(2.14)
	Loser	3.83***	4.37***	3.20***	2.78***
		(4.38)	(5.19)	(4.48)	(3.46)
	Contrarian	1.88***	2.02***	1.22*	0.78
		(3.21)	(2.91)	(1.91)	(1.19)

Note: *, ** and *** represent statistical significance at 10%, 5% and 1% level respectively.

and 5 per cent levels respectively. We find strong contrarian returns for Thailand throughout the ranking and holding periods. As the length of the holding period increases, so does the return to the contrarian portfolio. Contrarian portfolio returns range from 1.67 per cent to 3.88 per cent and are highly significant at the 1 per cent level except for 60 months, which is significant at 5 per cent. In general, the returns become progressively higher with increase in time. Contrarian strategy also seems to be profitable in Indonesia. The returns are significant with the exception of 60 months (J = K = 60). Moreover, returns for winner and loser portfolios are all positive and highly significant.

Consistent with the studies in Asia and the United States, we find similarly high levels of profitability for the long-term contrarian strategy in emerging ASEAN markets. The exception is the Malaysian market. There are weak returns for the contrarian strategy in Malaysia, particularly for the longer holding periods. The results for Malaysia do, in general, concur with the findings of Lai et al. (2003), where significant returns were only found for periods less than 15 months. However, Ahmad and Hussain (2001) have reported more significant contrarian returns for Malaysia. We anticipate the difference could be due to the survivourship bias as Ahmad and Hussain (2001) use only active stocks in their sample. This possibility is addressed further in the next section.

3.2 Does survivourship bias matter?

Several past studies have tended to rely on a sample of active stocks only (e.g., Ahmad & Hussain, 2001). By excluding dead stocks, survivourship bias is introduced into the analysis. The bias may distort the results and ultimately the findings of the study. We examine this possibility by replicating the analysis using a sample of active stocks. For each country, stocks are screened, and only stocks that are active at the end of the sample period are selected. Stocks that are de-listed during the sample period are excluded from the sample. Essentially, we are retesting the trading strategies using data plagued by survivorship bias.

Table 9.3 reports the investigation of the link between survivorship bias and momentum. Momentum strategy is implemented for a sample of active stocks only. De-listed stocks are removed from the sample. The average monthly returns are expressed in percentage. The associated t-statistics is presented in parentheses.

For the momentum strategy, the findings are mixed. The results are qualitatively similar for the Philippines irrespective of whether the full sample of active and de-listed stocks or the sample of only active stocks is used for the analysis. Similarly, Indonesia does not display much difference between the two sample sets. Though there is a decrease in momentum returns, essentially the findings of significant negative momentum remain unchanged.

For Malaysia, ignoring de-listed stocks causes a decrease in portfolio returns; thereby tilting the return to a more negative figure. The statistical significance of the momentum portfolio is also altered. Momentum strategy now yields a –0.95 per cent per month (significant at 5 per cent) and a marginally significant –1.12 per cent for 9 and 12 months respectively. The negative returns suggest that a contrarian strategy would be profitable in Malaysia. However, these are largely illusory returns fueled by survivorship bias. As evidenced by Table 9.1, momentum portfolio yields no significant returns in Malaysia, negative or positive. As in Malaysia, we also find a decrease in momentum returns for Thailand.

Table 9.3 Momentum strategy for sample with survivourship bias

Country	Portfolio	J = K = 3	J = K = 6	J = K = 9	J = K = 12
Malaysia	Winner	0.32	0.15	0.27	0.47
		(0.81)	(0.30)	(0.51)	(0.88)
	Loser	0.41	0.84	1.22	1.60*
		(0.74)	(1.13)	(1.63)	(1.86)
	Momentum	−0.09	−0.68	−0.95**	−1.12*
		(−0.24)	(−1.51)	(−2.02)	(−1.79)
Philippines	Winner	1.61**	2.06**	2.18***	2.00***
		(2.07)	(2.61)	(2.97)	(2.65)
	Loser	6.89**	7.21**	6.22***	5.52***
		(2.19)	(2.24)	(3.13)	(3.56)
	Momentum	−5.28*	−5.15*	−4.04**	−3.52**
		(−1.73)	(−1.66)	(−2.24)	(−2.59)
Thailand	Winner	2.20***	1.99***	2.00***	1.84***
		(3.39)	(2.92)	(2.90)	(2.62)
	Loser	1.69**	2.69***	3.03***	3.01***
		(2.17)	(3.16)	(3.47)	(3.39)
	Momentum	0.51	−0.70	−1.03	−1.16*
		(1.13)	(−1.10)	(−1.56)	(−1.70)
Indonesia	Winner	1.67**	1.62**	1.95***	1.78***
		(2.40)	(2.60)	(3.22)	(2.93)
	Loser	2.68***	2.76***	2.95***	3.02***
		(3.39)	(3.22)	(3.69)	(3.65)
	Momentum	−1.01*	−1.14*	−1.00*	−1.24**
		(−1.86)	(−1.82)	(−1.88)	(−2.38)

Note: *, ** and *** represent statistical significance at 10%, 5% and 1% level respectively.

Using the sample of active stocks, we find marginally significant negative return for the momentum portfolio for J = K = 60. Again, there are no significant returns with the full sample of stocks (Table 9.1).

Table 9.4 reports the returns for the contrarian strategy implemented on the sample afflicted by survivorship bias for the ranking and holding period ranging from 3 to 12 months. The average monthly returns for the winner, loser and 3 portfolios are presented along with the t-statistics in parentheses.

Survivorship bias does appear to distort contrarian portfolio returns as evidenced by the findings in Table 9.4. In general, we find an increase in contrarian returns when de-listed stocks are ignored in the analysis. There is a return differential as high as 0.79 per cent between the full sample and sample of only active stocks. The change in returns also affects

Table 9.4 Long-term contrarian strategy for sample with survivourship bias

Country	**Portfolio**	**J = K = 24**	**J = K = 36**	**J = K = 48**	**J = K = 60**
Malaysia	Winner	0.62	0.78	0.59	0.95
		(1.09)	(1.28)	(0.92)	(1.45)
	Loser	1.66**	2.22**	1.47**	1.70*
		(2.10)	(2.44)	(2.05)	(1.88)
	Contrarian	1.04*	1.44*	0.88**	0.75
		(1.73)	(1.90)	(2.07)	(1.46)
Philippines	Winner	3.35***	2.99***	3.22***	3.71**
		(3.29)	(3.11)	(2.70)	(2.64)
	Loser	5.12***	6.96***	7.27***	5.71***
		(4.14)	(4.78)	(4.53)	(4.08)
	Contrarian	1.78	3.97***	4.05**	2.00
		(1.44)	(2.88)	(2.44)	(1.39)
Thailand	Winner	1.43**	1.23*	0.64	1.31
		(2.07)	(1.68)	(0.80)	(1.45)
	Loser	3.37***	4.39***	5.53***	5.73***
		(3.72)	(4.01)	(3.57)	(3.19)
	Contrarian	1.94***	3.16***	4.89***	4.42**
		(2.75)	(3.38)	(3.44)	(2.62)
Indonesia	Winner	2.02***	2.51***	1.99**	2.07**
		(3.08)	(3.46)	(2.27)	(2.14)
	Loser	3.49***	4.03***	2.99***	3.08***
		(4.64)	(5.12)	(4.29)	(3.59)
	Contrarian	1.47***	1.52**	1.00	1.01
		(3.38)	(2.44)	(1.55)	(1.41)

Note: *, ** and *** represent statistical significance at 10%, 5% and 1% level respectively.

the conclusion. For example, Malaysia was reported as having significant returns only for 24 months. However, with the sample comprised of only active stocks, the results are altered. There are strong contrarian returns for 24, 36 and 48 months. Overall, long-term contrarian strategy appears to be highly profitable in Malaysia, but this is merely the product of the survivorship bias that was created as a result of ignoring de-listed stocks. In other words, the contrarian profits are illusory. This highlights the importance of taking survivorship bias into account when examining contrarian strategy.

3.3 Examining the January effect

Fu and Wood (2010) suggest that the absence of momentum in Asia is caused by seasonal factors. In other words, momentum is present in

Asian markets, but the profitability is masked by seasonality. In a recent study, Yao (2012) states that contrarian returns are caused solely by the January effect. Once the January effect is taken into account, contrarian returns cease to exist. As in Jegadeesh and Titman (1993), we evaluate the profitability of the two strategies in January and other months independently in order to evaluate whether the returns of the strategies are influenced by the January effect.

Table 9.5 reports the average monthly returns (per cent) and associated t-statistics for the momentum strategy for January (Jan) and February to December (Feb–Dec). For each country, the first row reports the returns solely for January. The second row reports the returns for February to December.

We find a clear distinction between returns for January and the rest of the months in the Malaysian market. January returns are higher and significant for winner and loser portfolios. In stark contrast, returns for February to December are economically and statistically insignificant. Additionally, the momentum portfolio has a higher absolute value for January than the rest of the months. For example at J = K = 6, January returns are 3.02 per cent, 5.33 per cent and −2.31 per cent for the winner, loser and momentum portfolio respectively; while the corresponding values for the remaining months of February to December are −0.05 per cent, 0.14 per cent and −0.19 per cent. Next, we compare the returns with overall returns in Table 9.1. Overall portfolio returns for Malaysia are not significant. This suggests that the higher returns in January are subsumed by the returns in the remaining months. As a result, the overall portfolio returns are not significant. In other words, the January effect does not seem to be influencing the returns of the overall momentum portfolio. For the Philippines, winner and loser portfolio returns are drastically higher in January. However, the returns for the winner portfolio are lower than the loser portfolio for months other than January. This results in significantly negative returns for the momentum portfolio. In comparison, momentum returns for January are not significant. The magnitude and significance of the February to December momentum returns are generally similar to that of the overall momentum return (Table 9.1). Thus, February to December returns appear to contribute to much of the overall momentum.

The winner portfolio does not perform well in the Thailand stock market for the month of January, with returns as low as 0.28 per cent (t-statistic = 0.14). On the other hand, returns for February to December are primarily large and significant. For the loser portfolio, returns are generally large, albeit insignificant, for January and highly significant

Table 9.5 January effect and momentum strategy

J = K		Malaysia			Philippines			Thailand			Indonesia		
		Winner	Loser	Mom	Winner	Loser	Mom	Winner	Loser	Mom	Winner	Loser	Mom
3	Jan	3.15*	4.73**	−1.57	5.60	9.34*	−3.75	2.14	3.97	−1.83	0.91	1.49	−0.58
		(2.03)	(2.52)	(−1.09)	(1.09)	(2.11)	(−1.33)	(0.84)	(1.30)	(−0.96)	(0.50)	(0.70)	(−0.25)
	Feb-Dec	0.09	−0.12	0.20	1.44*	6.68*	−5.24	2.03***	1.28	0.75	1.90**	2.66***	−0.76
		(0.15)	(−0.15)	(0.41)	(1.96)	(1.98)	(−1.59)	(3.11)	(1.58)	(1.51)	(2.54)	(3.19)	(−1.42)
6	Jan	3.02*	5.33**	−2.31	7.39	8.23**	−0.84	0.28	7.53	−7.26	1.16	0.54	0.61
		(2.09)	(2.90)	(−1.74)	(1.35)	(2.26)	(−0.21)	(0.14)	(1.62)	(−1.74)	(0.55)	(0.34)	(0.40)
	Feb-Dec	−0.05	0.14	−0.19	1.61**	7.45**	−5.84*	2.05***	1.86**	0.19	1.55**	3.13***	−1.59**
		(−0.09)	(0.18)	(−0.38)	(2.35)	(2.14)	(−1.74)	(2.93)	(2.33)	(0.36)	(2.36)	(3.40)	(−2.40)
9	Jan	3.10*	5.59**	−2.49*	6.05	10.17**	−4.12	0.37	6.92	−6.55	0.45	0.30	0.15
		(2.12)	(3.12)	(−1.89)	(1.32)	(2.79)	(−1.33)	(0.18)	(1.47)	(−1.60)	(0.26)	(0.17)	(0.14)
	Feb-Dec	−0.01	0.43	−0.44	1.83***	6.08***	−4.25**	1.95***	2.01**	−0.05	1.87***	3.38***	−1.50**
		(−0.02)	(0.53)	(−0.84)	(2.68)	(2.84)	(−2.18)	(2.76)	(2.61)	(−0.11)	(2.94)	(3.83)	(−2.48)
12	Jan	3.27*	5.00**	−1.72	5.65	7.32**	−1.67	0.34	2.83	−2.50***	−0.28	0.59	−0.86
		(2.11)	(2.83)	(−1.56)	(1.11)	(2.52)	(−0.50)	(0.15)	(1.25)	(−3.96)	(−0.15)	(0.26)	(−0.72)
	Feb-Dec	0.08	0.86	−0.78	1.59**	5.46***	−3.87***	1.81**	2.43***	−0.63	1.80***	3.39***	−1.59***
		(0.15)	(0.97)	(−1.25)	(2.30)	(3.32)	(−2.71)	(2.51)	(3.07)	(−1.16)	(2.85)	(3.84)	(−2.65)

Note: *, ** and *** represent statistical significance at 10%, 5% and 1% level respectively.

for other months. Momentum returns in those other months are positive for 3 and 6 months (J = K) and insignificantly negative for 9 and 12 months. On the other hand, we find strong negative returns to the momentum portfolio in January for 12 months (J = K = 12). The negative returns in January is in line with the results reported by Jegadeesh and Titman (1993). However, the negative returns in January are subsumed by the non-January returns as the overall momentum portfolio (Table 9.1) is insignificant. For Indonesia, we find very little evidence of a January effect influencing the portfolio returns. Winner and loser portfolios remain significant after excluding January. Moreover, momentum returns are still significantly negative for non-January months and closely resemble the overall momentum returns. January returns seem to have little or no effect on momentum strategy in the Indonesian market.

The analysis for the contrarian strategy and January effect is reported in Table 9.6. The average monthly returns (per cent) and t-statistics for winner, loser and contrarian portfolios for January (Jan) and the remaining months of February to December (Feb–Dec) are presented sequentially for each country.

For the Malaysian stock market, we find that the winner and loser portfolio returns are higher in January than other months. The contrarian portfolio returns are significant only for January. Upon comparison with the overall returns (Table 9.2), we find the contrarian return is no longer significant for J = K = 24 once the January returns are excluded. If contrarian strategy is not driven by the January effect then the returns should persist even after accounting for the January effect. Not only do the contrarian returns cease to exist after excluding January, the return for January alone is stronger and more significant than the overall return. In addition, returns for the overall contrarian strategy is insignificant for 60 months (J = K = 60), but the returns are significant for January with a return of 4.52 per cent per month. Thus we conclude that long-term contrarian returns in Malaysia are heavily influenced by the January effect.

Conversely, we find that returns to the contrarian portfolio are significant for February to December in the Philippines. Although January returns are noticeably higher, they are not statistically significant. In other words, the contrarian strategy remains profitable even after excluding January. Similarly, winner and loser portfolio returns are significant only for February to December. Based on the results, the January effect does not appear to influence winner, loser and contrarian portfolio returns in the Philippines. Similar results can be observed, in general, for Thailand. Winner portfolio returns are negative for January for all

Table 9.6 January effect and long-term contrarian strategy

J = K		Malaysia			Philippines			Thailand			Indonesia		
		Winner	Loser	Con	Winner	Loser	Con	Winner	Loser	Con	Winner	Loser	Con
24	Jan	2.77	4.52*	1.74*	3.90	5.75	1.85	−0.98	0.69	1.67	−0.21	2.09	2.30
		(1.72)	(2.25)	(2.10)	(0.88)	(1.56)	(1.01)	(−0.52)	(0.33)	(1.41)	(−0.11)	(0.65)	(0.99)
	Feb-Dec	0.31	1.14	0.83	3.13***	5.05***	1.93	1.45**	3.12***	1.67**	2.12***	3.97***	1.85***
		(0.54)	(1.42)	(1.45)	(3.09)	(4.16)	(1.57)	(2.05)	(3.68)	(2.58)	(3.08)	(4.37)	(3.04)
36	Jan	2.99	4.34	1.35	2.68	15.12	12.44	−1.37	3.15	4.52	0.76	5.82	5.06
		(1.42)	(1.67)	(0.76)	(0.64)	(1.73)	(1.58)	(−0.62)	(1.10)	(1.79)	(0.44)	(1.40)	(1.48)
	Feb-Dec	0.56	1.57*	1.01	2.95***	5.99***	3.04**	1.37*	3.97***	2.60***	2.48***	4.26***	1.77**
		(0.90)	(1.77)	(1.43)	(3.07)	(4.72)	(2.52)	(1.82)	(3.73)	(2.92)	(3.33)	(4.98)	(2.54)
48	Jan	3.10	5.71*	2.61	3.56	17.04	13.48	−0.99	8.18	9.17	0.08	4.38	4.30
		(1.45)	(1.96)	(1.59)	(0.77)	(1.52)	(1.26)	(−0.41)	(1.50)	(1.85)	(0.06)	(1.10)	(1.07)
	Feb-Dec	0.28	0.65	0.37	3.08**	6.05***	2.97**	0.70	4.16***	3.46**	2.12**	3.10***	0.98
		(0.42)	(0.91)	(0.88)	(2.63)	(4.47)	(2.07)	(0.85)	(2.81)	(2.55)	(2.37)	(4.36)	(1.59)
60	Jan	2.11	6.62	4.52*	0.53	10.80	10.28	−2.62	6.75	9.38*	−0.57	−0.99	−0.42
		(1.10)	(1.90)	(2.21)	(0.12)	(1.02)	(0.94)	(−1.29)	(1.29)	(2.46)	(−0.29)	(−0.61)	(−0.18)
	Feb-Dec	0.70	0.96	0.25	3.89***	4.73***	0.84	1.47	4.65***	3.19*	2.20**	3.08***	0.88
		(1.01)	(1.07)	(0.52)	(2.81)	(4.22)	(0.78)	(1.54)	(2.68)	(1.93)	(2.21)	(3.61)	(1.27)

Note: *, ** and *** represent statistical significance at 10%, 5% and 1% level respectively.

holding periods. Returns are positive only for February to December. The differences in winner portfolio returns between January and the remaining months are drastic. For example, winner returns for January are −0.98 per cent whereas February to December they are 1.45 per cent. Though loser portfolio returns are positive for January and February to December, the returns are significant only for February to December. Similarly, contrarian portfolio returns are significant only for February to December for all ranking and holding periods expect for 60 months. For the holding period of 60 months, contrarian returns are significant for both January and February to December. Nevertheless, as the contrarian strategy remains profitable even after excluding January, contrarian returns are not solely caused by the January effect. Overall, the evidence suggests that seasonality in January is not the primary cause of the profitability of long-term contrarian strategy in Thailand.

We find that returns for Indonesia also follow a similar trend. Winner portfolio returns are significant after excluding January returns. The highest returns of 2.48 per cent can be observed for 36 months ranking and holding period. In contrast, January returns are an insignificant 0.76 per cent per month. Loser portfolio returns for February–December are highly significant at the 1 per cent level for all periods. January loser portfolio returns are insignificant. We find significant returns for the contrarian portfolio only for February–December, indicating that the January effect does not influence returns to the contrarian strategy.

3.4 Global financial crisis

Our sample period of 2000 to 2011 incorporates the recent global financial crisis. The global crisis commenced in 2008 and the far-reaching effects of the crisis could have 'significantly larger impact on Asian economies than earlier global downturns' (Fidrmuc & Korhonen, 2010). Chui et al. (2003) show that momentum returns are positive before the 1997 Asian financial crisis, but returns turn negative following the onset of the crisis for our sample of ASEAN countries. Thus, we investigate whether our results are affected by the recent global financial crisis. In particular, it would be interesting to examine whether the negative momentum we observed in the Philippines and Indonesia are caused by the crisis. For this purpose, we split the sample periods into two: the pre-crisis period from 2000 to 2007; and after the crisis commences, which is from 2008 onwards.

For the momentum strategy, Table 9.7 reports the average portfolio returns, and the associated t-statistics are in parentheses. For each country, the first row provides the returns for the 2000 to 2007 period, while

Table 9.7 Global financial crisis and momentum strategy

J = K		Malaysia			Philippines			Thailand			Indonesia		
		Winner	Loser	Mom	Winner	Loser	Mom	Winner	Loser	Mom	Winner	Loser	Mom
3	2000-2007	0.29	0.05	0.24	2.08**	3.75***	−1.68**	2.15***	2.05**	0.10	1.88**	2.64***	−0.76
		(0.41)	(0.05)	(0.38)	(2.06)	(3.56)	(−2.03)	(2.75)	(2.10)	(0.15)	(2.14)	(2.74)	(−1.12)
	2008-2011	0.40	0.67	−0.27	1.16	12.89	−11.73	1.82*	0.41	1.41**	1.71	2.43*	−0.72
		(0.50)	(0.59)	(−0.44)	(0.95)	(1.45)	(−1.35)	(1.69)	(0.31)	(2.26)	(1.45)	(1.77)	(−0.90)
6	2000-2007	0.23	0.44	−0.21	2.43**	4.70***	−2.27**	2.57***	2.92***	−0.35	1.72**	2.91***	−1.19*
		(0.35)	(0.45)	(−0.34)	(2.34)	(4.03)	(−2.35)	(3.24)	(2.74)	(−0.41)	(2.20)	(3.04)	(−1.71)
	2008-2011	0.14	0.78	−0.64	1.42	12.73	−11.31	0.68	1.19	−0.51	1.13	2.96*	−1.82
		(0.17)	(0.63)	(−0.87)	(1.32)	(1.43)	(−1.31)	(0.57)	(0.92)	(−0.77)	(1.09)	(1.74)	(−1.49)
9	2000-2007	0.44	0.78	−0.34	2.39**	5.02***	−2.62***	2.59***	2.94***	−0.35	2.08***	3.25***	−1.17
		(0.69)	(0.77)	(−0.51)	(2.63)	(4.52)	(−3.39)	(3.23)	(2.82)	(−0.43)	(2.77)	(3.26)	(−1.65)
	2008-2011	−0.11	0.98	−1.10	1.78	8.92*	−7.13	0.45	1.45	−1.01	1.18	2.91*	−1.73*
		(−0.13)	(0.83)	(−1.57)	(1.45)	(1.72)	(−1.47)	(0.38)	(1.17)	(−1.65)	(1.16)	(1.99)	(−1.85)
12	2000-2007	0.62	1.22	−0.60	2.42**	4.35***	−1.93**	2.38***	2.82***	−0.44	1.91**	3.43***	−1.52**
		(0.97)	(1.06)	(−0.71)	(2.49)	(4.12)	(−2.37)	(2.82)	(2.92)	(−0.61)	(2.60)	(3.17)	(−2.02)
	2008-2011	−0.18	1.09	−1.28**	1.00	7.76**	−6.76**	0.50	1.85	−1.35**	1.17	2.73**	−1.56*
		(−0.20)	(0.97)	(−2.08)	(0.87)	(2.06)	(−2.02)	(0.43)	(1.55)	(−2.30)	(1.13)	(2.08)	(−1.89)

Note: *, ** and *** represent statistical significance at 10%, 5% and 1% level respectively.

the second row provides the returns for the 2008 to 2011 period. For Malaysia, winner portfolio returns appear to be generally higher in the pre-crisis period. For the loser portfolio, the opposite seems to be true. Nevertheless, we find that none of the returns are significant. Momentum portfolio returns are insignificant as well, except for the holding period of 12 months where there is evidence of negative momentum (significant at the 5 per cent level).

Interestingly, we find that winner portfolio returns are significant only for the pre-crisis period in the Philippines. Furthermore, significant returns for loser and momentum portfolios are also confined to the period before the crisis. The only exception is the 12-month holding period in which returns for both periods are significant. Thus, the negative momentum observed for the Philippines market is not caused by the recent crisis. For Thailand, winner and loser portfolio returns are generally highly significant at the 1 per cent level in the pre-crisis period. Surprisingly there is significant momentum for the 3 months holding period (J = K = 3) after the crisis. However, we also find negative momentum for the 12-month holding period after the crisis. Similar to the Philippines and Thailand, winner portfolio returns in Indonesia are significantly positive only prior to the crisis. Notably, all of returns for the loser portfolio are significantly positive regardless of the time period. Negative momentum can be observed before and after the crisis, particularly at 12 months (J = K = 12). Thus, the negative momentum reported in Table 9.1 is not confined to the period following the crisis.

Table 9.8 reports the portfolio returns for the contrarian strategy for the 2000 to 2007 period and 2008 to 2011 period in the first and second rows respectively. For the Malaysian market, we do not find much distinction between the periods, suggesting that the crisis does not affect contrarian returns. Winner, loser and contrarian portfolio returns are largely similar. The only exception is the holding period of 36 months (J = K = 36) in which higher and significant loser portfolio returns are evident for the pre-crisis period.

The winner portfolio is significant in the Philippines for the pre-crisis period, but not for the period after the crisis. Loser portfolio returns are consistently significant for all periods. We could observe significant contrarian returns in the pre-crisis period as well as in the period following the crisis. We find no discernable pattern in the winner portfolio returns for Thailand. Significant returns can be found for 2000 to 2007 as well as the 2008 to 2011 period for selected holding periods. Overall, loser portfolio returns are significant for both periods. For contrarian portfolios, the returns are notably higher and statistically significant in the

Table 9.8 Global financial crisis and long-term contrarian strategy

J = K		Malaysia			Philippines			Thailand			Indonesia		
		Winner	Loser	Con	Winner	Loser	Con	Winner	Loser	Con	Winner	Loser	Con
24	2000-2007	0.63	1.59	0.95	3.30***	5.84***	2.54	1.71*	3.38***	1.67*	2.68***	4.44***	1.76*
		(0.99)	(1.43)	(1.15)	(2.97)	(3.64)	(1.66)	(1.93)	(3.36)	(1.82)	(3.35)	(3.42)	(1.94)
	2008-2011	0.30	1.11	0.81	3.02	4.03**	1.01	0.62	2.29*	1.67**	0.86	2.92***	2.06***
		(0.30)	(1.19)	(1.63)	(1.65)	(2.50)	(0.59)	(0.60)	(1.74)	(2.61)	(0.78)	(2.91)	(3.68)
36	2000-2007	1.14	2.44*	1.30	4.07***	8.17***	4.10**	1.32	5.72***	4.40***	3.40***	6.23***	2.83**
		(1.66)	(1.81)	(1.17)	(3.39)	(4.22)	(2.24)	(1.39)	(3.71)	(3.05)	(4.01)	(4.76)	(2.58)
	2008-2011	0.25	0.95	0.71	1.53	4.83**	3.30*	0.98	1.68	0.70	1.06	2.09**	1.03
		(0.24)	(1.07)	(1.21)	(1.04)	(2.68)	(1.92)	(0.88)	(1.49)	(1.39)	(0.93)	(2.38)	(1.37)
48	2000-2007	0.49	1.00	0.51	4.56***	8.05***	3.50	−0.18	6.58**	6.75***	2.99***	4.41***	1.42*
		(0.62)	(0.94)	(0.93)	(2.76)	(3.64)	(1.57)	(−0.19)	(2.46)	(2.71)	(3.12)	(3.75)	(1.74)
	2008-2011	0.49	1.04	0.55	1.71	5.70***	3.99*	1.32	2.38**	1.06	0.98	2.01**	1.03
		(0.48)	(1.11)	(0.91)	(1.11)	(2.79)	(1.84)	(1.05)	(2.38)	(1.51)	(0.72)	(2.54)	(1.04)
60	2000-2007	1.04	1.50	0.46	5.61**	5.19***	−0.42	0.01	6.15**	6.14**	3.02**	4.56***	1.54
		(1.15)	(1.05)	(0.60)	(2.50)	(3.45)	(−0.28)	(0.01)	(2.36)	(2.51)	(2.60)	(3.07)	(1.61)
	2008-2011	0.63	1.27	0.64	2.21	5.15***	2.94	2.02	3.82*	1.81	1.26	1.49*	0.23
		(0.68)	(1.14)	(1.00)	(1.39)	(2.70)	(1.57)	(1.52)	(1.79)	(0.90)	(0.91)	(1.77)	(0.25)

Note: *, ** and *** represent statistical significance at 10%, 5% and 1% level respectively.

pre-crisis period of 2000 to 2007. For Indonesia, significant returns for the winner portfolio can only be found prior to the 2008 crisis. Loser portfolio returns are significant for all holding periods irrespective of the time period. Nevertheless, pre-crisis returns are drastically higher than after the crisis for the loser portfolio. Contrarian portfolio returns are significant prior to 2008 for all holding periods except 60 months.

4 Conclusion

In our investigation, we further confirm the absence of momentum in Malaysia and Thailand. More pertinently, we find significant negative momentum for the Philippines and Indonesia. The negative momentum returns were caused by the superior performance of the loser portfolio. We find that contrarian strategy is highly profitable in the long term for all markets except Malaysia, where there is only a marginally significant return. In particular, contrarian strategy is consistently profitable for the Thailand stock market. We recommend implementing a contrarian strategy with a ranking and holding period of less than 48 months. In short, investors may be better off adhering to a contrarian strategy for the intermediate and long term in the ASEAN stock markets.

In addition, we have also established that survivorship bias tends to inflate the contrarian return to point of altering the results of the study. Thus, there is a danger in using a sample restricted to only active stocks. Researchers should abstain from employing samples afflicted with survivorship bias because the results and, ultimately, the conclusions could be distorted. As for the January effect, we find no influence of seasonality on momentum in the Philippines and Indonesia. Though there is a difference in returns between January and the rest of the months in Malaysia and Thailand, the overall momentum portfolio returns seem to be unaltered by the returns in January. Thus, we conclude that the January effect does not influence momentum. On the contrary, contrarian returns in Malaysia are largely derived from the returns in January. Nevertheless, contrarian strategy is unaffected by January seasonality in the other ASEAN markets. In general, we also find that there is little evidence to suggest that contrarian and momentum strategy returns are influenced by the recent global financial crisis.

Acknowledgement

The authors gratefully acknowledges the support of Universiti Sains Malaysia Research University grant: 1001.PPAMC.816192.

References

Ahmad, Z. and Hussain, S. (2001) 'KLSE Long Run Overreaction and the Chinese New-Year Effect', *Journal of Business Finance & Accounting*, 28(1–2), 63–105.

Brown, S., Yan Du, D., Rhee, S. G. and Zhang, L. (2008) 'The Returns to Value and Momentum in Asian Markets', *Emerging Markets Review*, 9(2), 79–88.

Chae, J. and Eom, Y. (2009) 'Negative Momentum Profit in Korea and its Sources', *Asia-Pacific Journal of Financial Studies*, 38(2), 211–36.

Chiao, C. and Hueng, C. J. (2005) 'Overreaction Effects Independent of Risk and Characteristics: Evidence from the Japanese Stock Market', *Japan and the World Economy*, 17(4), 431–55.

Chui, A. C. W., Titman, S. and Wei, K. C. J. (2010) 'Individualism and Momentum around the World', *The Journal of Finance*, 65(1), 361–92.

Chui, A. C. W., Titman, S. and Wei, K. C. J. (2003) 'Momentum, Legal Systems And Ownership Structure: An Analysis Of Asian Stock Markets', *Working Paper* (Austin: University of Texas).

Click, R. W. and Plummer, M. G. (2005) 'Stock Market Integration in ASEAN after the Asian Financial Crisis', *Journal of Asian Economics*, 16(1), 5–28.

De Bondt, W. F. M. and Thaler, R. (1985). 'Does the Stock Market Overreact?' *Journal of Finance*, 40(3), 793–805.

De Bondt, W. F. M. and Thaler, R. H. (1987) 'Further Evidence on Investor Overreaction and Stock Market Seasonality', *Journal of Finance*, 42(3), 557–81.

Fidrmuc, J. and Korhonen, I. (2010) 'The Impact of the Global Financial Crisis on Business Cycles in Asian Emerging Economies', *Journal of Asian Economics*, 21(3), 293–303.

Fu, H.-P. and Wood, A. (2009) 'Momentum in Taiwan: Seasonality Matters!' *Applied Economics Letters*, 17(13), 1247–53.

Fung, A. K.-W. (1999) 'Overreaction in the Hong Kong Stock Market, *Global Finance Journal*, 10(2), 223–30.

Gaunt, C. (2000) 'Overreaction in the Australian Equity Market: 1974–1997', *Pacific-Basin Finance Journal*, 8(3–4), 375–98.

Griffin, J. M., Ji, S. and Martin, J. S. (2005) 'Global Momentum Strategies: A Portfolio. Perspective', *Journal of Portfolio Management*, 31, 23–39.

Griffin, J. M., Ji, X. and Martin, J. S. (2003). 'Momentum Investing and Business Cycle Risk: Evidence from Pole to Pole', *The Journal of Finance*, 58(6), 2515–47.

Hameed, A. and Kusnadi, Y. (2002) 'Momentum Strategies: Evidence from Pacific Basin Stock Markets', *Journal of Financial Research*, 25(3), 383–97.

Jegadeesh, N. and Titman, S. (1993) 'Returns to Buying Winners and Selling Losers: Implications for Stock Market Efficiency', *Journal of Finance*, 48, 65–91.

Lai, M. -M., Guru, B. K. and Nor, F. M. (2003) 'Do Malaysian Investors Overreact?' *Journal of American Academy of Business*, 2(2), 602–09.

Mun, J. C., Vasconcellos, G. M. and Kish, R. (1999) 'Tests of the Contrarian Investment Strategy Evidence from the French and German Stock Markets', *International Review of Financial Analysis*, 8(3), 215–34.

Mun, J. C., Vasconcellos, G. M. and Kish, R. (2000) 'The Contrarian/Overreaction Hypothesis: An Analysis of the US and Canadian Stock Markets', *Global Finance Journal*, 11(2), 53–72.

Naranjo, A. and Porter, B. (2007) 'Including Emerging Markets in International Momentum Investment Strategies', *Emerging Markets Review*, 8(2), 147–66.

Ramiah, V., Cheng, K. Y., Orriols, J., Naughton, T. and Hallahan, T. (2011) 'Contrarian Investment Strategies Work Better for Dually-Traded Stocks: Evidence from Hong Kong', *Pacific-Basin Finance Journal*, 19(1), 140–56.

Rouwenhorst, K. G. (1999) 'Local Return Factors and Turnover in Emerging Stock Markets', *Journal of Finance*, 54(4), 1439–64.

Sharma, S. C. and Wongbangpo, P. (2002) 'Long-Term Trends and Cycles in ASEAN Stock Markets', *Review of Financial Economics*, 11(4), 299–315.

Yao, Y. (2012) 'Momentum, Contrarian, and the January Seasonality', *Journal of Banking & Finance*, 36(10), 2757–69.

Zarowin, P. (1990) 'Size, Seasonality, and Stock Market Overreaction', *The Journal of Financial and Quantitative Analysis*, 25(1), 113–25.

10
Socially Responsible Investing Funds in Asia Pacific

Wei-Rong Ang and Hooi Hooi Lean

1 Introduction

The term socially responsible investing (SRI) is defined as an investment strategy that provides investors financial gain as well as contributes to society and the environment (Benson et al., 2008). SRI is also defined as an investment that integrates environmental, social and governance issues when forming the investment portfolio (Kiesel et al., 2010). As stated in Hamilton et al. (1993), SRI can be described as 'doing good while doing well' because the aim of SRI is to enhance the sustainability level in our surroundings besides providing financial returns to investors. Alternative terms include mission investing, responsible investing, double or triple bottom line investing, ethical investing, sustainable investing or green investing.[1] In total, there are four types of SRI portfolios: environmental, religious or ethical, social and corporate governance (Fung et al., 2010). SRI not only uses financial criteria solely to determine which investment to invest in but also takes into account the contribution and impact of that particular investment towards society, environment and people (Ballestero et al., 2011).

Due to the rapid growth and popularity of SRI funds, market players and investors are cognizant of and interested in investing in portfolios that are able – by taking into consideration social, environmental and ethical factors – to have a positive impact on society and the environment (Kiesel et al., 2010). In the United States, SRI assets comprise approximately \$3.07 trillion of the \$25.2 trillion in the investment market.[2] Säve-Söderbergh (2010) showed that for every eight investors in the market, one is found to be a socially responsible investor.

Broadly speaking, negative and positive screenings are normally and widely employed. These two screening methods are the first and second generations of SRI screening, respectively, whereas, the third generation of the screening process is an integrated approach of investing in companies based on the economic, environmental and social criteria by comprising both positive and negative screenings. The third generation is also known as the triple bottom line because it places emphasis on the impact of investment on people, planet and profit (Renneboog et al., 2008). Furthermore, the fourth generation is just combining the third generation with shareholder activism. In the fourth generation, the fund manager who specializes in granting ethical labels will influence the company's policy through direct dialogue with the management or voting right during its annual general meeting (Renneboog et al., 2008).

SRI is not a new investment concept in the Europe; it started as early as 1920 when the Methodist Church in the United Kingdom chose to avoid investing in so-called 'sinful stock' (Eurosif Report, 2003). This new investment strategy only spread to the rest of Continental Europe in the 1960s. SRI has undergone rapid development and progression as many people have begun to value the importance of SRI funds. SRI assets are growing tremendously. Many countries in the Europe have taken the initiative to promote SRI. Renneboog et al. (2008) revealed that United Kingdom was the first country to require disclosure of social, environmental and ethical investment policies for pension funds and charities. France was the first country to make social, environmental and ethical policies a mandatory reporting requirement for all listed companies in France.

Table 10.1 reports the total assets of SRI in selected countries. Total SRI assets are lead by the Europe which made up more than half of the total amount. Within two years, the increment was 87.06 per cent, whereas in the United States it only grew by 11.67 per cent. Total SRI assets

Table 10.1 Total SRI assets (€bn) in selected countries

Year	United States	Canada	Asia Pacific	Europe	Total
2006–2007	1917.3	333.6	46.9	2665.4	4963.20
	38.63%	6.72%	0.94%	53.71%	100%
2008–2010	2141	405	62	4986	7594
	28.19%	5.33%	0.82%	65.66%	100%

Source: Extracted from Eurosif 2008 Report and Eurosif 2010 Report and authors' own calculation in the Asia Pacific represent 0.82 per cent of total SRI assets in 2010. Although the proportion decreased after two years, the total amount of funds invested increased. In accordance with the statistics from Table 10.1, SRI funds in the Asia Pacific region are yet to be explored and are less developed in conjunction with Europe and North America. This small proportion indicates that SRI will become mainstream in the near future. Our study aims to fill this research gap since there is so far no study of the performance of SRI funds in the Asia Pacific region.

Unlike previous studies that investigated the performance of SRI funds compared to conventional funds, this study investigates the performance of a total of 32 SRI funds that invest in the Asia Pacific. We find that the mean return of SRI funds is higher than the average return of the U.S. T-bill rate. The performance period we investigated is January 2003 to June 2010, which includes the 2008 financial crisis. The positive return during the financial crisis indicates that SRI investment is able to withstand the downturn of the market.

The remainder of this chapter includes a literature review in the next section. Section 3 provides descriptions of data, and Section 4 discusses the methodology. Section 5 reports empirical results and, lastly, the conclusion is in Section 6.

2 Literature review

It is argued that SRI investors face the dubious dilemma of a financial penalty for imposing ethical constraints on the investment universe; that is, by avoiding certain assets for social, environmental and ethical reasons. SRI investors face a risk-return optimization problem that comes at the cost of portfolio performance. Likewise, Ballestero et al. (2011) found that conventional portfolios outperformed SRI portfolios in terms of the traditional mean–variance approach. For instance, a large body of research has investigated the social/environmental–financial performance by comparing the historical returns of SRI funds to those of conventional funds with respect to market indexes. In order to investigate how true are these arguments, many studies have been conducted using different methodologies, including (the most prominent) Sharpe (1966) ratio, Treynor (1965) ratio, Jensen's (1968) alpha, the unconditional regression method as well as the conditional regression model. This research seeks to evaluate, from different perspectives, the performance of SRI funds relative to conventional funds. The area that has been studied includes risk-adjusted returns performance from different countries, stock-selection ability, the impact of screening intensity, the cost of screening and the fund size that is expected will affect the performance of SRI funds.

Previous studies (for example, Hamilton et al., 1993; Sauer, 1997; Schröder, 2004; Bello, 2005; Bauer et al., 2005, 2006; Boasson et al., 2006; Benson et al., 2006; Galema et al., 2008; Renneboog et al., 2008; Cortez et al., 2009; Derwall et al., 2009) have shown that there is no significant difference between the performance of SRI funds and conventional funds/benchmarks in terms of risk-return, fund-selection ability and screening intensity. Moreover, there are studies that investigate the performance of the ethical index and the conventional index. Albaity and Ahmad (2008) measured the return performance and risk between the Kuala Lumpur Syariah Index (KLSI) and Kuala Lumpur Composite Index (KLCI) for the period 1999 to 2005. The study found no significant difference between the performances of both. However, there is a clear-cut evidence that screens indices required to bear higher cost and lesser diversification. This argument is supported by Bauer et al. (2006), who stated that screens portfolios tend to produce lower returns and lack diversification power because the portfolio is the subset of the market and constraint investment opportunity.

Analysis of SRI funds in Asia Pacific mainly focuses on Australia due to data availability. Cummings (2000) analyzed seven unlisted Australian ethical funds, which invested in Australian Securities Exchange (ASX) stock and operated from September 1986 to October 1994 on a risk-adjusted basis against the benchmark's performance. Consistent with previous studies, ethical funds tended to be smaller in market capitalization. The study concluded that incurring ethical constraints will not increase or decrease the return of the funds. Furthermore, there is no significant difference found between the return of funds and the indices.

For instance, Tippet (2001) investigated three Australian ethical funds (Tower Life fund, Tyndall fund & Australian Ethical fund) within a seven years' period, from June 1991 to June 1998. Two of them, Tower Life fund and Australian Ethical fund, show negative abnormal returns. Moreover, Australian funds are found to be underperforming 1.5 per cent per annum relative to risk-free assets. It is found that this underperformance is due to management fees and transaction costs.

Bauer et al. (2006) studied the performance of 25 Australian SRI funds over the period of 1992 to 2003, including dead funds to minimize the survivorship problem. Bauer et al. (2006) divided the period into three sub-periods: November 1992 to April 1996; May 1996 to October 1999; and November 1999 to April 2003. For the whole period of 1992–2003, there is no significant difference in performance between SRI funds and conventional funds. However, for domestic funds underperformance happened during November 1992 to April 1996, whereas international funds are outperformed the market for that period. Australian domestic funds are performed equally well with the conventional funds from May 1996 to October 1999.

Jones et al. (2008) investigated the performance of Australian SRI funds over 1986–2005. They found that 89 Australian SRI funds underperformed the market significantly over the period 2000–05. The annual underperformance is about 1.52 per cent in 2000–05 and 0.88 per cent for 1986–2005.

Humphrey and Lee (2011) investigated the performance and risk of 27 Australian SRI funds and 514 conventional funds within the period January 1996 to December 2008. They found no significant difference in performance between SRI funds and conventional funds. Regarding the effect of screening intensity on the funds' returns, they found little evidence of screening either positively or negatively affecting the performance, but a higher intensity of screening will lead to a higher risk-adjusted return. On the other hand, when positive screening increases, total and diversified risk are reduced. Likewise, negative screening definitely increased the risk to the portfolio. Overall, a curvilinear relation between the number of screens and risk is found, and negative screens will reduce the systematic risk as well.

From these studies (Cummings, 2000; Tippet, 2001; Humphrey & Lee, 2011), it was found that the performance of SRI funds in Australia is no different from the conventional funds for different lengths of period and sample size. We note that previous studies mainly focus on the funds in a single country. A literature search found no study of SRI funds in the Asia Pacific, as a whole region, in one study. Hence, this present study intends to fill this research gap by investigating the performance of SRI funds in the Asia Pacific region as a whole.

3 Data

This chapter uses data from the Eurekahedge database for the SRI funds category. Eurekahedge provides a funds database by compiling all investment funds into several categories, such as Islamic funds, Real Estate Investment Trust (REIT), SRI Funds, Commodity Trading Advisor funds, hedge funds and so forth. This database enabled us to collect all the required SRI funds at once. Moreover, Eurekahedge is the world's largest alternative investment funds research house which specializes in hedge fund research.[3]

There were 32 SRI funds in the Asia Pacific as of June 2010, excluding Islamic funds.[4] Thus, the analysis of this study does not take into account the effect of the religion component. The sample period is from January 2003 to June 2010. We chose this period for two reasons. First, the percentage of SRI funds launched and active within this period is at its highest. Second, the 2008 global financial crisis falls into this period. This allows us to study the performance of SRI funds during the crisis period. The risk-free rate used in this chapter is the U.S. T-bill. We agree with Hassan et al. (2010) that there is no better riskless asset than the U.S. T-bill. Hayat and Kraeussl (2011) used the same risk-free rate in their study. In order to employ the Fama–French (1993) model, the size effect (SMB) and value/growth effect variables (HML) are computed following the formulae in Kenneth French's website.[5] Six portfolios are taken from the Morgan Stanley Capital Investment (MSCI) website[6] to represent the six proxies, that is: small value, small neutral, small growth, big value, big neutral and big growth for SMB and HML proxy computation. We use market indexes that are summarized in Chegut et al. (2011). The ethical benchmark is the Dow Jones Sustainability World Index (DJSWI), which is one of the categories from the Dow Jones Sustainability Indexes (DJSI), a subset of the world equity market that tracks the price movement of portfolios of SRI stocks (Copp et al., 2010). We chose DJWSI because it consists of leading companies, based on SRI criteria and ability to represent the performance of the best SRI portfolios (Fung et al., 2010). The conventional index is MSCI All Country Asia Pacific Index (MSCIAP), which represents the performance of conventional portfolios in the Asia Pacific region[7]. For comparison, we add one more market proxy, the Eurekahedge SRI Funds Index (ESFI). Furthermore, we obtain the momentum (MOM) variable from Style Research Ltd when examining the Carhart (1997) model.

4 Methodology

This chapter employs performance-evaluation methods: that is, Sharpe ratio, Treynor ratio and Jensen's alpha, which are widely used in the mutual fund literature. The Sharpe (1966) ratio is the most conventional formula used in stocks and mutual funds performance measurement. The Sharpe ratio is defined as:

$$S_i = \frac{\overline{R}_i - \overline{R}_f}{\sigma_i} \tag{1}$$

where

$\overline{R}_i$ = average return of the fund
$\overline{R}_f$ = average risk-free rate
σ_i = standard deviation of the fund return.

Ideally, the larger the Sharpe ratio the better the performance of that stock or fund. In other words, the fund or stock with a higher value along the capital market line will have a higher Sharpe ratio.

Treynor (1965) ratio measures the performance of a stock or fund by taking into account the systematic risk or market volatility as its measure of risk instead of standard deviation. Treynor expressed the relationship of excess fund return with beta, which lies along the security market line as:

$$\mathrm{T_i} = \frac{\overline{R}_i - \overline{R}_f}{\beta_i} \qquad (2)$$

where

$\overline{R}_i$ = average return of the fund
$\overline{R}_f$ = average risk-free rate
β_i = beta

Beta is the fundamental trade-off of risk among excess fund return and the excess market return that lies along the securities characteristic line. Beta represents the systematic risk, where the risk cannot be diversified. It is obtained from the single index capital asset pricing model (CAPM). Mathematically, if beta is positive, it means that market return and fund return move along the same direction. If beta is negative when market return increases, fund return will decrease or vice versa. If beta is zero, there is no relationship between market return and fund return. Moreover, a fund with beta equal to one is considered neutral where the fund performs equally as well as the market. Beta greater than one and significant indicates the fund is considered as an aggressive or risky investment. When beta is less than one and significant, the fund is considered as a defensive or conservative investment.

Jensen's alpha is a measure of the difference between a portfolio's actual return and its expected return. It is computed from the below CAPM:

$$(R_{it} - R_{ft}) = \alpha_i + \beta_i(R_{mt} - R_{ft}) + \varepsilon_{it} \qquad (3)$$

where

R_{it} = return of the fund at time t
R_{ft} = return of risk-free rate at time t

α_i = Jensen's alpha
β_i = beta
R_{mt} = return of the market or benchmark
ε_{it} = error

Jensen's alpha is calculated to assess predictive ability in terms of the security-selection skill of a fund manager. For an active investment strategy, a fund manager is actively buying and selling stocks in order to achieve better performance in line with the fund's objective. A positive alpha indicates that the fund manager has a superior ability in security selection, which means that the manager is able to select undervalued stocks for the portfolio. Likewise, a negative alpha shows that the manager's investment strategy is poor; the manager is unable to include undervalued stocks in the portfolio. In other words, Jensen's alpha is the marginal return of the fund relative to the benchmark. For a passive investment strategy, the mutual fund is constructed to follow the movement of certain market benchmarks; thus, the alpha is theoretically zero where no out-performance or under-performance can be realized.

Funds with the same Jensen's alpha values may not have the same beta value, thus the performance within the funds is not consistent. Jensen's alpha cannot reveal an accurate ranking. In order to rank funds of different risk levels consistently, we also compute the adjusted Jensen's alpha by dividing it by its systematic risk (beta) as:

$$\text{Adjusted } J_i = \frac{\alpha_i}{\beta_i} \tag{4}$$

where

α_i = alpha value from the single index CAPM
β_i = beta

However, if the beta of different assets is almost the same, the adjusted Jensen's alpha is not needed, as it can be approximated by Jensen's alpha (Halem, 2003).

Apart from that, Basu (1977) found that high earning-price stocks have a higher future return. Banz (1981) also concluded that small size stock tends to have high average return. In line with that, Fama and French (1993) incorporated two more variables: small minus big (SMB) and high minus low (HML), where size effect and book-to-market value can be captured in explaining the return of a fund. SMB represents the difference of return between the small capitalization portfolio and large capitalization portfolio. HML represents the difference in return between a high book-to-market portfolio and low book-to-market portfolio. Hence, the excess return of the fund is defined as:

$$(R_{it} - R_{ft}) = \alpha_i + \beta_{0i}(R_{mt} - R_{ft}) + \beta_{1i}SMB_t + \beta_{2i}HML_t + \varepsilon_{it} \quad (5)$$

where

R_{it} = return of fund i at time t
R_{ft} = return of risk-free rate at time t
α_i = Fama–French alpha
SMB_t = difference in return between the small cap portfolio and large cap portfolio
HML_t = difference in return between a high book-to-market portfolio and a low book-to-market portfolio
ε_{it} = error term

However, the Fama–French (1993) model is not able to explain the cross-sectional variation in the momentum-sorted portfolio. Thereafter, Carhart (1997) proposed another variable to be added into the model: the momentum factor suggested by Jegadeesh and Titman (1993). The Carhart model is defined as:

$$(R_{it} - R_{ft}) = \alpha_i + \beta_{0i}(R_{mt} - R_{ft}) + \beta_{1i}SMB_t + \beta_{2i}HML_t + \beta_{3i}MOM_t + \varepsilon_{it} \quad (6)$$

where

R_{it} = return on fund i in month t
R_{ft} = return on one month T-bill in month t
α_i = Carhart alpha
β_i = beta
R_{mt} = return of the benchmark in month t
SMB_t = difference in return between a small cap portfolio and a large cap portfolio at time t
HML_t = difference in return at time t between a portfolio consisting of 'value' stocks (with a high book-to-market ratio) and one consisting of 'growth' stocks (with a low book-to-market ratio)
MOM_t (momentum) = difference in return between portfolios with high and low returns over the past twelve months:
ε_{it} = error

Jegadeesh and Titman (1993) found that a significant positive abnormal return is generated based on the strategy of buying past winners (the stock with the highest past return) and selling past losers (the stock with the lowest past return). It was found that the 4-factor Carhart model is expected to provide more reliable information on a fund's relative performance (Otten & Bams, 2004).

5 Results of analysis

First, we compute the descriptive statistic for all 32 SRI funds individually. The analysis is followed by investigating the risk-return behavior by an unconditional CAPM model and reward-to-risk volatility ratios. For every single CAPM regression, it is tested with the White test in order to detect the heteroscedasticity problem. The model is then treated with Newey–West (1987) heteroscedasticity and the autocorrelation consistent covariance matrix in order to minimize the heteroscedasticity problem.

Table 10.2 reports the descriptive statistics of 'all' SRI funds in Asia Pacific, U.S. T-bill and three market benchmarks. It is found that the mean of monthly returns of 'all' SRI funds is higher than the U.S. T-bill. However, the mean return of 'all' SRI funds is less than the three benchmarks and has higher risk. Moreover, the SRI funds also ranked the lowest according to the Sharpe ratio. This result is consistent with Jones et al. (2008), who found that the SRI funds under-perform the market benchmark of Australia. This indicates that the SRI funds in the Asia Pacific are in the process of development; it could be an attractive alternative investment for investors and market players in the future.

Results of the single-index CAPM, Fama–French model and Carhart model for each benchmark are summarized in Table 10.3. The SRI funds are found to be aggressive ($\beta > 1$) when the return is compared to the ESFI with CAPM and the Fama–French model. However, when the fund return is compared to MSCIAP and DJWSI, the funds are conservative ($\beta < 1$). With the Carhart model, the funds are found to be conservative regardless of the market benchmarks.

Table 10.2 Descriptive statistic of "all" fund return, U.S. T-Bill, benchmark indices

	"All" fund return	U.S. T-Bill	ESFI	MSCIAP	DJWSI
Mean	0.2600	0.1719	0.3701	0.4016	0.6331
Standard deviation	5.2333	0.1501	3.1702	5.0767	5.0308
Sharpe ratio	0.0168	–	0.0625	0.0452	0.0917

Table 10.3 Results of CAPM, Fama–French model and Carhart model

Model	CAPM		Fama–French				Carhart				
Market benchmark	Alpha	Beta	Alpha	Beta	SMB	HML	Alpha	Beta	SMB	HML	MOM
ESFI	−0.0157	1.0739***	0.0412	1.0417***	0.0300	−0.1938***	−0.0159	0.9831***	−0.0142	−0.1868***	3.8236*
MSCIAP	0.0606	0.6481***	0.0388	0.6563***	0.0028	0.0672	0.0724	0.6821***	0.0259	0.0737	−2.3813
DJWSI	−0.1033	0.6324***	0.0430	0.5962***	−0.0110***	−0.4288***	−0.0772	0.5121***	−0.0969*	−0.3934***	8.4338***

Note: *** significant at 1% , ** significant at 5% and * significant at 1%.

On the other hand, the insignificance alphas implies that there is no difference between the return of SRI funds and the market benchmarks. In other words, the SRI funds do not outperform the market. This also implies that the fund manager does not possess any predictive skill or stock selection ability by including undervalued stocks in the SRI funds.

We further investigate whether there are size and value/growth effects in the SRI funds. The size effect can only be seen with the DJWSI. However, the negative and significant estimated coefficient implies that SRI funds are tilted to large size. In other words, the return of the SRI funds is driven by the large size portfolio. Our finding is consistent with Bauer et al. (2006). Hence, we conclude that there is no small size effect in the SRI funds in Asia Pacific.

Besides, the estimated coefficients are negative and significant, showing that the growth effect is extant when the return is compared with ESFI and DJWSI for both Fama–French and Carhart models. In other words, the SRI funds in the Asia Pacific are more to the growth-orientated investment style. This infers that the return of SRI funds is likely to be driven by low book-to-market ratio stocks. The momentum effect can be seen when ESFI and DJWSI are used as market benchmarks. Bauer et al. (2006) also showed that momentum effect exists for the domestic SRI funds but Humphrey and Lee (2011) found no momentum effects in their study.

Consistent with previous studies, we find no significant difference between the performance of SRI funds and the market index. The SRI funds in our sample are more sensitive to ESFI where the beta is higher than the other benchmarks. Moreover, growth effect and momentum effect exist in the SRI funds in Asia Pacific.

We further investigate each SRI fund with its descriptive statistics in Table 10.4. The average mean return of the SRI funds is 0.28 per cent. We find that 68.75 per cent of the SRI funds have a positive mean return, but only 37.5 per cent of the funds have a mean return more than the average mean return. About half of the SRI funds have standard deviation greater than the average standard deviation. Fund No. 2 has the highest mean monthly return (2.0689) and a Sharpe ratio (0.3124), whereas Fund No. 13 has the lowest mean monthly return (−0.6087) and Sharpe ratio (−0.1318). The lowest standard deviation is from Fund No. 5, whereas the highest is Fund No. 25. In sum, we conclude that the SRI funds in Asia Pacific are still able to perform well with positive returns and are less volatile during the period of uncertainty.

In Table 10.5, when ESFI is used as the market index, about two thirds of SRI funds are found to be aggressive. However, only a small portion are

Table 10.4 Descriptive statistic of SRI funds

Fund no	Mean	Standard deviation	Sharpe ratio
1	0.1311	3.4864	−0.0117
2	2.0689	6.0962	0.3124
3	0.1731	2.5017	0.0005
4	0.6652	5.0613	0.0975
5	0.2583	1.0673	0.0810
6	0.4167	4.1564	0.0589
7	0.6652	5.0613	0.0975
8	0.1111	4.6729	−0.0130
9	0.0019	4.6888	−0.0362
10	−0.0243	4.9692	−0.0395
11	0.0107	4.6623	−0.0346
12	0.5579	5.8708	0.0670
13	−0.6087	5.4222	−0.1318
14	−0.3762	6.1934	−0.0917
15	0.4603	6.3288	0.0456
16	−0.3047	6.7028	−0.0754
17	1.3627	5.2296	0.2236
18	1.4109	5.2236	0.2331
19	0.6463	6.1836	0.0767
20	0.1396	5.2497	−0.0061
21	0.2298	5.8506	0.0099
22	−0.0282	5.4701	−0.0381
23	−0.0318	5.4017	−0.0393
24	−0.1851	4.2029	−0.0854
25	−0.1132	9.7566	−0.0139
26	0.2811	5.3282	0.0205
27	0.1626	5.0556	−0.0018
28	0.3323	5.1943	0.0290
29	0.5308	5.4000	0.0665
30	0.1082	8.5289	−0.0053
31	−0.0423	5.1599	−0.0415
32	−0.1578	5.4011	−0.0610
Average	0.2766	5.2993	0.0217

aggressive funds when the other two market benchmarks are used as market benchmarks. Consistent with our result from 'all' funds, the SRI funds in Asia Pacific tend to be aggressive when compared to ESFI. Regardless of market benchmarks, about half of SRI funds have a positive Treynor ratio, which indicates that these funds are good investment assets after the market risk has been diversified. Fund No. 2 has the highest Treynor ratio, and Fund No. 24 has the lowest Treynor ratio.

Table 10.5 Reward-to-volatility ratios

Benchmark	ESFI				MSCIAP				DJWSI			
Fund no	Beta	Treynor ratio	Jensen's alpha	Adjusted Jensen's alpha	Beta	Treynor ratio	Jensen's alpha	Adjusted Jensen's alpha	Beta	Treynor ratio	Jensen's alpha	Adjusted Jensen's alpha
1	0.8438	−0.0483	−0.2080	−0.2466	0.5122	−0.0795	−0.1584	−0.3092	0.4885	−0.0834	−0.2660	−0.5446
2	0.3533	5.3903	1.9925	5.6397	0.1308	14.5647	1.9929	15.2420	0.1995	9.5443	1.9623	9.8345
3	0.4948	0.0026	−0.0968	−0.1957	0.2710	0.0047	−0.0610	−0.2250	0.2909	0.0044	−0.1329	−0.4569
4	0.9405	0.5246	0.3069	0.3263	0.5269	0.9363	0.3723	0.7066	0.5251	0.9396	0.2512	0.4783
5	0.0199	4.3553	0.0826	4.1570	0.0111	7.8040	0.0840	7.5743	0.0137	6.3042	0.0802	5.8429
6	0.9301	0.2632	0.0604	0.0649	0.4904	0.4992	0.1322	0.2695	0.5243	0.4670	0.0030	0.0057
7	0.9405	0.5246	0.3069	0.3263	0.5269	0.9363	0.3723	0.7066	0.5251	0.9396	0.2512	0.4783
8	1.0756	−0.0565	−0.2740	−0.2548	0.6103	−0.0995	−0.2009	−0.3292	0.6325	−0.0960	−0.3525	−0.5573
9	1.2185	−0.1395	−0.4116	−0.3378	0.6610	−0.2571	−0.3218	−0.4868	0.7131	−0.2383	−0.4989	−0.6996
10	1.2475	−0.1572	−0.4800	−0.3847	0.6899	−0.2843	−0.3720	−0.5393	0.7193	−0.2726	−0.5478	−0.7616
11	1.2093	−0.1333	−0.4010	−0.3316	0.6585	−0.2447	−0.3124	−0.4745	0.7061	−0.2283	−0.4869	−0.6895
12	0.9366	0.4199	0.6269	0.6693	0.6903	0.5698	0.8608	1.2471	0.5950	0.6611	0.5660	0.9513
13	0.8792	−0.8126	−0.2265	−0.2576	0.6402	−1.1159	0.0117	0.0183	0.5245	−1.3622	−0.3590	−0.6845
14	1.4477	−0.3923	−0.6206	−0.4287	1.0403	−0.5460	−0.4779	−0.4594	0.8511	−0.6674	−0.6767	−0.7951
15	1.4432	0.1999	0.0023	0.0016	1.0162	0.2839	0.0550	0.0542	0.8795	0.3280	−0.1172	−0.1332
16	1.5744	−0.3210	−0.3541	−0.2249	1.0628	−0.4756	−0.3238	−0.3046	0.9753	−0.5183	−0.5147	−0.5278
17	1.1914	0.9816	1.3980	1.1734	0.7323	1.5971	1.5539	2.1221	0.7093	1.6488	1.2370	1.7440
18	1.1903	1.0231	1.4460	1.2148	0.7314	1.6648	1.6017	2.1897	0.7087	1.7183	1.2852	1.8135
19	1.5205	0.3121	0.4484	0.2949	0.9448	0.5023	0.4385	0.4641	0.8151	0.5821	0.2371	0.2909
20	0.7924	−0.0407	−0.0669	−0.0845	0.6409	−0.0503	−0.0709	−0.1106	0.2943	−0.1096	−0.1461	−0.4965

21	1.3106	0.0442	−0.2019	−0.1541	0.7178	0.0807	−0.1070	−0.1490	0.7603	0.0762	−0.2928	−0.3851
22	1.1878	−0.1755	−0.3336	−0.2808	0.6831	−0.3052	−0.2643	−0.3870	0.6866	−0.3036	−0.4343	−0.6325
23	1.2048	−0.1760	−0.3390	−0.2814	0.6984	−0.3037	−0.2693	−0.3855	0.7118	−0.2980	−0.4462	−0.6269
24	0.2422	−1.4819	−0.3058	−1.2627	0.1460	−2.4586	−0.2621	−1.7952	0.1681	−2.1344	−0.3181	−1.8916
25	1.7403	−0.0782	0.7539	0.4332	1.2347	−0.1102	1.5648	1.2673	1.0973	−0.1240	1.0725	0.9774
26	1.2909	0.0847	−0.1990	−0.1541	0.7403	0.1476	−0.1398	−0.1888	0.7741	0.1412	−0.3884	−0.5017
27	1.2487	−0.0074	−0.2569	−0.2057	0.7262	−0.0128	−0.1761	−0.2425	0.7481	−0.0124	−0.3544	−0.4737
28	1.0420	0.1447	0.0178	0.0171	0.5763	0.2616	0.1048	0.1818	0.6156	0.2449	−0.0480	−0.0779
29	1.1905	0.3015	0.1229	0.1032	0.6242	0.5750	0.2155	0.3453	0.7305	0.4914	0.0220	0.0301
30	1.8565	−0.0245	0.5321	0.2866	1.2531	−0.0364	0.9193	0.7336	1.1872	−0.0384	0.4050	0.3411
31	1.0907	−0.1964	−0.4305	−0.3947	0.6151	−0.3482	−0.3555	−0.5779	0.6361	−0.3367	−0.5076	−0.7980
32	1.0903	−0.3023	−0.5458	−0.5006	0.6144	−0.5365	−0.4708	−0.7662	0.6328	−0.5209	−0.6215	−0.9821

We also find that about 40 per cent of SRI funds are found to have positive alpha. This implies that the fund managers for these funds have ability in selecting undervalued stocks for the portfolio. Fund No. 14 has the lowest alpha value, whereas Fund No. 2 has the highest alpha and adjusted Jensen's alpha regardless of the market proxies. Fund No. 24 has the lowest adjusted Jensen's alpha regardless of the market proxies. Again, Fund No. 2 is ranked the highest based on Jensen's alpha and adjusted Jensen's alpha.

For the Fama–French model in Table 10.6, we find no significant difference in performance between the SRI funds and market benchmarks. Fund No. 2 again has the best stock selection among the rest. There is about a 2 per cent out-performance of the fund relative to the market benchmark. Moreover, Fund No. 30 is found to be is the most aggressive fund for all market benchmarks.

Only a small portion of SRI funds have a small-size effect. Fund No. 25 has the largest significant small-size effect with ESFI and DJWSI as benchmark while Fund No.12 shows the largest small-size effect, with the MSCIAP as the market benchmark. When the fund return is compared with ESFI, 21.88 per cent of funds are tilted to growth portfolio and 40.63 per cent of funds are found to be growth funds when compared against DJWSI. However, only one fund shows growth effect when the market benchmark is MSCIAP. Fund No. 13 shows the highest magnitude of growth among the other 31 funds. In sum, growth effect is just moderate among the SRI funds in Asia Pacific.

The result of Carhart model is reported in Table 10.7. Obviously, there is about 10 per cent of the funds show significant alpha. Fund No. 2 is still the most outstanding fund when the ESFI and DJWSI are market benchmarks. However, Fund No. 17 has the largest significant alpha value when the return compared against MSCIAP. Consistence with the result of the Fama–French model, when the fund return is compared with ESFI, more than half of the funds are found to be aggressive. However, only 12.5 per cent of the funds are aggressive when the market benchmark is MSCIAP and there is no aggressive fund found with DJWSI.

There is no small size effect with ESFI and DJWSI and the effect can only be found for Fund No. 14 and 15 when the market proxy is MSCIAP. We also find that 18.75 per cent and 37.5 per cent of the SRI funds show growth effect when the market benchmarks are ESFI and DJWSI respectively. However, one fund show growth effect when MSCIAP is the market benchmark.

Table 10.6 Results of Fama–French model

Benchmarks	ESFI				MSCIAP				DJWSI			
Fund no	Alpha	Beta	SMB	HML	Alpha	Beta	SMB	HML	Alpha	Beta	SMB	HML
1	−0.3893	0.8954***	0.2023	0.3769*	−0.4144	0.5818***	0.1819	0.6168***	−0.3567	0.4947***	0.1655	0.1401
2	2.1146**	0.3156	−0.1255	−0.3353	2.1380**	0.0744	−0.0627	−0.5378	2.1096**	0.1753	−0.1428	−0.3963
3	−0.1462	0.5149***	0.0171	0.1314	−0.1299	0.2948***	0.0094	0.1963	−0.1328	0.2913***	−0.0051	0.0035
4	0.3304	0.9599***	−0.1898	0.0756	0.3528	0.5599***	−0.2052	0.2157	0.3765	0.5164***	−0.2271	−0.1949
5	0.1389	0.0009	−0.0447	−0.1310	0.1430	−0.0047	−0.0441	−0.1405	0.1355	0.0048	−0.0453	−0.1261
6	−0.0274	0.9875***	−0.1051	0.3371	0.0184	0.5465***	−0.1179	0.4269	0.0178	0.5340***	−0.1439	0.0621
7	0.3304	0.9599***	−0.1898	0.0756	0.3528	0.5599***	−0.2052	0.2157	0.3765	0.5164***	−0.2271	−0.1949
8	−0.1770	1.0535***	−0.1429	−0.1753	−0.1506	0.6122***	−0.1596	−0.0258	−0.1554	0.6034***	−0.1895	−0.4284
9	−0.4661	1.2358***	0.0499	0.1218	−0.4135	0.6900***	0.0332	0.2454	−0.4330	0.6978***	−0.0032	−0.1869
10	−0.5064	1.2575***	0.0136	0.0665	−0.4476	0.7166***	0.0024	0.2188	−0.4483	0.6988***	−0.0319	−0.2614
11	−0.4608	1.2286***	0.0527	0.1350	−0.4114	0.6898***	0.0358	0.2650	−0.4262	0.6918***	0.0003	−0.1743
12	0.6491	0.6902***	1.2954***	−1.0790**	0.7260	0.5587***	1.1720***	−0.5937	0.6317	0.4315***	1.2222***	−1.1256**
13	−0.0470	0.5897***	0.7622**	−1.5957***	0.0501	0.4615***	0.6311**	−1.1773***	−0.0725	0.3271***	0.7269**	−1.7181***
14	−0.3852	1.3123***	−0.0122	−0.8191**	−0.4697	1.0391***	−0.0347	−0.0195	−0.3791	0.7503***	−0.0427	−1.0845***
15	0.0045	1.4009***	0.2594	−0.2038	−0.1543	1.0652***	0.2116	0.4559	0.0099	0.8318***	0.1929	−0.5051
16	−0.2573	1.5102***	−0.0731	−0.4431	−0.4274	1.1255***	−0.0821	0.4857*	−0.3713	0.9286***	−0.2105	−0.6200
17	1.5346***	1.0926***	0.1888	−0.5723*	1.5798***	0.7053***	0.1292	−0.1574	1.4302***	0.6388***	0.1243	−0.7206**
18	1.5825***	1.0915***	0.1879	−0.5722*	1.6277***	0.7045***	0.1284	−0.1580	1.4783***	0.6382***	0.1234	−0.7203**
19	0.7561	1.3612***	−0.5699**	−0.7001	0.5943	0.9053***	−0.5151*	−0.2745	0.7969	0.6289***	−0.5984*	−1.2872***
20	0.0897	0.6968***	−0.1447	−0.4072	−0.1656	0.6890***	−0.0717	0.3003	0.2414	0.1539	−0.1852	−0.9621*
21	−0.0869	1.2797***	−0.1401	−0.2303	−0.0282	0.7092***	−0.1569	−0.1121	−0.0514	0.7212***	−0.1949	−0.5517
22	−0.1582	1.1178***	−0.1513	−0.4740	−0.1358	0.6534***	−0.1999	−0.3080	−0.1587	0.6280***	−0.1720	−0.7558**
23	−0.1414	1.1251***	−0.1634	−0.5378	−0.1219	0.6627***	−0.2130	−0.3615	−0.1540	0.6499***	−0.1861	−0.7999**
24	−0.2617	0.2396	−0.1301	−0.0920	−0.2355	0.1510	−0.1382	−0.0260	−0.2759	0.1715	−0.1609	−0.0726
25	0.5640	1.3961***	1.6445***	−1.4179*	1.3912	1.0786***	0.7802	−0.7554	1.1106	0.9006***	1.2603***	−1.5434**
26	−0.0649	1.2348***	0.0209	−0.3580	−0.1007	0.7256***	0.0213	−0.1127	−0.1341	0.7255***	−0.0382	−0.6056*
27	−0.1612	1.2020***	0.0157	−0.2923	−0.1440	0.7152***	−0.0050	−0.0911	−0.1482	0.7031***	−0.0396	−0.5634*
28	−0.0331	1.0463***	0.1771	0.0869	0.0115	0.5998***	0.1532	0.2417	−0.0254	0.5977***	0.1746	−0.1457
29	−0.1402***	1.2957***	0.1027	0.6921*	−0.0836	0.7216***	0.0854	0.8184**	−0.1298	0.7624***	0.0423	0.4052
30	0.5274	1.6508***	1.1851***	−0.8530*	0.7104	1.1942***	0.9718***	−0.0383	0.4752	1.0534***	0.9856***	−0.9332**
31	−0.3422	1.0756***	−0.1609	−0.1359	−0.3131	0.6222***	−0.1776	0.0115	−0.3152	0.6098***	−0.2075	−0.4018
32	−0.4518	1.0648***	−0.1128	−0.1892	−0.4204	0.6125***	−0.1290	−0.0497	−0.4226	0.6004***	−0.1585	−0.4563

Note: *** significant at 1%, ** significant at 5% and * significant at 10%.

Table 10.7 Results of Carhart model

Benchmarks	ESFI					MSCIAP					DJWSI				
Fund no	Alpha	Beta	SMB	HML	MOM	Alpha	Beta	SMB	HML	MOM	Alpha	Beta	SMB	HML	MOM
1	−0.5847**	0.6918***	0.0646	0.4017**	13.4366**	−0.5015*	0.5094***	0.1175	0.5882***	6.5841	−0.6733**	0.2737***	−0.0474	0.2349	22.6295***
2	2.65976**	0.7684	0.3432	−0.4934	−29.2107	1.9534	−0.0282	−0.1910	−0.5608	9.0926	2.7051**	0.5027	0.3200	−0.5880	−32.6784
3	−0.1078	0.5549***	0.0442	0.1266	−2.6382	−0.1147	0.3074***	0.0207	0.2013	−1.1509	−0.1206	0.2998***	0.0031	−0.0002	−0.8730
4	0.3154	0.9442***	−0.2004	0.0775	1.0337	0.2963	0.5129**	−0.2470	0.1971	4.2720	0.2175	0.4055**	−0.3340	−0.1473	11.3596
5	0.1256	−0.0130	−0.0541	−0.1293	0.9190	0.1038	−0.0373	−0.0731	−0.1533	2.9602	0.1333	0.0033	−0.0468	−0.1255	0.1583
6	0.2178	1.2430***	0.0677	0.3059	−16.8651*	0.2228	0.7166***	0.0333	0.4940	−15.4584	0.1624	0.6349***	−0.0466	0.0188	−10.3379
7	0.3154	0.9442***	−0.2004	0.0775	1.0337	0.2963	0.5129**	−0.2470	0.1971	4.2720	0.2175	0.4055**	−0.3340	−0.1473	11.3596
8	0.0513	1.2915***	0.0180	−0.2043	−15.7024	0.1306	0.8464***	0.0485	0.0665	−21.2752	0.0643	0.7567***	−0.0417	−0.4942	−15.6995
9	−0.3183	1.3899***	0.1541	0.1030	−10.1697	−0.3633	0.7317***	0.0704	0.2619	−3.7979	−0.3437	0.7601***	0.0568	−0.2137	−6.3769
10	−0.2432	1.5338***	0.1996	0.0333	−18.2037*	−0.1643	0.9508***	0.2114	0.3109	−21.2953	−0.2516	0.8349***	0.1000	−0.3201	−13.9617
11	−0.3230	1.3721***	0.1498	0.1175	−9.4732	−0.3601	0.7325***	0.0737	0.2818	−3.8811	−0.3543	0.7420***	0.0486	−0.1959	−5.1426
12	−0.3535	−0.1427	0.4332	−0.7883*	53.7325***	0.0220	0.1675	0.6829	−0.6813	34.6719*	−0.4964	−0.1886	0.3456	−0.7624*	61.8998***
13	−0.7085	0.0191***	0.1417	−1.3558***	37.3911***	−0.5066	0.1422	0.2513	−1.2650***	27.9370	−1.1086**	−0.2579	−0.1270	−1.3165***	58.8289***
14	−0.5887	1.0917***	−0.1716	−0.7866**	14.1240	0.1308	1.5086***	0.4428**	0.1690	−42.7263***	−0.7128	0.4972**	−0.3031	−1.0012**	24.3638
15	−0.3457	1.0359***	0.0126	−0.1593	24.0873*	0.2344	1.3888***	0.4992*	0.5836*	−29.4006**	−0.3589	0.5746***	−0.0550	−0.3947	26.3517*
16	−0.6631	1.1643***	−0.3519	−0.3933	21.5427	0.1117**	1.4746***	0.3213	0.6682**	−31.1623***	−0.7452	0.7020***	−0.4533*	−0.5513	21.5122
17	1.2273***	0.8458***	−0.0265	−0.5239	15.5025	1.1143**	0.4418**	−0.1577	−0.2869	22.8396	0.9734*	0.3755**	−0.1940	−0.6269*	25.4271*
18	1.2759***	0.8453***	−0.0270	−0.5239*	15.4696	1.1620	0.4408**	−0.1587	−0.2876	22.8514	1.0227**	0.3756**	−0.1941	−0.6268*	25.3629*
19	0.2918	0.8918***	−0.8079***	−0.5236*	34.2408**	0.4789	0.8018***	−0.5942**	−0.2865	10.2888	0.0055	−0.0338	−1.0938***	−0.8618*	69.1559***
20	−0.0998	0.5052	−0.2418	−0.3352	13.9756	0.4683	1.2574***	0.3629	0.3662	−56.5263***	−0.3883	−0.3734	−0.5793	−0.6237*	55.0205**
21	−0.2105	1.1509***	−0.2273	−0.2146	8.5046	−0.3945	0.4043*	−0.4279	−0.2324	27.7057	−0.2815	0.5607***	−0.3497	−0.4828	16.4456
22	0.1337	1.4455***	0.0858	−0.4908	−20.9152	0.1229	0.8676***	0.0041	−0.2142	−19.6097	0.1605	0.8783***	0.0953	−0.8310**	−24.5349
23	0.0628	1.3543***	0.0025	−0.5495	−14.6333	0.0413	0.7978***	−0.0843	−0.3023	−12.3737	0.1225	0.8667***	0.0454	−0.8650**	−21.2497
24	−0.5878	−0.0221	−0.3893	−0.0061	16.8205	−0.8190	−0.1625	−0.5270	−0.0986	27.7759	−0.4753	0.0653	−0.3111	−0.0106	10.6117
25	0.2240	0.7162*	0.6252	−1.3317*	44.8859*	0.7220	0.6036*	0.2607	−0.9819	39.9810	0.9248	0.7665**	1.0029	−1.4967**	13.8081
26	−0.0030	1.2957***	0.0604	−0.3693	−3.9858	−0.0364	0.7808***	0.0696	−0.0920	−4.9361	−0.0844	0.7615***	−0.0054	−0.6230*	−3.6216
27	−0.1252	1.2395***	0.0411	−0.2968	−2.4745	−0.0825	0.7663***	0.0405	−0.0709	−4.6466	−0.1103	0.7296***	−0.0142	−0.5747*	−2.7074
28	0.2520	1.3757***	0.4061	0.0620	−20.9519*	0.2143	0.7682***	0.3126	0.3141	−15.4288	0.3153	0.8662***	0.4589	−0.2300	−26.3582
29	−0.1529	1.2825***	0.0938	0.6937**	0.8710	−0.2789	0.5591***	−0.0590	0.7543*	14.7711	−0.1344	0.7592***	0.0393	0.4065	0.3277
30	−0.7928	0.5909**	0.0828	−0.4938	−0.4938***	−0.3224	0.6398***	0.2813	−0.1651	48.8558***	−0.6939	0.4316**	0.1051	−0.5724	61.8535***
31	−0.0418	1.3886***	0.0508	−0.1741	−20.6595*	0.0601	0.9329***	0.0985	0.1340	−28.2268*	−0.0328	0.8068***	−0.0175	−0.4864	−20.1820
32	−0.1583	1.3707***	0.0940	−0.2265	−20.1872	−0.0698	0.9044***	0.1304	0.0654	−26.5186	−0.1575	0.7854***	0.0198	−0.5357	−18.9464

Note: *** significant at 1%, ** significant at 5% and * significant at 10%.

We find that 18.75 per cent and 28.13 per cent of SRI funds show momentum effect when the return is compared against ESFI and DJWSI respectively. On the other hand, only 6.25 per cent of SRI funds show a momentum effect when MSCIAP is the market benchmark. As indicated by Otten and Bams (2004), the Carhart model is the best unconditional model to explain the fund's performance – thus, we came to the conclusion based on this model.

6 Conclusion

This chapter evaluates the performance of SRI funds, both at the aggregate level and individual level. The comparison of a fund's performance is conducted against the conventional and ethical benchmarks. Consistent with many other's literature, we find no significant difference in the performance of SRI funds against the benchmarks. Furthermore, we find the SRI funds are still profitable, although they are restricted from investing in certain sectors with a positive monthly return of 0.26 per cent on average, which is a better performance than the U.S. T-bill, but underperform when measured against the market benchmarks.

In general, we find no small-size effect, but there are growth and momentum effects in the SRI funds in Asia Pacific. Our results contradict Otten and Bams (2002), who found European mutual funds prefer small stocks with high book-to-market value. In general, the SRI funds seem prefers to invest in the stocks with low book-to-market ratio and momentum strategy. Hence, we suggest that the SRI funds in Asia Pacific can be an alternative investment to conventional investors who believed that SRI funds tend to produce lower returns. Furthermore, our study shows that SRI funds have growth investment style that the stocks under these funds are believed to produce high earning persistently or high return on capital as explained in Fama and French (1993). Moreover, with the momentum strategy found in SRI funds, the funds are believed to produce positive abnormal return when a strategy based on buying past winner's stocks and selling past loser's stock is implemented.

A study by Hong and Kacperczyk (2009) proved that non-ethical stocks such as tobacco and the alcohol industry are able to generate higher returns. But, as the business world shifted towards sustainable directions, many companies are opting to employ the sustainability concept in business and governance as well. These show that there are a lot of sustainable investing opportunities to be explored in the future, which indicates that SRI funds can be developed as an attractive alternative option for investment in the Asia Pacific region.

Notes

1. Detail definition of SRI in Social Investment Forum website, http://ussif.org/resources/sriguide/srifacts.cfm
2. The statistic of SRI assets in the United States, http://ussif.org/resources/sriguide/
3. http://www.eurekahedge.com/database/
4. Islamic funds are categorized as another individual category.
5. http://mba.tuck.dartmouth.edu/pages/faculty/ken.french/Data_Library/f-f_bench_factor.html
6. The data to construct SMB and HML are obtained from http://www.msci.com/products/indices/size/standard/performance.html?undefined
7. http://www.msci.com/resources/factsheets/index_fact_sheet/msci-ac-asia-pacific-index.pdf

References

Albaity, M. and Ahmad, R. (2008) 'Performance of Syariah and Composite Indices: Evidence from Bursa Malaysia', *Asian Academy of Management Journal of Accounting & Finance*, 4(1), 23–43.

Ballestero, E., Bravo, M., Peérez-Gladish, B., Arenas-Parra, M., and Plà-Santamaria, D. (2012). Socially Responsible Investment: A Multicriteria Approach to Portfolio Selection Combining Ethical and Financial Objectives, *European Journal of Operational Research*, 216(2), 487–94.

Banz, R. W. (1981) 'The Relationship Between Return and Market Value of Common Stocks', *Journal of Financial Economics*, 9(1), 3–18.

Basu, S. (1977) 'Investment Performance of Common Stocks in Relation to Their Price-Earnings Ratios: A Test of the Efficient Market Hypothesis', *Journal of Finance*, 32(3), 663–82.

Bauer, R., Koedijk, K. and Otten, R. (2005) 'International Evidence on Ethical Mutual Fund Performance and Investment Style', *Journal of Banking & Finance*, 29(7), 1751–67.

Bauer, R., Otten, R. and Rad, A. T. (2006) 'Ethical Investing in Australia: Is There A Financial Penalty?', *Pacific-Basin Finance Journal*, 14(1), 33–48.

Bello, Z. Y. (2005) 'Socially Responsible Investing and Portfolio Diversification', *Journal of Financial Research*, 28(1), 41–57.

Benson, K., Brailsford, T. and Humphrey, J. (2006) 'Do Socially Responsible Fund Managers Really Invest Differently?' *Journal of Business Ethics*, 65(4), 337–57.

Benson, K. L. and Humphrey, J. E. (2008) 'Socially Responsible Investment Funds: Investor Reaction to Current and Past Returns', *Journal of Banking & Finance*, 32(9), 1850–59.

Boasson, E., Boasson, V. and Cheng, J. (2006) 'Investment Principles and Strategies of Faith-Based Funds', *Managerial Finance*, 32, 837–45.

Carhart, M. M. (1997) 'On Persistence in Mutual Fund Performance', *Journal of Finance*, 52(1), 57–82.

Chegut, A., Schenk, H. and Scholtens, B. (2011) 'Assessing SRI Fund Performance Research: Best Practices in Empirical Analysis', *Sustainable Development*, 19(2), 77–94.

Copp, R., Kremmer, M. L. and Roca, E. (2010) 'Should Funds Invest in Socially Responsible Investments During Downturns? Financial and Legal Implications of the Fund Manager's Dilemma', *Accounting Research Journal*, 23(3), 254–66.
Cortez, M., Silva, F. and Areal, N. (2009) 'The Performance of European Socially Responsible Funds', *Journal of Business Ethics*, 87(4), 573–88.
Cummings, L. S. (2000) 'The Financial Performance of Ethical Investment Trusts: An Australian Perspective', *Journal of Business Ethics*, 25(1), 79–92.
Derwall, J. and Koedijk, K. (2009) 'Socially Responsible Fixed-Income Funds', *Journal of Business Finance & Accounting*, 36(1–2), 210–29.
Fama, E. F. and French, K. R. (1993) 'Common Risk Factors in the Returns on Stocks and Bonds', *Journal of Financial Economics*, 33(1), 3–56.
Fung, H. G., Law, S. A. and Yau, J. (2010) *Socially Responsible Investment in a Global Environment*, 25–43 (Cheltenham, UK, and Northampton, MA: Edward Elgar Publishing Limited).
Galema, R., Plantinga, A. and Scholtens, B. (2008) 'The Stocks at Stake: Return and Risk in Socially Responsible Investment', *Journal of Banking & Finance*, 32(12), 2646–54.
Hassan, M. K., Khan, A. N. F. and Ngow, T. (2010) 'Is Faith-Based Investing Rewarding? The Case for Malaysian Islamic Unit Trust Funds', *Journal of Islamic Accounting and Business Research*, 1(2), 148–71.
Halem, J. A. (2003) *Mutual Funds: Risk and Performance Analysis for Decision Making*, 252 (Malden, MA: Blackwell Publishing).
Hamilton, S., Jo, H. and Statman, M. (1993) 'Doing Well While Doing Good? The Investment Performance of Socially Responsible Mutual Funds', *Financial Analysts Journal*, 49(6), 62.
Hayat, R. and Kraeussl, R. (2011) 'Risk and Return Characteristics of Islamic Equity Funds', *Emerging Markets Review*, 12(2), 189–203.
Hong, H. and Kacperczyk, M. (2009) 'The Price of Sin: The Effects of Social Norms on Markets', *Journal of Financial Economics*, 93(1), 15–36.
Humphrey, J. and Lee, D. (2011) 'Australian Socially Responsible Funds: Performance, Risk and Screening Intensity', *Journal of Business Ethics*, 102(4), 519–35.
Jegadeesh, N. and Titman, S. (1993) 'Returns to Buying Winners and Selling Losers: Implications for Stock Market Efficiency', *Journal of Finance*, 48(1), 65–91.
Jensen, M. C. (1968) 'The Performance of Mutual Funds in the Period 1945–1964', *Journal of Finance*, 23(2), 389–416.
Jones, S., Van der Laan, S., Frost, G. and Loftus, J. (2008) 'The Investment Performance of Socially Responsible Investment Funds in Australia', *Journal of Business Ethics*, 80(2), 181–203.
Kiesel, R., Scherer, M. and Zagst, R. (Eds) (2010) *Alternative Investments and Strategies. Chapter 1: Socially Responsible Investments*, 3–20 (World Scientific Publishing Co. Pte. Ltd).
Newey, W. K. and West, K. D. (1987) 'A Simple, Positive Semi-Definite, Heteroskedasticity and Autocorrelation Consistent Covariance Matrix', *Econometrica*, 55(3), 703–08.
Otten, R. and Bams, D. (2002) 'European Mutual Fund Performance', *European Financial Market*, 8(1), 75–101.
Otten, R. and Bams, D. (2004) 'How to Measure Mutual Fund Performance: Economic Versus Statistical Relevance', *Accounting & Finance*, 44(2), 203–22.

Renneboog, L., Ter Horst, J. and Zhang, C. (2008) 'Socially Responsible Investments: Institutional Aspects, Performance, and Investor Behavior', *Journal of Banking & Finance*, 32(9), 1723–42.

Sauer, D. A. (1997) 'The Impact of Social-Responsibility Screens on Investment Performance: Evidence from the Domini 400 Social Index and Domini Equity Mutual Fund', *Review of Financial Economics*, 6(2), 137–49

Säve-Söderbergh, J. (2010) 'Who Lets Ethics Guide His Economic Decision-making? An Empirical Analysis of Individual Investments in Ethical Funds', *Economics Letters*, 107(2), 270–72.

Schröder, M. (2004) 'The Performance of Socially Responsible Investments: Investment Funds and Indices', *Financial Markets and Portfolio Management*, 18(2), 122–42.

Sharpe, W. (1966). 'Mutual Fund Performance', *Journal of Business*, 39(1), 119–38.

Tippet, J. (2001) 'Performance of Australia's Ethical Funds', *Australian Economic Review*, 34(2), 170–78.

Treynor, J. L. (1965) 'How to Rate Management of Investment Funds', *Harvard Business Review*, 43(1), 63–7.

Part V
Corporate Finance and Banking

11
Capital Structure of Southeast Asian Firms

Razali Haron, Khairunisah Ibrahim, Fauzias Mat Nor and Izani Ibrahim

1 Introduction

The relationship between capital structure and firm value has been widely studied and analysed theoretically and empirically by researchers past and present. This is because a firm's financing behaviour will consequently affect the value of the firm. In tackling the issue of capital structure, two main questions have to be addressed: how firms choose their capital structure to finance their operation, and how the choice of capital structure financing affects the value of the firm.

Despite the extensive research done in the area of capital structure since Modigliani and Miller in 1958 and ever since Myers (1977) published his article on the determinants of corporate borrowing, understanding in the area is still inconclusive (Harris & Raviv, 1991; Gill et al., 2009; Sheikh & Wang, 2011; Al-Najjar & Hussainey, 2011; Gwatidzo & Ramjee, 2012). Empirical work in this area, according to Titman and Wessels (1988), has lagged behind the theoretical research. This is, perhaps, because the relevant firm attributes are expressed in terms of fairly abstract concepts that are not directly observable. Deesomsak et al. (2004) find that empirical evidence on the effect of determinants on leverage is mixed and inconsistent. A fairly recent work done by Beattie et al. (2006) documents the same results showing that understanding in the area remains incomplete. They further argue that neither theory is able, independently, to explain the complexity encountered in capital structure practice.

The issue of incompleteness and inconclusiveness of the understanding in the debated area is also reported by Al-Najjar and Taylor (2008). Through their findings, they notice that theoretical explanation is still lacking and empirical results are not yet sufficiently consistent to resolve the capital structure issues as to how firms choose between the different methods of financing. Boateng (2004) adds to the literature, saying that capital structure decision making is even more complicated when it is examined in an international context, particularly in developing countries where markets are characterized by controls and institutional constraints. Margaritis and Psillaki (2009) put forward that corporate-financing decisions are quite a complex process, and existing theories can at best explain only certain facets of the diversity and complexity of financing choices. Myers (2001) stresses that there is no universal theory of debt-equity choice and no reason to expect one. The reason may be because these theories differ in their emphasis.

The literature has been recording cases of inconclusiveness by researchers throughout the years. Nevertheless this issue of inconsistent sign reading keeps on recurring as no one particular study has been done to tackle this unresolved issue. In response, this chapter looks into the issue of inconclusiveness by analysing the impact of the use of different definitions of leverage as well as the use of different models in examining the determinants of leverage. Therefore, three Southeast Asian countries are selected for this study: Malaysia, Thailand and Singapore. We use 790 firms for the Malaysian sample, 269 for Thailand and 546 for Singapore. This study uses a ten-year period of data, from 2000 to 2009. We employed two models, the static model and the dynamic partial adjustment model which were estimated based on the Fixed Effect Model and the Generalized Method of Moments (GMM), respectively, in order to analyse the issue of inconsistent results in the study of capital structure.

This chapter is organized in this manner: Section 2 briefly lays out the dominant theories behind capital structure study, followed by Section 3 discussing the issue of inconclusiveness in capital structure studies. Section 4 is on data and methodology. The findings of our analysis are discussed in Section 5 and section 6 concludes the chapter.

2 Overview of capital structure theories

The most prominent theories of capital structure being studied in the literature explaining firms' financing behaviour are the trade-off, pecking order, agency and market timing theories. Despite the emergence of different feasible capital structure theories, there is still no conclusive guidance for the corporate managers in deciding between debt and equity in financing their operations (Collins & Sekely, 1983; Myers, 1984).

2.1 The trade-off theory

The trade-off theory of capital structure states that optimal capital structure can be achieved if the net tax advantage of debt financing balances with leverage-related costs. The trade-off of the costs and benefits of borrowing determines the optimal debt ratio. Examples of leverage-related costs taken into account in some empirical corporate financing investigations can be found in Scott (1977), who incorporates bankruptcy costs; in Jensen and Meckling (1976), on agency costs, and in De Angelo and Masulis (1980), on loss of non-debt tax shield.

2.2 The pecking order theory

The pecking order theory suggests that investments are first financed by internal funds, then external debt and, as a last resort, external equity (Myers & Majluf, 1984). The pecking order theory is an alternative to the trade-off theory which has emerged based on asymmetric information problems. These problems occur when one party, for example the manager of a firm, has better quality information than do the other parties, such as outside investors and creditors. In such cases the financing method can serve as a signal to outside investors. Facing information asymmetry between inside and outside investors, firms end up having a financial hierarchy. Equity is issued only when firms have no more debt capacity (Myers, 1984; Myers & Majluf, 1984).

2.3 The agency theory

The agency theory is based on another problem resulting from information asymmetry. Minimizing the costs arising from conflicts between the parties involved can result in the optimal capital structure. Jensen and Meckling (1976) argue that agency costs play an important role in financing decisions due to the conflict that may exist between shareholders and debt holders. The conflict arises when there is moral hazard inside the firm, which is called the agency costs of equity. It is suggested that the use of debt financing can also help in mitigating the agency cost of equity, as debts can discipline managers (Jensen, 1986; Stulz, 1990). The optimal capital structure can be achieved by trading off the agency costs, which include the monitoring expenditure by the principal, the bonding expenditure by the agent and the residual loss, against the benefits of debt.

2.4 The market timing theory

Baker and Wurgler (2002) propose the market timing theory of capital structure, arguing that current capital structure is the cumulative outcome of past attempts to time the equity market. In this theory, there is no optimal capital structure, and market valuation has a persistent impact on capital structure. However, Leary and Roberts (2005) provide evidence contradicting the implications of market timing theory. They show that the persistent effect of shocks on leverage is more likely due to the presence of adjustment costs than to an indifference towards capital structure.

3 Issues of inconclusiveness in capital structure studies

The issues of inconclusiveness have long been recognized in the studies of capital structure. The capital structure puzzle, as referred to by Myers (1984) still remains unanswered today (Al-Najjar & Hussainey, 2011; Gwatidzo & Ramjee, 2012). Various issues have been put forward in explaining this phenomenon throughout the period of capital structure studies. Among the issues discussed are the various definitions of leverage used in capital structure studies and the different models employed in the studies. It is worth noting that this chapter does not intend to investigate in depth the relationships between leverage and firms as well as country-specific factors. Our main objective is to highlight the impact of models employed and different definitions of leverage used in capital structure studies that are found to be responsible in the inconsistent results and inconclusive findings documented throughout the capital structure studies, past and present.

3.1 Definitions of leverage

Many empirical definitions of leverage have been used, and opinions differ on which is a better measure of leverage. Referring to past studies, different definitions of leverage produced different results. This observation is supported by Bevan and Danbolt (2002), who find that results are highly dependent upon the precise definition of gearing being examined. Rajan and Zingales (1995) add that the definition of leverage should depend on the objective of the analysis being carried out

Being the proxy to capital structure, it is crucial to have a clear-cut definition of the term leverage. Despite hundreds of capital structure studies in the literature, Dissanaike and Markar (2009) state that none has clearly defined, in accounting terms, what is meant by leverage. An appropriate leverage measure in one country may not be appropriate in another due to institutional and accounting differences between the countries. Some leverage measures, according to these authors, may be more appropriate than others for evaluating particular capital structure theories. For instance, Rajan and Zingales (1995) argue that the debt relative to firm value would be the relevant measure of leverage for study done on agency theory relating to conflicts based on how a firm has been previously financed. Studies related to agency problems would use debt-to-firm value ratio as the definition of leverage. Studies on leverage and financial distress would prefer the interest-coverage ratio as the definition. Other definitions of leverage include total liabilities-to-total assets, debt-to-total assets, debt-to-net assets, and debt-to-capitalization. Debt could also be divided into its various components, and the numerator and denominator could be measured in book-value and market-value terms. Debt-to-assets (or debt-to-capital) is frequently used as a measure of leverage in empirical studies. Some previous research studies (Titman & Wessels, 1988; Chung, 1993; Pandey et al., 2000) also use different measures of leverage.

Another question regarding definition of leverage is whether to use book value of leverage or market value of leverage. Both book-value leverage and market-value leverage have their own advocates. Being unaffected by volatility of market prices, book-value leverage offers a better reflection of the management's target capital structure. Market value leverage, on the other hand, is unable to reflect the underlying alterations initiated by a firm's decision maker because it is dependent on several factors which are not in direct control of the firm. Book value leverage is referred to as a 'plug number' (Frank & Goyal, 2009) by those who are in favour of market-value leverage, because it (rather than a managerially relevant number) is used to balance the left-hand and right-hand sides of the balance sheet (Welch, 2004). Welch also argues that book-value leverage can take negative values. It is backward-looking and measures what has already taken place. Market value leverage, on the other hand, is forward-looking. The different nature of book value leverage and market value leverage may consequently produce different results (Frank & Goyal, 2009) thus making it more unfeasible to solve the puzzle.

It is also recorded in the literature that the use of different leverage definitions has an impact on the results, even though the same models are employed in the studies. For example, Bevan and Danbolt (2002), Mukherjee and Mahakud (2010) and Caglayan (2010) have reported on different results derived from the use of different leverage definitions. Arguments put forward above show how highly important leverage definition is in determining and examining both the level of leverage (Rajan & Zingales, 1995; Bevan & Danbolt, 2001) and the determinants of leverage (Chittenden et al., 1996; Michaelas et al., 1999; Bevan & Danbolt, 2002) as different leverage definition used may yield different results thus leads to inconclusive findings in the capital structure studies.

3.2 Different models employed

Another issue is the impact of employing different models in analysing the determinants of capital structure. This phenomenon has also been experienced by many researchers. Many earlier studies on the determinants of capital structure decisions have tended to concentrate on the static model. Only recently have researchers started to look into the dynamic aspect of capital structure, using the dynamic model. In contrast to the static model, Rasiah and Kim (2011), state that there are relatively fewer studies on capital structure employing the dynamic model. The contrasting nature of these two models (static and dynamic) is that the static model assumes the observed leverage ratio to be the optimal. The dynamic model, on the other hand, does not assume firms being in equilibrium; rather it relies on a more realistic assumption of partial or incomplete adjustment. Myers and Majluf (1984) suggested that the observed leverage ratio may differ from the optimal level predicted by the static trade-off model between the marginal costs and benefits of debt.

These different aspects of the two models have somewhat contributed to the inconclusiveness of capital structure studies. The impact of the static and the dynamic models on the determinants vary and the results are inconsistent throughout the studies of capital structure. There are cases in which different models working with the same leverage definition record inconsistencies in the coefficient signs. For example, Serrasqueiro and Nunes (2008) encountered different signs of parameter estimation derived from static and dynamic models employed in their studies of capital structure. They compared the uses of different estimators on determinants of capital structure of Portuguese companies and recorded different signs of parameter estimates on the Non-debt Tax Shield (NDTS), tangibility and growth between the static and dynamic models. Kim et al. (2006), in their studies on capital structure in Korea, report that results for growth and NDTS on leverage show differing signs and magnitudes between the static and dynamic models. Banerjee et al. (2004) detect significant positive influence of growth on speed of adjustment in their studies on the UK firms using the static model, but significant negative influence according to the dynamic model. A more dramatic conclusion by Reinhard and Li (2010) in their study of non-financial Indonesian firms, alleges that capital structure models, whether static or dynamic, fail to differentiate between trade-off and pecking order theories. Thus, the debate on which one better explains the financing behaviour of firms is far from over.

These reported findings highlight the notion that different models can lead to inconsistent results on the impact of leverage on factors. Hence, this contributes to the unresolved issue of the inconclusiveness in capital structure studies. Unfortunately, there is no unified model of leverage currently available that can directly account for the factors affecting capital structure decisions (Frank & Goyal, 2009).

4 Data and methodology

4.1 Data and period of study

This study employs panel data. Firms from the financial sector, such as banks, insurance and finance companies, are excluded from the sample firms. This is mainly because of the different accounting categories and rules practiced by these firms. This practice is in line with Rajan and Zingales (1995), Wiwattanakantang (1999), De Miguel and Pindado (2001) and De Jong et al. (2008). Therefore, after excluding these firms, the final sample of firms under study consists of 790 firms for the Malaysian sample, 269 for Thailand and 546 for Singapore. This study uses a ten-year period of data, from 2000 until 2009, in which firm-level data is sourced from the Datastream database while country data is from the World Bank database. For observation purposes, only firms with a minimum of three consecutive observations towards the end of the period under study are included in the data set (Deesomsak et al., 2009). This means that for this study the firms should at least be listed on the stock exchange from the year 2007. After removing the outliers, the numbers of observation are 6531, 2368 and 4170 for Malaysia, Thailand and Singapore respectively. Table 11.1 presents in detail the structure of the panel data on sample firms for this study.

4.2 Measures of leverage

Despite having a vast literature on various studies of capital structure, we realize that there is no clear-cut definition of leverage being referred to.

Table 11.1 The structure of panel data

No. of annual Observations for each firm	No. of records on each firm			No. of observations		
	Malaysia	Thailand	Singapore	Malaysia	Thailand	Singapore
3	34	3	34	102	9	102
4	14	2	35	56	8	140
5	30	1	16	150	5	80
6	48	6	52	288	36	312
7	63	25	61	441	175	427
8	40	22	51	320	176	408
9	92	16	50	828	144	450
10	469	194	247	4690	1940	2470
Total	790	269	546	6875	2493	4389

Source: Datastream.
Note: 3 annual observations refer to the minimum listing period of 2007–09.

Being the proxy to capital structure, it is crucial to have a clear-cut definition of the term leverage. Referring to past studies, different definitions of leverage produce different results, and no universally accepted definition of leverage exists in the literature (Wanzenried, 2006). In relation to this, there are basically two questions facing a researcher in defining leverage; which particular leverage ratio to choose, and whether to use book value of leverage or market value of leverage.

To define leverage, and so cater to the needs of this study, six measures of leverage are used. Following Titman and Wessels (1988), leverage is defined as the ratio of total debt, long-term debt and short-term debt to total assets at book value (termed as book-value leverage) and to total debt plus total equity at market value (termed as market-value leverage). Both market-value and book-value leverage are incorporated in order to observe any inconsistent results as argued by past researchers. However, since the market value of debt is not available, quasi-market leverage will be used where the book value of equity will be replaced by the market value of equity but debt, in this case, will be valued at its book value. The six measures are also used to check the robustness of the results obtained in this study. Although the strict notion of capital structure refers exclusively to long-term debt, short-term debt is used in the definition of leverage because of the significant proportion of short-term debt in the total debt of firms in the samples of this study.

4.3 Explanatory variables

Most empirical studies on capital structure determinants propose a list of variables likely to affect capital structure choices as suggested by Harris and Raviv (1991) in their theory review: fixed assets, non-debt tax shields, investment opportunities, firm size, earnings volatility, default risk, profitability, advertising expenditures, R&D expenditures and product uniqueness. Harris and Raviv even suggest that available studies 'generally agree' on these determinants, although Titman and Wessels (1988) find no significant impact on leverage of non-debt tax-shields, volatility, collateral value or future growth. These ambiguous and contradictory empirical findings on the impact of determinants on leverage can be traced in the literature as far back as the Modigliani and Miller (1958) period. However, recently consensus has been reached on variables influencing capital structure decisions.

We have incorporated 13 explanatory variables, divided according to firm, and country-specific to determine their relationship with leverage. Country-specific variables are incorporated in this study because firm leverage is also influenced by country–specific aspects, not merely firm-specific aspects (Demirguc-Kunt & Maksimovic, 1996; De Jong et al., 2008; Kayo & Kimura, 2011). Furthermore, a misleading result would be reported if critical country-specific differences were ignored (Fan et al., 2011). The choices of these determinants follow those commonly cited in the literature. The selection of variables and proxies is also according to past literature. Table 11.2 summarizes the explanatory variables and proxies used in the study.

4.4 Methodology

We employed two models, the static model and dynamic model, to determine the relationship between leverage and explanatory variables and to observe any discrepancies and inconsistent readings derived from the use of the two models. The Fixed Effect Model and Partial Adjustment Model are employed to represent the static and dynamic model respectively.

Fixed-effect model

The model allows for heterogeneity among firms by allowing each entity to have its own intercept value. The differences across firms in the respective countries may be due to the special features of each firm, such as managerial style, managerial philosophy or the type of market each firm is serving (Gujarati & Porter, 2009). This study hypothesized that leverage is a linear function of a set of k explanatory variables, and the relationship

Table 11.2 Explanatory variables and proxies

No	Explanatory variable	Proxy
	Firm Specific	
1	Non-debt tax shield	Annual depreciation expenses over total assets
2	Tangibility	Net fixed assets over total assets
3	Profitability	EBIT over total assets
4	Business risk	Yearly change on firm EBIT
5	Firm size	Natural logarithm of total assets
6	Growth opportunities	Market value of equity to book value of equity
7	Liquidity	Current assets over current liabilities
8	Share price performance	First difference of the year-end share price
	Country-Specific	
9	Stock market development	Stock market capitalization over GDP
10	Bond market development	Total bond market capitalization over GDP
11	Economic growth	Annual percentage changes in GDP
12	Interest rates	Lending rate
13	Country governance	Aggregate governance indicators, comprised of six indicators (voice and accountability, political stability and absence of violence, government effectiveness, regulatory quality, rule of law and control of corruption)

can be expressed as follows,

$$Y_{it} = \alpha_i + \beta_k X_{kit} + \varepsilon_{it} \tag{1}$$

Since the model allows for heterogeneity among firms by allowing each entity to have its own intercept value, the dummy variables are included as additional regressors to allow for the fixed effect intercept to vary between firms. After adding the dummy variables to equation (1), this study obtains

$$Y_{it} = \sum_{i=1}^{N-1} \alpha_i d_i + \beta_k X_{kit} + \varepsilon_{it} \tag{2}$$

Dynamic model

Using the framework of the partial adjustment model, which is similar to Jalilvand and Harris (1984), Shyam-Sunder and Myers (1999), De Miguel and Pindado (2001) and Hovakimian et al. (2001), this study assumes that the optimal (target) leverage ratio for a firm is a function of sets of explanatory variables as in Equation (3):

$$Y_{it}^{*} = F(X_{it}, X_i, X_t) \tag{3}$$

Where Y_{it}^{*} is the optimal leverage ratio of firm*i*, at time t, X_{it} is a vector of firm and time variant determinants of the optimal leverage, X_i andX_t are unobservable firm-specific and time-specific effects which are common to all firms and can change over time.

In a perfectly frictionless world with no adjustment cost, the firm would immediately respond with complete adjustment to variations in the independent variables by varying its existing leverage ratio to equalize its optimal leverage. Thus, at any point in time, the observed leverage of firm i at time $t(Y_{it})$ should not be different from the optimal leverage, that is, $Y_{it} = Y_{it}^{*}$. This implies that the change in actual leverage from the previous to the current period should be exactly equal to the change required for the firm to be at its optimum at time t, that is, $Y_{it} - Y_{it-1} = Y_{it}^{*} - Y_{it-1}$. In practice, however, the existence of significant adjustment costs means that the firm will not completely adjust its actual leverage to Y^{*}. In other words, only partial adjustment takes place in order to be at the optimal leverage and not complete adjustment due to the presence of significant adjustment cost. Thus, with partial adjustment, the firm's observed leverage ratio at any point in time would not equal its optimal leverage ratio. This can be represented by a partial adjustment model, as in Equation (4).

$$Y_{it} - Y_{it-1} = \delta_{it}(Y_{it}^{*} - Y_{it-1}) \tag{4}$$

Where δ_{it}, is known as the coefficient of adjustment or the speed of adjustment, it is representing the magnitude of desired adjustment between two subsequent periods, or the rate of convergence of Y_{it}, to its optimal value. The effects of adjustment costs are represented by the restriction that $|\delta_{it}| < 1$, which is a condition that $Y_{it} \rightarrow Y_{it}^{*}$ as $t \rightarrow \infty$. Leverage values that are not at their optimal level will be referred to as sub-optimal. In other words, Equation (4) states that the extent to which the desired adjustment depends on its adjustment parameter value. First, if $\delta_{it} = 1$, then the entire adjustment is made within one period and the firm at time *t* is at its target leverage. Since δ_{it} can vary across firms as well as over time for the same firm, only if $\delta_{it} = 1$ for all *t* shall a firm consistently be at its target leverage. Second, if δ_{it}<1, then the adjustment from year *t*–*1* to *t*falls short of the adjustment required to attain the target. Third, if δ_{it}>1, this means that the firm over-adjusts in the sense that it makes more adjustment than necessary and is still not at the optimal. Since δ_{it} represents the degree of adjustment per period or the speed of adjustment, a higher δ_{it} denotes a higher speed of adjustment. Further, the model assumes that the firm's long-term target is a linear function of all the explanatory variables that this study has identified earlier. The firm's behaviour can be represented by Equation (4) below.

$$Y^*_{it} = \sum_{n=1}^{N} \beta_k X_{kit} + \varepsilon_{it} \tag{5}$$

Combining Equations (4) and (5), we derive

$$Y_{it} = Y_{it-1} + \delta_{it}(Y^*_{it} - Y_{it-1}) \tag{6}$$

$$Y_{it} = Y_{it-1} + \delta_{it} Y^*_{it} - \delta_{it} Y_{it-1} \tag{7}$$

$$Y_{it} = (1 - \delta_{it}) Y_{it-1} + \delta_{it} \left(\sum_{n=1}^{N} \beta_k X_{kit} + \varepsilon_{it} \right) \tag{8}$$

$$Y^*_{it} = (1 - \delta_{it}) Y_{it-1} + \sum_{n=1}^{N} \delta_{it} \beta_k X_{kit} + \delta_{it} \varepsilon_{it} \tag{9}$$

To simplify, Equation (9) can also be written as

$$Y^*_{it} = \lambda_0 Y_{it-1} + \sum_{n=1}^{N} \lambda_k X_{kit} + \mu_{it} \tag{10}$$

where $\lambda_0 = 1 - \delta_{it}, \lambda_k = \delta_{it}\beta_k,$ and $\delta_{it}\varepsilon_{it} = \mu_{it}$ (where μ_{it} has the same properties as ε_{it}).

Equation (10) above is the dynamic capital structure model, which this study is intended to estimate using the Generalized Method of Moments (GMM) estimation technique suggested by Arellano and Bond (1991). The GMM estimator is designed for situations with 'small T, large N' panel data, meaning few time periods and many individual firms (Roodman, 2006). That situation is very much applicable to this study.

5 Findings

Inconsistencies in the capital structure issues are still unresolved despite countless studies having been done. This is due, as discussed in the earlier section, to the variations of leverage definitions (Sheikh & Wang, 2011) and also to the models used in explaining the impacts of factors on leverage. Responding to the above issue, we will, firstly, compare the signs of the significant determinants derived from the use of the different models, that is the static model and dynamic model, within the same definition of leverage. Following that we will then look into the signs of the significant determinants derived from the use of different definitions of leverage based on the use of the same model. The following Table 11.3 (Different models, same leverage definition) and Table 11.4 (Different leverage definitions, same model) show the summary derived from the regression output (refer to Appendices A.4 and A.5 for details).

5.1 Different models (same leverage definitions)

When comparisons are made on the use of different models (same leverage definitions), it is clearly shown from the Table 11.3 that, despite some similarities in the signs of coefficients, there are cases where, different models yield different signs. For instance, looking at variable tangibility for Malaysia, leverage according to definitions Lev2 (Long Term Debt at Book Value), Lev4 (Total Debt at Market Value) and Lev5 (Long Term Debt at Market Value), the use of static model yields negative relationship in contrast to the positive relationship using the dynamic model. The implication from this is that different signs would lead to different theoretical argument to support the finding. A positive relationship under dynamic

Table 11.3 Different models (same leverage definition)

Independent variable	Book value						Market value					
	FE	GMM	FE	GMM	FE	GMM	FE	GMM	FE	GMM	FE	GMM
	Lev1		Lev2		Lev3		Lev4		Lev5		Lev6	
Malaysia												
NDTS			–	–	–				–	–		
Tangibility	–		–	+	–		–	+	–	+	–	
Profitability	–	–		–	–	–		–				–
Risk			+		–		+		+		–	
Size	–		+	+	–		+	+	+	+	+	+
Growth			+	+			–	–	–		–	–
Liquidity	–		+		–	–	–	–	+		–	–
SPP		–	+			–	–	–	–	–	–	–
Stock		–	–				+				+	
Bond		+	+				–		–		–	
Eco growth		+	+				–		–		–	
Interest		+					–		–		–	
Governance		+	+				–		–		–	

Continued

Table 11.3 Continued

Independent variable	Book value						Market value					
	FE	GMM	FE	GMM	FE	GMM	FE	GMM	FE	GMM	FE	GMM
	Lev1		Lev2		Lev3		Lev4		Lev5		Lev6	
Thailand												
NDTS				−	−		+				−	
Tangibility	−		−		−	−	−		−		−	
Profitability		−				−		−		−		−
Risk	+						+		−			
Size		+	+				+	+	+	+	+	
Growth												
Liquidity					−	−					−	
SPP		+	−	+		−	−	−			−	−
Stock	−		−	−		−	−	−	−	−	−	−
Bond	+						−	−	−	−	+	
Eco Growth	+	+	+			+	−		−			
Interest	+						−	−	−	−	−	
Governance	+	+	+				−	−	−			
Singapore												
NDTS												
Tangibility					−	−	−	+	−	+		
Profitability					+	−		−	+	−		
Risk						+	+		+			
Size					−		+	+	+	+	+	+
Growth		−										
Liquidity	−				−		−		+	+	−	−
SPP							−	−	−	−	−	−
Stock	−		−		+		−	−	−	−	−	−
Bond					−		−			+	−	
Eco Growth						+	−	−	−		−	−
Interest							−	−	−		−	−
Governance	−		−				+	+	+		+	+

Notes: Model FE = Fixed effect model (Static model); GMM = Generalized method of moments (Estimator of dynamic partial adjustment model); Leverage definitions: Book value leverage [Lev1 = Total debt/Total asset; Lev2 = Long-term debt/Total assets; Lev3 = Short-term debt/Total assets]; Market value leverage [Lev4 = Total debt/(Total debt + Total equity); Lev5 = Long-term debt/(Total debt + Total equity); Lev6 = Short-term debt/(Total debt + Total equity)].

model supports the trade-off theory. Since tangible assets of a firm represent real guarantees to its creditors, the importance of those assets among total assets influences the level of debt issued by lenders to firms. Therefore, the greater the proportion of tangible assets on the balance

Fixed effect model estimation						
MALAYSIA (N = 6531)						
Independent variable	**Book value**			**Market value**		
	Lev1	**Lev2**	**Lev3**	**Lev4**	**Lev5**	**Lev6**
C	3.5804	−1.3376***	2.5219	3.5167***	0.3863	8.9290***
	[0.4149]	[−4.0925]	[0.3157]	[3.5941]	[0.5355]	[2.7911]
NDTS	−1.0257	−0.18506*	−1.2104**	0.0205	−0.2710*	−0.2210
	[−0.9952]	[−1.7955]	[−2.1539]	[0.0646]	[−1.7387]	[−0.2829]
TANG	−0.3583***	−0.0854***	−0.3754***	−0.0706***	−0.0263***	−0.0658*
	[−11.0092]	[−14.5344]	[−7.4471]	[−3.8272]	[−3.2349]	[−1.7877]
PROFIT	−0.0002***	0.0000	−0.0002**	0.0001	0.0001	0.0002
	[−8.7925]	[0.9227]	[−2.2787]	[0.5520]	[1.1682]	[1.0195]
RISK	0.0145	0.0944***	−0.1879***	0.1611***	0.1662***	−0.2141***
	[0.2469]	[5.0679]	[−2.7734]	[3.9608]	[7.3750]	[−2.4614]
SIZE	−0.2202***	0.0539***	−0.2592**	0.1116***	0.0857***	0.0851*
	[−3.0626]	[7.1281]	[−2.0525]	[5.2649]	[8.6558]	[1.8180]
GROWTH	−0.0025	0.0016***	−0.0080	−0.0067**	−0.0035**	−0.0233**
	[−0.8154]	[3.1361]	[−1.5702]	[−2.0983]	[−2.0790]	[−2.3182]
LIQUIDITY	−0.0012***	0.0005*	−0.0027***	−0.0008***	0.0006**	−0.0041**
	[−2.7254]	[1.6359]	[−3.1311]	[−3.7192]	[2.1970]	[−2.4109]
SPP	−0.0064	0.0024**	−0.0147	−0.0178***	−0.0034**	−0.0361***
	[−0.6903]	[2.1686]	[−1.0877]	[−2.6079]	[−2.1926]	[−5.9762]
STOCK MKT	0.0001	−0.0004**	−0.0009	0.0021***	0.0005	0.0049***
	[0.0152]	[−2.0984]	[−0.2261]	[4.2992]	[1.4290]	[2.9571]

Continued

Appendix A.4 Continued

Fixed effect model estimation						
MALAYSIA (N = 6531)						
Independent variable	**Book value**			**Market value**		
	Lev1	**Lev2**	**Lev3**	**Lev4**	**Lev5**	**Lev6**
BOND MKT	−0.3893	0.5285**	0.7442	−3.4075***	−0.9875**	−6.7875***
	[−0.0662]	[2.1980]	[0.1608]	[−5.8919]	[−2.2197]	[−3.5204]
ECON	−0.0039	0.0194**	0.0379	−0.1224***	−0.0352**	−0.2497***
	[−0.0196]	[2.3749]	[0.2343]	[−6.1445]	[−2.3496]	[−3.6832]
INT	−0.0023	0.0155	0.0595	−0.0988***	−0.0361**	−0.2210***
	[−0.0100]	[1.4337]	[0.3106]	[−3.9745]	[−1.9026]	[−2.6800]
GOV	−0.2712	0.2972**	0.3648	−1.5772***	−0.4409*	−3.4573***
	[−0.0889]	[2.2194]	[0.1458]	[−5.0898]	[−1.8438]	[−3.2947]
R-sq	0.6332	0.7939	0.7074	0.8926	0.7881	0.6664
Adj-R sq	0.5414	0.7424	0.6341	0.8658	0.7351	0.5829
F-stat	6.8982***	15.3959***	9.6527***	33.2189***	14.8628***	7.9765***
DW	1.2951	2.0912	1.9813	1.8811	2.0236	1.6773
Wald (Joint) χ^2	55.1233***	32.6974***	89.6730***	182.8504***	43.8925***	71.9218***
AR(1)	0.3044	0.4344***	0.5686**	0.5116***	0.3783***	0.1538
	[0.9129]	[3.9260]	[1.9258]	[9.3009]	[4.1173]	[1.1718]

Notes: ***, ** and * denotes significant at 1%, 5% and 10% respectively. The heteroskedastic effects are corrected using the White's heteroscedasticity-corrected Standard Errors; *t*-statistics in parentheses are the *t*-values adjusted for White's heteroscedasticity consistent standard errors; Wald test statistic refers to the null hypothesis that all coefficients on the determinants of leverage are jointly equal zero.

Appendix A.4 THAILAND

Fixed effect model estimation						
THAILAND (N = 2368)						
Independent variable	**Book value**			**Market value**		
	Lev1	**Lev2**	**Lev3**	**Lev4**	**Lev5**	**Lev6**
C	−0.4914	−0.0073	0.3814	−1.4212***	−0.1365	−1.9997***
	[−0.5153]	[−0.0677]	[0.3401]	[−2.6125]	[−0.6483]	[−3.0549]
NDTS	−0.0477	−0.1514	−0.5977***	0.5559***	0.1718	−1.3791*
	[−0.1689]	[−1.1035]	[−3.6517]	[2.7466]	[0.7876]	[−1.7164]
TANG	−0.1944***	−0.0108*	−0.5080***	−0.2543***	−0.0656**	−0.4478***
	[−7.2601]	[−1.6188]	[−4.3592]	[−4.7321]	[−2.0408]	[−3.3586]
PROFIT	0.0001	0.0000	0.0001	−0.0002	0.0000	−0.0002
	[1.2237]	[1.2656]	[0.6019]	[−1.4599]	[0.3974]	[−1.0211]
RISK	0.0108*	0.0008	−0.0130	0.0090*	−0.0104**	0.0059
	[1.8524]	[0.5132]	[−1.2671]	[1.7657]	[−2.3821]	[1.0839]
SIZE	0.0440	0.0109*	−0.0079	0.1381***	0.0374***	0.1610***
	[0.7088]	[1.6046]	[−0.1092]	[3.9032]	[2.9956]	[3.5932]
GROWTH	0.0002	0.0000	0.0002	0.0002	0.0000	0.0001
	[0.8999]	[0.0575]	[1.2077]	[0.6458]	[−0.0714]	[0.1222]
LIQUIDITY	−0.0018	0.0005	−0.0070***	−0.0018	0.0007	−0.0069**
	[−1.1807]	[1.4061]	[−4.3026]	[−1.1394]	[1.5662]	[−2.2609]
SPP	−0.0001	−0.0001***	0.0000	−0.0003*	0.0000	−0.0004*
	[−1.2222]	[−3.7337]	[−0.4374]	[−1.8153]	[−1.0042]	[−1.7003]
STOCK MKT	−0.0004***	−0.0002***	−0.0001	−0.0015***	−0.0008***	−0.0025***
	[−7.3662]	[−4.3336]	[−0.6048]	[−17.5463]	[−10.3942]	[−16.4279]

Continued

Appendix A.4 Continued

Fixed effect model estimation						
THAILAND (N = 2368)						
Independent variable	**Book value**			**Market value**		
	Lev1	**Lev2**	**Lev3**	**Lev4**	**Lev5**	**Lev6**
BOND MKT	0.1287**	−0.0445	0.2155	−0.3499***	−0.3387***	0.7210***
	[2.3076]	[−0.7710]	[1.6483]	[−4.0510]	[−5.6802]	[2.9791]
ECON	0.0096***	0.0035**	0.0071	−0.0116***	−0.0088***	0.0023
	[6.4293]	[2.2412]	[1.4872]	[−4.4564]	[−4.8098]	[0.3335]
INT	0.0040**	−0.0005	0.0015	−0.0137***	−0.0085***	−0.0165***
	[2.3602]	[−0.5611]	[1.0183]	[−9.5213]	[−7.0551]	[−6.3086]
GOV	0.1031***	0.0855***	−0.0334	−0.1163***	−0.0449**	0.0029
	[8.0105]	[4.5181]	[−0.7407]	[−4.8366]	[−2.3156]	[0.0453]
R-sq	0.8807	0.8686	0.7990	0.8746	0.8212	0.8209
Adj-R sq	0.8499	0.8347	0.7471	0.8422	0.7751	0.7747
F-stat	28.6133***	25.6194***	15.4033***	27.0260***	17.8055***	17.7687***
DW	1.9400	2.0319	1.8395	1.8550	1.9487	1.9011
Wald (Joint) χ^2	124.6948***	48.1047***	154.1371***	191.9180***	68.1000***	110.1685***
AR(1)	0.5783***	0.5185***	0.3477***	0.3683***	0.2672***	0.3283*
	[5.9804]	[5.1441]	[4.5391]	[3.6528]	[4.1900]	[1.8080]

Notes: ***, ** and * denotes significant at 1%, 5% and 10% respectively. The heteroskedastic effects are corrected using the White's heteroscedasticity-corrected Standard Errors; *t*-statistics in parentheses are the *t*-values adjusted for White's heteroscedasticity consistent standard errors; Wald test statistic refers to the null hypothesis that all coefficients on the determinants of leverage are jointly equal zero.

Appendix A.4 SINGAPORE

Fixed effect model estimation						
SINGAPORE (N = 4170)						
Independent variable	**Book value**			**Market value**		
	Lev1	**Lev2**	**Lev3**	**Lev4**	**Lev5**	**Lev6**
C	9.1949	1.3210	8.5466	24.4507***	3.6447***	51.7788***
	[0.9927]	[0.3132]	[1.1941]	[13.7553]	[4.4648]	[7.1328]
NDTS	−4.0197	−1.4647	−2.5416	0.0533	−0.0787	−0.0865
	[−0.8116]	[−0.7042]	[−1.4541]	[0.2060]	[−0.4574]	[−0.0981]
TANG	−0.9748	−0.3662	−0.9312***	−0.0555***	−0.0219***	−0.0597
	[−1.4012]	[−1.2234]	[−3.7107]	[−4.7717]	[−2.9278]	[−1.1610]
PROFIT	0.0006	0.0002	0.0005*	0.0000	0.0000**	0.0001
	[1.1485]	[1.1717]	[1.7800]	[−0.1185]	[−2.4448]	[0.2930]
RISK	−0.4044	−0.0547	−0.7884	0.2742***	0.2611***	−0.0400
	[−0.7530]	[−0.2511]	[−1.4588]	[5.2354]	[6.6008]	[−0.7322]
SIZE	−0.1742	−0.0447	−0.4186***	0.1127***	0.0599***	0.0726**
	[−0.8781]	[−0.4988]	[−2.9697]	[11.9771]	[6.3787]	[2.1399]
GROWTH	−0.0053	−0.0016	−0.0050	−0.0007	0.0002	−0.0024
	[−1.5642]	[−1.1400]	[−1.5366]	[−1.0612]	[0.7735]	[−1.0551]
LIQUIDITY	−0.0105**	0.0004	−0.0229***	−0.0032**	0.0035**	−0.0151***
	[−2.1523]	[0.1533]	[−4.7265]	[−2.3833]	[2.2445]	[−7.5352]
SPP	0.0183	0.0098	−0.0151	−0.0199***	−0.0064***	−0.0452***
	[0.7823]	[0.8310]	[−0.7896]	[−4.8727]	[−2.8590]	[−6.5667]
STOCK MKT	−0.0009**	−0.0003*	0.0005*	−0.0006***	−0.0002***	−0.0012***
	[−2.0833]	[−1.6603]	[1.6695]	[−4.2082]	[−3.2404]	[−4.7256]

Continued

Appendix A.4 Continued

Fixed effect model estimation						
SINGAPORE (N = 4170)						
Independent variable	**Book value**			**Market value**		
	Lev1	**Lev2**	**Lev3**	**Lev4**	**Lev5**	**Lev6**
BOND MKT	−0.0591	0.2509	−2.4879**	−4.0766***	−0.2778	−7.2780**
	[−0.0814]	[0.8385]	[−1.8513]	[−5.7864]	[−1.4376]	[−2.3260]
ECON	0.0016	0.0031	−0.0043	−0.0278***	−0.0049***	−0.0557***
	[0.2632]	[1.1773]	[−0.6445]	[−19.4063]	[−10.9214]	[−6.1265]
INT	−0.9625	0.0015	−0.1433	−4.5324***	−0.8066***	−9.3830***
	[−0.4493]	[0.0016]	[−0.0894]	[−11.7421]	[−4.7630]	[−8.6734]
GOV	−0.7576*	−0.4538**	−0.3282	0.6948***	0.1071**	1.6479***
	[−1.6578]	[−2.2302]	[−0.9466]	[5.8672]	[2.2018]	[15.8147]
R-sq	0.4009	0.4093	0.5230	0.8415	0.7414	0.7037
Adj-R sq	0.2262	0.2371	0.3842	0.7952	0.6660	0.6175
F-stat	2.2945***	2.3762***	3.7683***	18.1992***	9.8329***	8.1630***
DW	2.4097	2.4318	2.2675	1.9594	2.1563	1.9703
Wald (Joint) χ^2	17.7048***	11.6711***	40.2523***	57.4148***	22.9741***	25.7757***
AR(1)	0.1044	0.0753	0.2082	0.4894***	0.2631**	0.3548**
	[0.6282]	[0.4617]	[0.9886]	[5.1062]	[2.1060]	[1.9658]

Notes: ***, ** and * denotes significant at 1%, 5% and 10% respectively. The heteroskedastic effects are corrected using the White's heteroscedasticity-corrected Standard Errors; *t*-statistics in parentheses are the *t*-values adjusted for White's heteroscedasticity consistent standard errors; Wald test statistic refers to the null hypothesis that all coefficients on the determinants of leverage are jointly equal zero.

Appendix A.5 MALAYSIA

Generalized method of moments (GMM) – First difference estimation						
MALAYSIA (N = 6531)						
Independent variable	**Book value**			**Market value**		
	Lev1	**Lev2**	**Lev3**	**Lev4**	**Lev5**	**Lev6**
Lev(−1)	0.4300***	0.6534***	0.4389***	0.4612***	0.5746***	0.0266**
	[7.8788]	[5.5707]	[4.5856]	[7.1235]	[7.4328]	[2.1854]
NDTS	−0.7179	−0.4923***	0.0975	−0.3297	−0.5387***	−0.0373
	[−0.6322]	[−2.7282]	[0.1060]	[−1.1790]	[−2.4543]	[−0.0405]
TANG	0.1150	0.0688*	−0.1010	0.1680***	0.1507***	−0.0892
	[1.5529]	[1.8941]	[−0.9452]	[4.8934]	[4.2689]	[−1.1896]
PROFIT	−0.4232***	−0.0834***	−0.4823***	−0.0793***	−0.0016	−0.0792**
	[−11.01]	[−3.5405]	[−10.2294]	[−2.7688]	[−0.0961]	[−2.0701]
RISK	−0.0004	0.0001	−0.0005	−0.0001	0.0001	0.0002
	[−1.0980]	[0.9090]	[−1.5394]	[−0.4043]	[0.8364]	[1.3152]
SIZE	−0.1727	0.0305**	−0.2436	0.1297***	0.0712***	0.1841**
	[−1.0964]	[2.8189]	[−1.3320]	[5.7611]	[4.0846]	[2.0572]
GROWTH	−0.0017	0.0032*	−0.0062	−0.0038**	−0.0010	−0.0164**
	[−0.8452]	[1.7537]	[−1.2980]	[−2.3030]	[−0.5018]	[−2.4303]
LIQUIDITY	−0.0015	0.0004	−0.0041**	−0.0010***	0.0006	−0.0038**
	[−1.3430]	[0.8534]	[−2.0019]	[−3.8293]	[1.0197]	[−2.1855]
SPP	−0.0196**	0.0024	−0.0320***	−0.0264***	−0.0057**	−0.0402***
	[−2.1222]	[0.8944]	[−3.6920]	[−4.2949]	[−2.0051]	[−4.3232]
STOCK MKT	−0.0062*	−0.0016	−0.0101	−0.0005	−0.0017	−0.0039
	[−1.8973]	[−1.5087]	[−1.2307]	[−0.3967]	[−1.2038]	[−0.5368]

Continued

Appendix A.5 Continued

Generalized method of moments (GMM) – First difference estimation						
MALAYSIA (N = 6531)						
Independent variable	**Book value**			**Market value**		
	Lev1	**Lev2**	**Lev3**	**Lev4**	**Lev5**	**Lev6**
BOND MKT	7.5830*	1.8765	12.0634	−0.4220	1.5563	3.5717
	[1.9091]	[1.4576]	[1.2348]	[−0.2576]	[0.9296]	[0.4035]
ECON	0.2638**	0.0665	0.4152	−0.0172	0.0539	0.0995
	[1.9811]	[1.5665]	[1.2575]	[−0.3147]	[0.9621]	[0.3387]
INT	0.3025*	0.0664	0.5377	−0.0039	0.0505	0.2432
	[1.8147]	[1.2211]	[1.2949]	[−0.0561]	[0.7144]	[0.6489]
GOV	3.7165*	0.9697	6.0991	−0.0292	0.8554	1.9729
	[1.8476]	[1.4615]	[1.2340]	[−0.0345]	[0.9815]	[0.4294]
1st Order Cor.	−0.3887***	−0.1950***	−0.2561***	−0.2427***	−0.3718***	−0.2632***
2nd Order Cor.	0.0207	0.3901***	−0.1761***	0.1039***	−0.0470***	0.0155
Wald (joint)χ^2	63.3091***	569.4434***	508.4449***	647.2911***	248.0277***	78.9032***
J-Statistic	24.5782	130.3220***	85.6978***	151.3819***	131.0562***	20.1826

Notes: Each variable is in its first difference form. ***, ** and * denotes significant at 1%, 5% and 10% level respectively. The *t*-statistics in parentheses are the *t*-values adjusted for White's heteroscedasticity consistent standard errors; (a) Wald test statistic refers to the null hypothesis that all coefficients on the determinants of the target debt ratio are jointly equal zero. (b) Second order correlation refers to the null of no second order correlation in the residuals. (c) The *J* test statistic for the null that the over identifying restrictions are valid.

Appendix A.5 THAILAND

Generalized method of moments (GMM) – First difference estimation						
THAILAND (N = 2368)						
Independent variable	**Book value**			**Market value**		
	Lev1	**Lev2**	**Lev3**	**Lev4**	**Lev5**	**Lev6**
Lev(−1)	0.7196***	0.6937***	0.3298**	0.3590***	0.3193***	0.0573
	[5.9748]	[5.4157]	[2.3259]	[5.6137]	[4.2039]	[0.3932]
NDTS	−0.3102	−0.3609**	−0.4755	0.0073	−0.1967	−0.8172
	[−0.7532]	[−2.2800]	[−1.5124]	[0.0211]	[−1.1588]	[−0.5966]
TANG	0.0128	−0.0001	−0.0204*	0.0145	−0.0030	0.0096
	[0.9185]	[−0.0139]	[−1.8205]	[1.1371]	[−0.4366]	[0.4607]
PROFIT	−0.3654***	−0.1481	−0.3979***	−0.2301***	−0.0487*	−0.2772***
	[−3.2063]	[−1.5370]	[−3.6386]	[−3.4467]	[−1.7292]	[−3.0575]
RISK	0.0001	0.0001	0.0000	−0.0002	0.0001	−0.0002
	[0.4936]	[1.2758]	[0.0722]	[−1.1258]	[0.6607]	[−0.7604]
SIZE	0.1266***	0.0289	0.0434	0.1730***	0.0453***	0.1339
	[2.6368]	[1.4771]	[0.5992]	[4.7098]	[2.5255]	[1.5537]
GROWTH	0.0001	−0.0003	0.0002	0.0001	−0.0003	0.0004
	[0.3356]	[−1.0837]	[1.1680]	[0.3905]	[−1.3168]	[1.1140]
LIQUIDITY	−0.0010	0.0026	−0.0068*	−0.0014	0.0023	−0.0057
	[−0.7397]	[1.2322]	[−1.8012]	[−0.9719]	[1.5258]	[−1.5136]
SPP	0.0002***	0.0000***	0.0002**	−0.0005***	0.0000	−0.0005***
	[3.0442]	[−2.5281]	[2.1143]	[−7.2677]	[−1.1132]	[−4.2557]
STOCK MKT	−0.0006	−0.0005*	−0.0007**	−0.0024***	−0.0014***	−0.0038***
	[−1.5446]	[−1.6140]	[−1.9535]	[−6.4283]	[−3.7503]	[−5.1933]

Continued

Appendix A.5 Continued

Generalized method of moments (GMM) – First difference estimation

THAILAND (N = 2368)

Independent variable	Book value			Market value		
	Lev1	Lev2	Lev3	Lev4	Lev5	Lev6
BOND MKT	0.3501	0.1724	0.2725	−0.5516**	−0.3915*	0.6404
	[1.5806]	[0.7648]	[1.1073]	[−2.3518]	[−1.6845]	[1.3143]
ECON	0.0149*	0.0092	0.0120*	−0.0035	−0.0018	0.0108
	[1.8005]	[1.2860]	[1.6605]	[−0.4163]	[−0.2557]	[0.8882]
INT	0.0054	−0.0022	0.0037	−0.0321***	−0.0184***	−0.0045
	[0.8662]	[−0.3795]	[0.5561]	[−3.8234]	[−2.5288]	[−0.3192]
GOV	0.1711**	0.1157	−0.0108	−0.2213***	−0.0926	−0.0146
	[2.2914]	[1.4910]	[−0.1277]	[−2.4538]	[−1.0351]	[−0.1014]
1st Order Cor.	−0.2363***	−0.3063***	−0.1699***	−0.2850***	−0.3208***	−0.1035***
2nd Order Cor.	−0.0659**	0.0029	0.0262	0.0413	0.0250	0.0116
Wald (joint) χ^2	90.7645***	177.3935***	154.7685***	424.5110***	159.6277***	438.1869***
J-Statistic	60.4067***	28.8222	33.1122	32.2300	122.3711***	276.0285***

Notes: Each variable is in its first difference form. ***, ** and * denotes significant at 1%, 5% and 10% level respectively. The *t*-statistics in parentheses are the *t*-values adjusted for White's heteroscedasticity consistent standard errors; (a) Wald test statistic refers to the null hypothesis that all coefficients on the determinants of the target debt ratio are jointly equal zero. (b) Second order correlation refers to the null of no second order correlation in the residuals. (c) The *J* test statistic for the null that the over identifying restrictions are valid.

Appendix A.5 SINGAPORE

Generalized method of moments (GMM) – First difference estimation						
SINGAPORE (N = 4170)						
Independent variable	**Book value**			**Market value**		
	Lev1	**Lev2**	**Lev3**	**Lev4**	**Lev5**	**Lev6**
Lev(−1)	0.3454	0.5270	0.6918***	0.3052***	0.4039***	0.3008***
	[0.8044]	[1.1339]	[2.5904]	[11.8288]	[7.4044]	[8.1106]
NDTS	−5.8855	−3.0082	−5.3965	−0.2826	−0.0108	−0.9329
	[−0.9953]	[−0.9733]	[−1.3169]	[−1.2728]	[−0.0591]	[−0.7647]
TANG	−0.6876	−0.1843	−1.1271*	0.2352***	0.2234***	−0.0957
	[−0.9046]	[−0.5146]	[−1.8229]	[6.1463]	[4.5239]	[−0.8083]
PROFIT	−1.7150	−0.8326	−2.0886***	−0.0706***	−0.0240***	−0.0958
	[−1.3097]	[−1.3048]	[−3.7777]	[−4.1715]	[−5.6534]	[−1.4874]
RISK	0.0009	0.0005	0.0008*	0.0000	0.0000	0.0000
	[1.2640]	[1.3396]	[1.5796]	[−0.3842]	[0.0254]	[−0.2883]
SIZE	0.0789	0.0349	−0.0807	0.1232***	0.0659***	0.1259**
	[1.1623]	[0.8786]	[−0.4191]	[9.2876]	[6.5647]	[1.9711]
GROWTH	−0.0034**	0.0012	−0.0022	0.0000	0.0004	−0.0010
	[−2.0927]	[0.9080]	[−0.9376]	[−0.0634]	[1.1490]	[−0.8535]
LIQUIDITY	−0.0051	0.0028	−0.0091	−0.0014	0.0039**	−0.0120***
	[−1.0159]	[1.4509]	[−1.0592]	[−1.1693]	[2.2733]	[−2.9616]
SPP	0.0147	0.0104	−0.0492	−0.0279***	−0.0094***	−0.0669***
	[0.9056]	[1.0715]	[−1.0174]	[−4.1423]	[−4.6083]	[−3.2456]
STOCK MKT	−0.0014	−0.0006	0.0006	−0.0009***	−0.0002*	−0.0016***
	[−1.5178]	[−1.2665]	[0.4674]	[−6.8487]	[−1.7539]	[−4.6258]

Continued

Appendix A.5 Continued

Generalized method of moments (GMM) – First difference estimation						
SINGAPORE (N = 4170)						
Independent variable	**Book value**			**Market value**		
	Lev1	**Lev2**	**Lev3**	**Lev4**	**Lev5**	**Lev6**
BOND MKT	1.9099	1.0339	1.7225	0.0444	0.3285*	−0.0757
	[1.3327]	[1.5219]	[1.0908]	[0.1958]	[1.7110]	[−0.0739]
ECON	0.0073	0.0047	0.0144**	−0.0091***	−0.0011	−0.0194***
	[1.2228]	[1.4980]	[2.1068]	[−6.2196]	[−0.8399]	[−5.3424]
INT	−2.0019	−0.5685	1.7688	−2.3174***	−0.1495	−4.8777***
	[−1.3618]	[−0.6779]	[0.6714]	[−7.2920]	[−0.6160]	[−6.1346]
GOV	−0.7154	−0.4857	−0.4586	0.8113***	0.0727	1.7481***
	[−0.9140]	[−1.2720]	[−0.7580]	[7.8353]	[0.9208]	[6.4559]
1st Order Cor.	−0.2885***	−0.3591***	−0.3274***	−0.2976***	−0.3313***	−0.3747***
2nd Order Cor.	−0.1834***	−0.1014***	−0.1393***	0.0232	0.0019	0.0580***
Wald (joint)χ^2	383.2576***	320.8692***	77.22856***	318.8110***	392.4942***	604.1809***
J-Statistic	26.8903	28.5957***	601.0097***	30.2149	33.0180	336.8049***

Notes: Each variable is in its first difference form. ***, ** and * denotes significant at 1%, 5% and 10% level respectively. The *t*-statistics in parentheses are the *t*-values adjusted for White's heteroscedasticity consistent standard errors; (a) Wald test statistic refers to the null hypothesis that all coefficients on the determinants of the target debt ratio are jointly equal zero. (b) Second order correlation refers to the null of no second order correlation in the residuals. (c) The *J* test statistic for the null that the over identifying restrictions are valid.

sheet, lenders should be more willing to supply loans and as a result leverage should be higher (see for examples, Harris & Raviv, 1991; Rajan & Zingales 1995, Gaud et al., 2005, Sheikh & Wang, 2011). While negative relationship under static model supports the agency theory. According to Titman and Wessels (1988), higher debt level will increase bankruptcy risk thus diminishes the managers' tendency to squander. This is because being highly levered, debtholder will monitor them very closely. To monitor the investment activities of firms with less collateralizable assets is more difficult. This means that the costs associated with this agency relation may be higher relative to firms with high collateralizable assets. This is why, as argued by Titman and Wessels (1988), firms with less collateralizable assets may choose higher debt levels to limit their managers' consumption of perquisites. Other studies also reported negative relationship between tangibilty and leverage (see, for examples, Booth et al., 2001; Bauer, 2004; Mazur, 2007; Karadeniz et al., 2009; Sheikh & Wang, 2011). These valid arguments, looking through contrasting theoretical lenses, further enhance what this paper intends to prove which is, still there is no concrete consensus regarding the influence of factors on leverage, especially when different models are put at work. We can see that fundamental assumptions from these capital structure theories are at work and do influence the overall results of the studies (Kayo & Kimura, 2011).

Referring to Singapore, for variable profitability, leverage by definition Lev3 (Short Term Debt at Book Value) and Lev5 (Long Term debt at Market Value), the static model leads to positive relationship in contrast to the negative relationship using dynamic model. While for variable tangibility, inconsistencies are reported for Lev4 (Total Debt at Market Value) and Lev5 (Long Term Debt at Market Value) in which the static model reported negative relationship in contrast to a positive relationship by the dynamic model. The same is detected for Thailand Lev2 (Long Term Debt at Book Value), for variable share price performance. Our findings therefore reveal that, results are sensitive to models employed. The different methodology of the two models in examining the impact of factors on leverage lead to different coefficient signs yielded thus making the results not conclusive.

5.2 Different leverage definitions (same model)

Using different leverage definitions could also lead to different results despite employing the same model. As an example, referring to Table 11.4 above, variable liquidity for Malaysia, based on the static model, we find

Table 11.4 Different leverage definitions (same model)

Independent variable	Lev1	Lev2	Lev3	Lev4	Lev5	Lev6	Lev1	Lev2	Lev3	Lev4	Lev5	Lev6
	Fixed effect model						GMM					
					Malaysia							
NDTS		−	−		−			−			−	
Tangibility	−	−	−	−	−	−		+		+	+	
Profitability	−		−				−	−	−	−		−
Risk		+	−	+	+	−						
Size	−	+	−	+	+	+		+		+	+	+
Growth		+		−	−	−		+		−		−
Liquidity	−	+	−	−	+	−			−	−		−
SPP		+		−	−	−	−		−	−	−	−
Stock		−		+		+	−					
Bond		+		−	−	−	+					
Eco growth		+		−	−	−	+					
Interest				−	−	−	+					
Governance		+		−	−	−	+					
					Thailand							
NDTS			−	+		−		−				
Tangibility	−	−	−	−	−	−			−			
Profitability							−		−	−	−	−
Risk	+			+	−							
Size		+		+	+	+	+			+	+	
Growth												
Liquidity			−			−			−			
SPP		−		−		−	+	+	−	−		−
Stock	−	−		−	−	−		−	−	−	−	−
Bond	+			−	−	+				−	−	
Eco growth	+	+		−	−		+		+			
Interest	+			−	−	−				−	−	
Governance	+	+		−	−		+			−		
					Singapore							
NDTS												
Tangibility			−	−	−				−	+	+	
Profitability			+		+				−	−	−	
Risk				+	+				+			
Size			−	+	+	+				+	+	+
Growth							−					
Liquidity	−		−	−	+	−					+	−
SPP				−	−	−				−	−	−

Continued

Table 11.4 Continued

Independent variable	Lev1	Lev2	Lev3	Lev4	Lev5	Lev6	Lev1	Lev2	Lev3	Lev4	Lev5	Lev6
	Fixed effect model						GMM					
Stock	−	−	+	−	−	−				−	−	−
Bond			−	−		−					+	
Eco growth				−	−	−			+	−		−
Interest				−	−	−				−		−
Governance	−	−		+	+	+				+		+

Notes: Model FE = Fixed effect model (Static model); GMM = Generalized method of moments (Estimator of dynamic partial adjustment model); Leverage definitions: Book value leverage [Lev1 = Total debt/Total asset; Lev2 = Long-term debt/Total asset; Lev3 = Short-term debt/Total asset]; Market value leverage [Lev4 = Total debt/(Total debt + Total equity); Lev5 = Long-term debt/(Total debt + Total equity); Lev6 = Short term debt/(Total debt + Total equity)].

negative coefficients for Lev1 (Total Debt at Book Value), Lev3 (Short Term Debt at Book Value), lev4 (Total Debt at Market Value) and Lev6 (Short Term Debt at Market Value) in contrast to positive coefficients for Lev2 (Long Term Debt at Book Value) and Lev5 (Long Term Debt at Market Value). Inconsistencies are also detected for bond market development and governance. As for Thailand, inconsistencies are detected on business risk under static model in which leverage defined as Lev1 (Total Debt at Book Value) and Lev4 (Total Debt at Market Value) lead to positive coefficients in contrast to the negative coefficients under Lev5 (Long Term Debt at Market Value). The same is also detected for country-specific variables with the exception of stock market development. Inconsistencies are also depicted in our results for Singapore, that is, stock market development and governance. The findings thus conclude that results are sensitive to the various definitions of leverage despite employing the same model. Welch (2010) justifies this phenomenon by claiming that there may not be one best measure (leverage definition) in the capital structure literature as it depends on the question being asked.

5.3 Summary of inconsistencies

To illustrate even further, a summary of inconsistencies of coefficient signs in relationship between leverage and independent variables is presented in Table 11.5. We can see how different models employed working with the same leverage definition yield differing results, and also how the

Table 11.5 Summary of inconsistencies of coefficient signs in relationship

Model	**Definition**	**Country**	**Inconsistencies in coefficient signs of variables**						
Different	Same	M'sia	Tang						
		Thai	SPP						
		S'pore	Tang	Profit					
Same	Different	M'sia	Size	Growth	SPP	Stock	Bond	Econ	Govern
		Thai	NDTS	Risk	SPP	Bond	Econ	Interest	Govern
		S'pore		Liquid	Stock	Econ	Govern		

Notes: Tang = Tangibility, SPP=Share price performance, Profit = Profitability, Size = Firm size, NDTS = Non-debt tax shield, Growth = Growth opportunities, Liquid = Liquidity, Stock = Stock market development, Bond = Bond market development, Econ = Economic growth, Interest = Interest rates, Govern = Governance.

same models being put to work with different leverage definitions give different results.

Table 11.5 above shows the summary of the inconsistencies found in the coefficient signs of relationship according to the use of first, different, models with the same leverage definition, and second, different, leverage definitions with the same model employed. From the summary, we can emphasize that inconsistencies are more pervasive in the use of different leverage definitions with the same model employed as compared to different models with the same leverage definition. To our knowledge, no study has really highlighted this interesting evidence, and we see the urgent need to further investigate this finding. Since no one universal leverage definition is to be found in the literature so far (Wanzenried, 2006), this scenario is expected to be repeated in the studies of capital structure. This scenario would, consequently, lead to the unresolved issue of inconclusive findings in the capital structure study. The findings of this study enhance and reinforce what has been put forward by Al-Najjar and Hussainey (2011) that the effect of the different definitions (of leverage) that can be used by different studies may complicate or even flaw any comparisons of findings made between studies that have been done.

6 Conclusion

Tremendous research has been done in studies of capital structure but, nevertheless, one concrete and conclusive answer has yet to be put forward. There is still no single answer to the question of what is the perfect debt-to-equity ratio for a firm to finance its operations and potential investments that would eventually maximize firm value. Inconclusiveness is still an issue in capital structure studies to date. The question of 'How do firms choose their capital structures?' posed by Myers (1984, p. 575) remains unanswered.

Our study, based on data from three Southeast Asian countries, namely Malaysia, Thailand and Singapore, derived the same conclusion: that capital structure is still a puzzle because there is still no clear explanation, theoretically or empirically, as to how firms within each country choose among the different methods of financing. What is clear is that theoretical puzzles still remain and that empirical results are not yet sufficiently consistent to resolve them (Al-Najjar & Taylor, 2008). Our study finds that the different leverage definitions used in capital structure studies throughout the years have their significant impact on the inconsistent results derived from the analysis. Bevan and Danbolt (2002) assert that different definitions of leverage give different results and, as proved by the evidence, our study agrees with this assertion and thus confirms that capital structure study is still inconclusive to date.

Employing different models is also identified as another contributing factor for inconclusiveness in capital structure studies. The contrasting nature of the static and dynamic models influence the results of findings on which each model yields a different coefficient sign and thus leads to different theoretical argument underlying it. Banerjee et al. (2004) and Serrasqueiro and Nunes (2008) also encounter a similar scenario when employing different models in their studies. Thus, the findings from our study support the argument that different models employed, though with the same leverage definitions, will lead to inconclusiveness in capital structure studies.

Evidence is more pervasive when different leverage definitions are put to work with the same model. Our study proves the notion that when the same model is working with different leverage definitions different signs are yielded and, hence, inconsistent results are recorded.

Although having been debated and studied for decades, studies on capital structure still represent one of the main unsolved issues in the corporate finance literature. Countless theoretical studies, as well as empirical research, have tried to address these issues, yet no one theory stands out to explain accurately the corporate financing behaviour of firms past and present. Indeed, what makes the capital structure debate so exciting is that only a few of the developed theories have been tested by empirical studies, and the theories themselves lead to different – not mutually exclusive, and sometimes opposed – results and conclusions (Gill et al., 2009). And we would conclude this study by agreeing that (which appears to be witnessed by the literature) empirical evidence indicates that the capital structure choice lies at the very heart of corporate financial decision making (Drobetz & Wanzenried, 2006).

References

Al-Najjar, B. and Taylor, P. (2008). 'The Relationship between Capital Structure and Ownership Structure. New Evidence from Jordanian Panel Data', *Managerial Finance*, 34(12), 919–33.

Al-Najjar, B. and Hussainey, K. (2011) 'Revisiting the Capital Structure Puzzle: UK Evidence', *The Journal of Risk Finance*, 12(4), 329–38.

Arellano, M. and Bond, S. R. (1991) 'Some Tests of Specification for Panel Data, Monte Carlo Evidence and Application to Employment Equations', *Review of Economic Studies*, 58(2), 277–97.

Baker, M. and Wurgler, J. (2002) 'Market Timing and Capital Structure', *Journal of Finance*, 57, 1–32.

Banerjee, S., Heshmati, A. and Wihlborg, C. (2004) 'The Dynamics of Capital Structure', *Research in Banking & Finance*, 4, 275–97.

Beattie, V., Goodacre, A. and Thomson, S. J. (2006). 'Corporate Financing Decision UK Survey Evidence'. *Journal of Business Finance & Accounting*, 33(9–10), 1402–34.

Bauer, P. (2004) 'Determinants of Capital Structure: Empirical Evidence from the Czech Republic', *Czech Journal of Economics & Finance*, 54, 2–21.

Bevan, A. and Danbolt, J. (2002) 'Capital Structure and Its Determinants in the UK: A Decompositional Analysis', *Applied Financial Economics*, 12, 159–70.

Boateng, A. (2004) 'Determinants of Capital Structure: Evidence from International Joint Ventures in Ghana', *International Journal of Social Economics*, 31(1), 56–66.

Booth, L., Aivazian, V., Demirguc-Kunt, A. and Maksimovic, V. (2001) 'Capital Structure in Developing Countries', *Journal of Finance*, 56(1), 87–130.

Caglayan, E. and Sak, N. (2010) 'The Determinants of Capital Structure: Evidence from the Turkish Banks', *Journal of Money, Investment & Banking*, 15, 57–65.

Chittenden, F., Hall, G. and Hutchinson, P. (1996) 'Small Firm Growth, Access to Capital Markets and Financial Structure. Review of Issues and an Empirical Investigation', *Small Business Economics*, 8, 59–67.

Chung, K. H. (1993) 'Asset Characteristics and Corporate Debt Policy: An Empirical Test', *Journal of Business, Finance & Accounting*, 20(1), 83–98.

Collins, J. M. and Sekely, W. S. (1983) 'The Relationship of Headquarters Country and Industry Classification to Financial Structure', *Financial Management*, 12, 45–51.

De Jong, A., Kabir, R. and Nguyen, T. T. (2008) 'Capital Structure Around The World. The Roles of Firm and Country-Specific Determinants', *Journal of Banking & Finance*, 32, 1954–69.

De Angelo, H. and Masulis, R. (1980) 'Optimal Capital Structure under Corporate and Personal Taxation', *Journal of Financial Economics*, 8, 3–29.

Deesomsak, R., Paudyal, K. and Pescetto, G. (2004) 'The Determinants of Capital Structure: Evidence from the Asia Pacific Region', *Journal of Multinational Financial Management*, 14, 387–405.

Deesomsak, R., Paudyal, K. and Pescetto, G. (2009) 'Debt Maturity Structure and the 1997 Asian Financial Crisis', *Journal of Multinational Financial Management*, 19, 26–42.

De Miguel, A. D. and Pindado, J. (2001) 'Determinant of Capital Structure: Evidence from Spanish Panel Data', *Journal of Corporate Finance*, 7, 77–99.

Demirguc-Kunt, A. and Maksimovic, V. (1996) 'Stock Market Development and Firms' Financing Choices', *World Bank Economic Review*, 10, 341–69.

Dissanaike, G. and Makar, I. (2009) 'Corporate Financing in East Asia before the 1997 Crash', *Journal of International Business Studies: Palgrave Macmillan*, 40(6), 990–1004.

Drobetz, W. and Wanzenried, G. (2006) 'What Determines the Speed of Adjustment to the Target Capital Structure?' *Applied Financial Economics*, 16, 941–58.

Fan, J. P. H., Wei, K. C. J. & Xu, X. (2011) 'Corporate Finance and Governance in Emerging Markets: A Selective Review and an Agenda for Future Research', *Journal of Corporate Finance*, 17, 207–14.

Frank, M. Z. and Goyal, V. K. (2009) 'Capital Structure Decisions: Which Factors are Really Important?', *Financial Management*, 38(1), 1–37.

Gaud, P., Jani, E., Hoesli, M. and Bender, A. (2005) 'The Capital Structure of Swiss Companies: An Empirical Analysis Using Dynamic Panel Data', *European Financial Management*, 11(1), 1–28.

Gill, A., Biger, N., Pai, C. and Bhutani, S. (2009) 'The Determinants of Capital Structure in the Service Industry: Evidence from the United States', *The Open Business Journal*, 2, 48–53.

Gujarati, D. N. and Porter, D. C. (2009) *Basic Econometrics*. New York, McGraw-Hill.

Gwatidzo, T. and Ramjee, A. (2012) 'Dynamics in Capital Structure Determinants in South Africa', *Meditary Accountancy Research*, 20(1), 52–67.

Hall, G., Hutchinson, P. and Michaelas, N. (2004) 'Determinants of the Capital Structures of European SMEs', *Journal of Business Finance & Accounting*, 31, 711–28.

Harris, M. and Raviv, A. (1991) 'The Theory of Capital Structure', *Journal of Finance*, 46(1), 297–355.

Hovakimian, A., Opler, T. and Titman, S. (2001) 'The Debt Equity Choice', *Journal of Financial & Quantitative Analysis*, 36, 1–24.

Jalilvand, A. and Harris, R. S. (1984) 'Corporate Behaviour in Adjusting to Capital Structure and Dividends Targets: An Econometric Study', *Journal of Finance*, 39, 127–45.

Jensen, M. C. and Meckling, W. (1976) 'Theory of the Firm, Managerial Behavior, Agency Costs and Ownership Structure', *Journal of Financial Economics*, 3, 305–60.

Jensen, M. C. (1986) 'Agency Costs of Free Cash Flow, Corporate Finance and Takeovers', *American Economic Review*, 76, 323–29.

Karadeniz, E., Kandir, S. Y., Balcilar, M. and Onal, Y. B. (2009) 'Determinants of Capital Structure: Evidence from Turkish Lodging Companies', *International Journal of Contemporary Hospitality Management*, 21(5), 594–609.

Kayo, E. K. and Kimura, H. (2011) 'Hierarchical Determinants of Capital Structure', *Journal of Banking & Finance*, 35, 358–71.

Kim, H., Heshmati, A. and Aoun, D. (2006) 'Dynamics of Capital Structure: The Case of Korean Listed Manufacturing Companies', *Asian Economic Journal*, 20(3), 275–302.

Leary, M. T. and Roberts, M. R. (2005) 'Do Firms Rebalance Their Capital Structures?' *Journal of Finance*, 60(6), 2575–619.

Margaritis, D. and Psillaki, M. (2010) 'Capital Structure, Equity Ownership and Firm Performance', *Journal of Banking & Finance*, 34(3), 621–32.

Mazur, K. (2007) 'The Determinants of Capital Structure Choice : Evidence from Polish Companies', *International Advances in Economic Research*, 13, 495–514.

Michaelas, N., Chittenden, F. and Poutziouris, P. (1999) 'Financial Policy and Capital Structure Choice in the U.K. SMEs: Empirical Evidence from Company Panel Data', *Small Business Economics*, 12, 113–30.

Modigliani, F. and Miller, M. (1958) 'The Cost of Capital, Corporation Finance, and the Theory of Investment', *American Economic Review*, 48, 261–97.

Mukherjee, S. and Mahakud, J. (2010) 'Dynamic Adjustment Towards Target Capital Structure: Evidence from Indian Companies', *Journal of Advances in Management Research*, 7(2), 250–66.

Myers, S. C. (1977) 'Determinants of Corporate Borrowing', *Journal of Financial Economics*, 5, 147–75.

Myers, S. C. (2001) 'Capital Structures', *Journal of Economic Perspectives*, 15, 81–102.

Myers, S. C. (1984) 'The Capital Structure Puzzle', *Journal of Finance*, 39, 575–92.

Myers, S. C. and Majluf, N. S. (1984) 'Corporate Financing and Investment Decisions when Firms have Information that Investors Do Not Have', *Journal of Financial Economics*, 13, 187–221.

Pandey, I. M., Chotigeat, T. and Ranjit, M. K. (2000) 'Capital Structure Choices in An Emerging Capital Market: the Case of Thailand', *Management & Change*, 4(1), 1–14.

Rajan, R. G. and Zingales, L. (1995) 'What Do We Know about Capital Structure? Some Evidence from International Data', *Journal of Finance*, 50(5), 1421–60.

Rasiah, D. and Kim, P. K. (2011) 'A Theoretical Review on the Use of the Static Trade Off Theory, the Pecking Order Theory and the Agency Cost Theory of Capital Structure', *International Research Journal of Finance and Economics*, 63, 150–9.

Reinhard, L. and Li, S. (2010) 'A Note on Capital Structure Target Adjustment – Indonesian Evidence', *International Journal of Managerial Finance*, 6(3), 245–59.

Roodman, D. (2006) *An Introduction to "Difference" and "System" GMM in STATA*. CGDEV Working Paper No. 103.

Scott, J. H. (1977) 'Bankruptcy, Secured Debt and Optimal Capital Structure', *Journal of Finance*, 32, 1–19.

Serrasqueiro, Z. and Nunes, P. M. (2008) 'Determinants of Capital Structure, Comparison of Empirical Evidence from the Use of Different Estimators', *International Journal of Applied Economics*, 5(1), 14–29.

Shyam-Sunder, L. and Myers, S. (1999) 'Testing Static Trade-Off against Pecking Order Models of Capital Structure', *Journal of Financial Economics*, 51, 219–44.

Stulz, R. M. (1990) 'Managerial Discretion and Optimal Financing Policies', *Journal of Financial Economics*, 26, 3–28.

Sheikh, N. A. and Wang, Z. (2011) 'Determinants of Capital Structure: An Empirical Study of Firms in the Manufacturing Industry of Pakistan', *Managerial Finance*, 37(2), 117–33.

Titman, S. and Wessels, R. (1988) 'The Determinants of Capital Structure Choice', *Journal of Finance*, 43, 1–19.

Wanzenried, G. (2006) 'Capital Structure Dynamics in the UK and Continental Europe', *The European Journal of Finance*, 12(8), 693–716.

Welch, I. (2004) 'Capital Structure and Stock Returns', *Journal of Political Economy*, 112(1), 106–31.

Welch, I. (2010) 'Two Common Problems in Capital Structure Research: The Financial-Debt-to-Asset Ratio and Issuing Activity versus Leverage Changes', *International Review of Finance*, 11(1), 1–17.

Wiwattanakantang, Y. (1999) 'An Empirical Study on the Determinants of the Capital Structure of Thai Firms', *Pacific-Basin Finance Journal*, 7, 371–403.

12
Determinants of Bank Profits and Net Interest Margins

Rubi Ahmad and Bolaji Tunde Matemilola

1 Introduction

The increase in the number of bank crises coupled with the important roles of the banking sector in the economy have stimulated extensive research focusing on banks. A systemic banking crisis would make costs to the economy rise as high as 55 per cent of GDP (Caprio & Klingebile, 2003). Consequently, the study on determinants of bank performance has received more attention in the literature, with the intention of developing a stable financial system.

Most studies of banking profit and interest margins have been conducted on U.S. and European banking institutions (Ho & Saunders, 1981; Bourke, 1989). However, little is known of the determinants of bank profits in the post–financial-crisis era in Asia (Park & Weber, 2006). Demirguc-Kunt and Huizinga (1999) investigated the determinants of bank interest margins in 80 countries, including countries in East Asia, during the period 1988–95. In addition, Demirguc-Kunt and Huizinga used a sample time period before the Asian financial crisis.

This chapter extends the existing literature on the determinants of banks' profits and net interest margins by using larger sample of banks from four countries in East Asia that successfully revamped after the Asian financial crisis. The chapter uses both bank-unique characteristics and selected macroeconomic indicators. Specifically, we investigate the determinants of banks' profits and net interest margins in the post–financial-crisis era in Asia. East Asia experienced systemic banking crises in the 1990s. The crisis affected East Asia at the end of that decade (most notably, Indonesia, South Korea, Thailand, Philippines and Malaysia during 1997–98).

Furthermore, over the last two decades these banks have faced many challenges, including going through major transformations in their operating environments and institutional structures (restructuring and recapitalization, privatization, liberalization, etc.). However, this chapter does not examine how successful the financial reforms have been in enhancing bank profits. Rather, it investigates the determinants of bank profits and net interest margins in the post–financial-crisis era in Asia. Incorporating both bank-specific factors and country-specific factors as independent variables, our results help to identify the characteristics of successful banks. In addition, our results will assist regulators in formulating the right banking policies and regulations that would enhance the overall performance of their banks.

The rest of this chapter is organized as follows: Section 2 reviews relevant literature. Section 3 explains the methodology and data. Section 4 discusses the results, while Section 5 concludes the chapter.

2 Literature review

The importance of bank profitability at both the micro and macro levels has motivated research on factors that influence the level of bank profits. The two most common proxies for bank profits are after-tax profits and net interest margins. Most research on banking focuses either on the determinants of bank profits or net interest margins separately, but it is difficult to find studies that investigate the determinants of bank profits and net interest margins together in a single study. However, Demirguc-Kunt and Huizinga (1999) are among the very few who analyse the underlying determinants of both bank profits and net interest margins. The results of their study reveal that well-capitalized banks have higher net interest margins and are more profitable, while official reserves and overhead reduce bank profits. Furthermore, they find that in developing countries, foreign banks have higher interest margins and profits compared to domestic banks.

In a related paper, Demirguc-Kunt and Huizinga (2000) examined the impact of financial development on bank profits and bank margins, and were the first to examine the impact of financial structure (i.e., the development of banks versus development of markets) on banks' profits. They found that in developed financial systems, bank profits and net interest margins are not statistically different across bank-based and market-based systems. Moreover, as bank development increases, greater competition among banks leads to increased efficiency and lower bank profits as well as lower net interest margins. Similarly, Abreu and Mendes (2001) investigate the determinants of interest margins and profitability of banks in four European Union (EU) countries. Their findings reveal that the determinants of net interest margins and bank profits are not the same. However, loan-to-assets and equity-to-assets ratios have positive impacts on net interest margins and profits.

Turning to studies of bank profits and net interest margins in a specific country, Ben Naceur and Goaeid (2003) examined factors that had an impact on the profits of ten Tunisian banks over the period 1980–2000. Their panel regression results show that individual bank characteristics explain a substantial part of the within-country variation in bank interest margins and net profits. On financial structure indicators, concentration has a negative and significant impact on net interest margins, which suggests that concentration is less beneficial (in terms of profits) to Tunisian commercial banks than competition. Also, Ben Naceur and Goaeid (2003) research results show that stock market development has a positive effect on bank profits, which implies that banks and stock markets complement each other.

In Latin America, Barajas et al. (1999) examined the determinants of high intermediation spreads in Colombia's banking sector over two decades (1974–96), covering pre- and post-liberalization periods. They note that average spreads remained unchanged even after banks in Colombia went through financial reforms. Barajas et al. (1999) found non-performing loans, financial taxation and operating cost to be the main determinants of bank net interest margins. Afanasieff et al. (2002) studied the determinants of interest margins in Brazil and found that macroeconomic variables are the main determinants of net interest margins in Brazil.

In the Philippines, Unite and Sullivan (2003) examined the relaxation of foreign bank entry regulations on the interest rate spreads and profits of 16 commercial banks in operation during the 1990–98 period. Their findings show that with foreign bank entry, interest rate spreads and profits of domestic banks narrow with the increased competition. However, interest rate spreads and profits of domestic banks that are affiliated with a family business group are less affected by foreign bank entry. In the study of Korean banks for the period 1992–2002, Park and Weber (2006) examined their profitability by testing the market structure (or structure-conduct performance) hypothesis against the efficient structure hypothesis. In the market structure hypothesis, through market power, banks in concentrated markets can charge higher loan rates, pay lower deposit rates and have lower collusion costs, thus generating more profits. Conversely, the efficient structure hypothesis states that efficient banks obtain higher profits and greater market share, which lead to a more concentrated market.

Park and Weber (2006) find that the major determinants of banks' profitability in Korea changed between the pre- and post-financial-crisis periods in East Asia. For the entire period, Park and Weber (2006) found that concentration has a negative impact on bank profits, which goes against the market structure hypothesis. Conversely, during the crisis period (1997–99) and the recovery period (2000–02), market concentration and market power became less significant, and the efficiency variable became the primary factor affecting bank profits. The results of this study indicate that bank efficiencies have significant effect on bank profits and support the efficiency structure hypothesis.

A recent strand of literature focuses on the relation between banks' profits and the business cycle. Biker and Hu (2002) analyse the degree of correlation between banks' profits and the business cycle of 26 OECD countries for the period 1979–2000. They found real GDP growth to be the single most useful indicator of the business cycle. Profits appear to move up and down with the business cycle, allowing for accumulation of capital in boom periods. Similarly, Athanasoglou et al. (2008) examined the relationship between bank profits and the business cycle of Greek banks during the period 1985–2001. Their results reveal the effects of the business cycle to be asymmetric because profit is positively correlated with the business cycle only when output is above trend. It is not within the scope of this chapter to cover the effects of business cycles on banks profits, due to the small time period (2003–08) under study.

In East Asia, studies that investigate the determinants of bank profits and net interest margins in the banking sector are few compared to the United States and Europe. Ben Naceur and Goaeid (2003), in their paper on bank performance in Tunisia, cite the works of Guru et al. (2002) on 17 Malaysian commercial banks over the period 1986–95. Among the internal factors, efficient expenses management is the most significant factor that explains high bank profits in Malaysia. For external factors, high interest ratio is associated with low bank profits, and inflation has a positive effect on bank profits. Also, Rosly and Bakar (2003) studied the performance of Islamic counters of mainstream banks in Malaysia during the period 1996–2001. Rosly and Bakar (2003) found that the higher return on assets (ROA) of the Islamic banks is due to lower overhead expenses, as the Islamic banking scheme utilizes the overheads of mainstream banks.

In this chapter, we expand the previous literature on the determinants of bank profits and net interest margins by relying on a larger set of countries in East Asia that are badly affected by the financial crisis, but which successfully revamped after the Asian financial crisis. The next section describes the empirical method that is used to investigate the determinants of bank profits and net interest margins. The study period (2003–08), which is after the Asian Financial crisis (1997–98), was chosen to reduce systemic shock that would affect the results.

3 The research model and data

This study investigates the determinants of bank profits and net interest margins in the post–financial-crisis era in Asia by specifying the following models:

$$\begin{aligned}\text{Profit}_{ijt} = {} & \beta_0 + \beta_1\text{Capital adequacy}_{ijt} + \beta_2\text{Management efficiency}_{ijt} \\ & + \beta_3\text{Liquidity}_{ijt} + \beta_4\text{Credit quality}_{ijt} + \beta_5\text{SIZE}_{ijt} \\ & + \beta_6\text{GDP}_{jt} + \beta_7\text{Inflation}_{jt} + \beta_8\text{Concentration}_{jt} + \varepsilon_{ijt} \qquad (1)\end{aligned}$$

$$\begin{aligned}\text{Net Interest Margin}_{ijt} = {} & \beta_0 + \beta_1\text{Capital adequacy}_{ijt} \\ & + \beta_2\text{Management efficiency}_{ijt} + \beta_3\text{Liquidity}_{ijt} \\ & + \beta_4\text{Credit quality}_{ijt} + \beta_5\text{SIZE}_{ijt} + \beta_6\text{GDP}_{jt} \\ & + \beta_7\text{Inflation}_{jt} + \beta_8\text{Concentration}_{jt} + \varepsilon_{ijt} \qquad (2)\end{aligned}$$

where:

Profit = Return on average assets of bank i in country j at t time
Net interest margin = Net interest margin of bank i in country j at time t
Capital adequacy = Equity to total assets of bank i in country j at time t
Management efficiency = Costs-to-income ratio of bank i in country j at time t
Liquidity = Net loans to customers and short-term fund ratio of bank i in country j at time t
Credit quality = Loan loss reserve to gross loan ratio of bank i in country j at time t
Size = Natural log of total assets of bank i in country j at time t
GDP = Annual change in real GDP of country j at time t
Inflation = Annual inflation rate of country j at time t

Concentration = Assets of three largest banks to the assets of all banks in country j at time t
β_0 = Bank-specific fixed effects constant term in the regression models
$\beta_1 - \beta_8$ = Parameters to be estimated
ε_{ijt} = Random variable.

The models specified above include internal and external factors that determine bank profits. The dependent and explanatory variables are chosen based on the works of Kosmidou (2008), who studies bank profits in Greece, and Ben Naceur and Goaied (2003) who study bank net interest margins and profits in Tunisia.

For the dependent variable, we follow standard indicators of ex-post bank profits commonly use in the literature, which are return on average assets (profit) and net interest margins (NIM). Bank profit is measured as net profit before tax divided by total average assets. As in Kosmidou (2008) and Athanasoglou et al. (2008), average assets of two consecutive years is used instead of end-year values, since profits are flow variables generated during the year. Return on average assets measures the overall profitability of the bank, or the profits earned per dollar of assets and reflects how well bank management use the banks' real investment resources to generate profits (Ben Naceur & Goaied, 2003).

The inclusion of net interest margins as another dependent variable is an attempt to gauge the cost of financial intermediation (Brock & Rojas-Suarez, 2000). NIM reflects pure operational efficiencies of the bank and the competitive nature of the banking markets (Demirguc-Kunt et al., 2004). According to Demirguc-Kunt and Huizinga (1999), the efficiency of bank intermediation can be measured using both ex-ante (contractual rates charged on loans less deposit rates) and ex-post spreads (interest revenue less interest expense). However, ex-post spread is a more useful measure as it takes into account loan defaults due to high-yield and risky credits. In this study, NIM is calculated by net interest income divided by average earning assets. NIM is a summary measure of banks' net interest return, an important component of bank profits (Angbazo, 1997). As an accounting identity, the bank net interest margin equals (pre-tax) profits plus bank operating costs, plus loan loss provisioning, minus non-interest income (Demirguc-Kunt & Huizinga, 2000).

Internal determinants of profits are measured by five bank-unique characteristics. They are ratio of equity to total assets (capital adequacy), costs-to-income ratio (management efficiency), ratio of banks' loans to customer and short-term funding (bank liquidity), ratio of loan loss reserves to gross loans (credit quality) and finally, banks' total assets which represent size (Ben Naceur & Goaied, 2003; Kosmidou, 2008).

The ratio of equity to total assets is used as a measure of capital adequacy. Capital adequacy measures how sufficient is the amount of equity to absorb any shocks that the bank may experience (Kosmidou, 2008). Berger (1995a) finds the return on equity and the capital asset ratio are positively related for a sample of U.S. banks for the 1983–89 time period. Similarly, Demirguc-Kunt and Huizinga (1999) find a positive relationship between capital adequacy and net interest income as well as positive relationship between capital adequacy and banks' profits. It is expected that well-capitalized banks (i.e., banks with higher equity-to-assets ratios) have higher interest margins on assets which increases profits (Abreu & Mendes, 2001). In addition, well-capitalized banks can charge more for loans and pay less on deposits because they face a lower risk of going bankrupt, and the need for external funding is lower (Demirguc-Kunt et al., 2004).

The management efficiency ratio measures the overhead, or cost, of running the bank, including staff salaries and benefits, occupancy expenses and other expenses such as office supplies, as a percentage of income. However, salaries, as percentage of income are commonly used to provide information on variation of bank costs over the banking system (Pasiouras & Kosmidou, 2007; Kosmidou, 2008). Banks with higher operating costs are expected to have higher net interest margins and lower profits (Abreu & Mendes, 2001). Athanasoglou et al. (2008) note that operating expenses can be viewed as the outcome of bank management, and management efficiency (costs-to-income ratio) is expected to be negatively related to profits. Since improved management of these expenses will increase efficiency and, therefore, raise profits.

However, Molyneux and Thornton (1992) and Ben Naceur and Goaied (2003) find a positive relationship between management efficiency and bank profits. Specifically, Molyneux and Thornton (1992) find staff expenses are positively related with bank profits, which suggest that high profits earned by firms in a regulated industry may be appropriated in the form of higher payroll expenditures. In this study, we expect a positive relationship between net interest margins and management efficiency, while the relationship between bank profits and management efficiency could be positive or negative (mixed) based on the literature.

Liquidity measures how liquid banks are to meet short-term maturing obligations. To avoid insolvency problems, banks often hold liquid assets, which can be easily converted to cash. This ratio shows the relationship between comparatively illiquid assets (i.e., loans) and comparatively stable funding sources (i.e., deposits and other short-term funding). Higher ratios indicate lower liquidity, while lower ratios indicate more liquidity for the bank. As liquid assets are associated with lower rates of return, higher liquidity would be associated with lower profits. A positive relationship is expected between profits and liquidity (Pasiouras & Kosmidou, 2007; Kosmidou, 2008).

Credit quality is proxy by the ratio of loan loss provisions to gross loans (Angbazo, 1997). Credit quality measures how much of the total portfolio has been provided for but not charged off, and it is used as a measure of a bank's credit quality. A positive impact of credit quality on profits implies better credit quality of loans that increase interest income and reduce provisioning costs. Conversely, a negative impact of credit quality on bank profits would imply poor quality of loans that reduce interest income and increase provisioning cost (Kosmidou, 2008). Athanasoglou et al. (2008) find negative relationship profits and credit quality as the theory suggests that increased exposure to credit risk is normally associated with a decrease in firm's profits. Conversely, Angbazo (1997) finds a positive relationship between credit risk and net interest margin, as risky loans require higher net interest margins to compensate for the higher risk of default. Hence, we expect a negative relation between bank profits and credit quality, but a positive relationship between net interest margin and credit quality.

Size is a variable that takes into account economies or diseconomies of scale. In most studies on banking, total assets of the bank are used as a proxy for size to account for size-related economies or diseconomies of scale. The effect of growing size on bank profits is initially positive to a certain extent, after which the effect is expected to be negative for banks that become too large, due to its bureaucracy. We use the log of total assets (LNSize) to proxy for size (Demirguc-Kunt et al., 2004; Athanasoglou et al., 2008). Demirguc-Kunt and Huizinga (1999) find that bank size has a significant and positive effect on interest margins, while Kosmidou (2008) finds a positive relationship between profits and size for Greek banks during the period of European Union (EU) integration. Conversely, other researchers report a negative correlation between net interest margin and size (Ben Naceur & Goaeid, 2003) and negative correlation between bank profits and size (Pasiouras & Kosmidou, 2007). We expect the results to be mixed (positive or negative) for both bank profits and interest margins.

The literature suggests that the environments in which commercial banks operate do influence how well they perform. Annual growth in real gross domestic product (GDP) and annual growth in the consumer price index (CPI) are two of the most commonly used macroeconomic indicators. GDP measures the total economic activity within an economy and is expected to show a positive relationship with bank profits (Biker & Hu, 2002; Kosmidou, 2008). However, growth has no significant effect on profits and net interest margins in studies on banks in 80 countries (Demirguc-Kunt & Huizinga, 1999) and also in Tunisia (Ben Naceur & Goaied, 2003).

Another macroeconomic variable in our regression model is the consumer price index, which represents inflation. According to Pasiouras and Kosmidou (2007), if banks anticipate inflation, profit will be positive because banks can adjust interest rates in a timely manner, which results in revenue rising faster than costs. However, if banks fail to anticipate inflation (unanticipated inflation), then the impact on bank profits could be negative. The reason is because banks may be slow in adjusting their interest rates, resulting in a faster increase in costs than in revenues. Studies by Bourke (1989) and Molyneux and Thornton (1992) find that profit is positively related to inflation. Demirguc-Kunt and Huizinga (1999) report that inflation is associated with higher interest margins and higher profits. Conversely, Abreu and Mendes (2001) examine banks in Portugal, Spain, France and Germany over the period 1986–99. Abreu and Mendes (2001) find a negative relationship between inflation and profits as well as a negative relationship between inflation and net interest margin because banks' costs increase more than revenues. Based on the literature, the effect of inflation on bank profits and net interest margins could be either positive or negative.

The last explanatory variable is the concentration ratio, which refers to the extent to which the banking industry is dominated by a few big banks (Park & Weber, 2006). Most of the earlier research on concentration was based on structure-conduct-performance (SCP), or market-power. The traditional SCP argues that prices are less favourable to consumers (lower deposit rates and higher loan rates) in more concentrated markets as a result of competitive imperfections in these markets (Berger, 1995b). In contrast, the efficient market hypothesis (EMH) argues that banks with superior management or production technologies have lower costs, and therefore higher profits. In addition, as these banks gain market share, the structure will become more concentrated due to efficiency gains. Most studies in the banking literature find a significant positive relationship between concentration and profits (see Bourke, 1989; Molyneux & Thornton, 1992; Demirguc-Kunt & Huizinga, 1999). Conversely, Park and Weber (2006) find that concentration has a negative impact on bank profits for Korean banks, contrary to the market structure hypothesis, while the Ben Naceur and Goaied (2003) study indicates a negative relationship between concentration and net interest margin. We expect a mixed (positive or negative) relationship between concentration and bank profits and a negative relationship between concentration and net interest margin.

As with previous studies (see Demirguc-Kunt & Huizinga, 1999), it is not the intention of this paper to explain which hypothesis best explains the positive profit-structure relationship; rather, concentration is included because the literature suggests that it is an important variable. There are at least two measurements of concentration, the Herfindahl-Hirschman (HH) index and concentration ratios. The HH index considers the largest banks and includes all banks. The HH index is the squared sum of market share of each bank's assets ($\sum [MS_i]^2$) in a given year. Conversely, concentration ratios include only the share of the market held by the two or three largest banks. We chose the share of the three largest banks, which is in line with previous studies (see Kosmidou et al., 2007; Garcia-Herrero et al., 2007). In our study, concentration is calculated by dividing the total assets of the three largest banks in the market with the total assets of all banks based on the sample obtained from the Bankscope Database of Bureau van Dijk's company.

Our data consist of a time series and cross-section of bank data. Hence, we use panel data. The use of the panel method improves the efficiency of econometric estimates and provides more flexibility in controlling for unobservable firm-specific effects. Moreover, since it is hard to capture the obvious differences across firms, panel data analysis provides the technique to control for those variables that are time invariant via firm-specific fixed effects (Baltagi, 2005). The model is first evaluated for the statistical significance of the estimated fixed effects using the redundant fixed effects likelihood ratio. If the result is significant, the model is then tested with the Hausman test to confirm the choice between the fixed effects and random effects models. Finally, we control for cross-section heteroskedasticity to obtain a robust coefficient by including in our estimation White cross-section standard errors and covariance (no d.f. correction).

Bank level data are obtained from the Bankscope database, supplemented by macroeconomic data from: International Financial Statistics, August 2009; International Monetary Fund; World Development Indicators, 2009, and the World Bank. Only banks with accounting statements from 2003–08 from the Bankscope database are included in the sample.

Our initial sample consists of 142 banks for the 4 countries (see Table 12.1) with information on standard ratios calculated based on a

Table 12.1 Crisis-hit Asian countries and number of banks

			After inspection			
	Initial sample	Missing values	Management efficiency >100%	Liquidity >200%	Final sample	Share %
Malaysia	34	14	2	–	20	59
Thailand	20	6	2	1	12	60
Indonesia	69	34	–	1	32	46
Korea	19	4	4	2	14	74
Total	142	58	–		78	55

Management efficiency = Cost/Income ratio; Liquidity = Net loans/Customers and Short-term funds.
Source: Data Collected from Bankscope.

global summary format. The banks are inspected for missing values and outliers. The outliers pertain specifically to costs-to-income ratio (management efficiency) and net loans to customer and short-term funding (liquidity). In our study, only banks with management efficiency within the ratio of 0 per cent–100 per cent are included. We then decide on whether the same criteria of 0 per cent–100 per cent should be applied to liquidity because there are a substantial number of banks with a liquidity ratio above 100 per cent. Using the same criteria would mean a further reduction of more banks. A review of the data show that quite a number of South Korean banks have a liquidity ratio above 100 per cent, with one Korean bank having a ratio of 213.29 per cent. This is consistent with the 26 March 2010 press release of the Financial Services Commission and South Korea's financial regulator reports that the South Korean domestic banking industry loan-to-deposit ratio is 127.1 per cent at end 2007, and 110.4 per cent as of end January 2010. Hence, we used South Korean banks as the benchmark, and decided to include banks with ratios of net loans to customer and short-term funding below 200 per cent in order not to reduce further the sample size. After deleting missing data and outliers, we have a balanced panel of 78 banks (55 per cent of the original number of banks) as shown in Table 12.1.

4 Results

This section focuses on the results of the study. The study uses a balanced panel of 84 banks from 4 countries, namely, Malaysia, Thailand,

Indonesia and South Korea for the period 2003–08. These countries are selected because they were badly affected by the Asian financial crisis but, successfully revamped post crisis. Summary statistics of these countries are presented in Table 12.2.

Table 12.2 reveals that mean return on profit is 1.93 while mean of net interest margin (NIM) is 4.40. The higher mean for NIM (which measure banks operational efficiency) compare to profit (which measure banks profitability) could mean that banks in impacted Asian countries place more emphasis on operational efficiency than profitability. Moreover, profit has standard deviation (1.45) compared to NIM (2.29). The low standard deviation of profit compared to NIM indicates that profit is less volatile when compared to NIM. Also, Table 12.2 reveals that of all the independent variables, bank concentration ratio has the highest mean, while credit quality has the lowest mean. Moreover, GDP has the lowest standard variation (1.87) among the independent variables, while liquidity has the highest standard deviation (25.59) among the independent variables. This result indicates that GDP is the least volatile and liquidity is the most volatile among the independent variables.

In this study, simple correlation coefficient between explanatory variables is used to examine multicollinearity. Multicollinearity is a concern if the absolute value of simple correlation coefficients exceeds 0.80 (Studenmund, 2006). Table 12.3 shows the pair-wise correlation matrix with all correlation coefficients which are less than 0.80. Low correlation coefficients between the variables suggest that there is little risk of multicollinearity in the data.

Capital adequacy regression coefficient is statistically significant and positively related to banks' profit in crisis-hit Asian countries (see Table 12.4). The significant positive relation between capital adequacy and banks' profits implies that well capitalized banks would increase their profits. This result supports the findings of Berger (1995a) that report a positive relation between profits and capital adequacy. Similarly, the inflation regression coefficient is statistically significant and positively related to banks' profits. The result suggests that bank managements in crisis-hit Asian countries have correctly anticipated the effects of inflation, and interest rates have been adjusted to achieve higher profits. This result is consistent with findings of Bourke (1989) and Boyd et al. (2001), who report a positive relation between profits and inflation. Conversely, the result is inconsistent with Kosmidou (2008), who reports a negative relation between profits and inflation.

Table 12.2 Crisis-hit Asian countries (78 Banks) – descriptive statistics (%) (2003–08) period

	Profit	NIM	Capital adequacy	Management efficiency	Liquidity	Credit quality	Size	GDP	Inf.	Con.
Mean	1.93	4.40	11.08	49.56	74.70	4.16	8.36	5.27	5.44	55.05
Median	1.68	3.72	8.45	49.22	76.10	3.07	8.55	5.30	4.68	55.99
Maximum	8.28	19.32	46.43	99.73	170.02	52.38	12.38	7.10	13.11	64.65
Minimum	−1.97	0.92	3.24	10.65	1.47	0.74	4.32	2.20	0.99	45.09
Std. Dev.	1.45	2.29	7.16	14.56	25.59	4.17	1.87	1.07	3.42	5.30
Skewness	1.46	2.47	1.71	0.11	−0.02	5.71	−0.04	−1.02	0.81	−0.01
Kurtosis	6.40	12.37	5.88	3.55	4.11	54.28	2.02	4.13	2.67	2.52
Jarque-Bera	391.6	2188	388.19	6.96	24.12	5382.15	18.70	106.26	52.90	9.74
Probability	0.00	0.00	0.00	0.03	0.00	0.00	0.00	0.00	0.00	0.01
Sum	905	2060	5188	23193	34961	1945	3911	2467	2548	25762
Sum Sq. Dev.	984	2455	23935	99042	305922	8122	1638	535	5454	13126
Observation	468	468	468	468	468	468	468	468	468	468

Notes: Profit = Return on average assets; NIM = Net interest margins; Capital adequacy = Equity/Total assets; Management efficiency = Cost/Income; Liquidity = Net loans/Customers and Short-term funding; Credit quality = Loan loss reserves/Gross loans; Size = LN Size; GDP = Real gross domestic product annual growth rate; Inflation (Inf) = Consumer price index; Concentration (Con) = Assets of 3 largest banks/assets of all banks in sample.

Table 12.3 Crisis-hit Asian countries (78 Banks) – independent variables correlation

	Capital adequacy	**Management efficiency**	**Liquidity**	**Credit quality**	**Size**	**GDP**	**Inflation**	**Concentration**
Capital adequacy	1							
Management efficiency	−0.3407	1						
Liquidity	0.0613	−0.1585	1					
Credit quality	0.3743	−0.0035	−0.0855	1				
Size	−0.6386	0.0046	0.1699	−0.0770	1			
GDP	0.2359	−0.0544	−0.1465	0.2121	−0.2887	1		
Inflation	0.1992	0.1359	0.0040	−0.1741	−0.4430	0.0460	1	
Concentration	0.0214	0.2146	0.1424	−0.0563	−0.2235	−0.2679	0.4551	1

Notes: Capital adequacy = Equity/Total assets; Management efficiency = Cost/Income; Liquidity = Net loans/Customers and Short-term funding; Credit quality = Loan loss reserves/Gross loans; Size = LN Size; GDP = Real gross domestic product annual growth rate; Inflation = Consumer price index; Concentration = Assets of 3 largest banks/assets of all banks in sample.

Table 12.4 Dependent variable – profit results

Variables	Panel fixed effects results
C	2.0473* (1.2095)
Capital adequacy	0.1407*** (0.0179)
Management efficiency	−0.0427***
Liquidity	0.0044 (0.0036)
Credit quality	−0.0362***
Size	−0.0462
GDP	0.1382*** (0.0219)
Inflation	0.0273*** (0.0096)
Concentration	0.0702*** (0.0112)
N	78
Observation	468
R^2	0.8819
Adjusted R^2	0.8556
F-statistics	33.5520
Probability (F-statistics)	0.0000

Notes: Profit = Return on average assets; Capital adequacy = Equity/Total assets; Management efficiency = Cost/Income; Liquidity = Net loans/Customers and Short-term funding; Credit quality = Loan loss reserves/Gross loans; Size = LN Size; GDP = Real gross domestic product annual growth rate; Inflation = Consumer price index; Concentration = Assets of 3 largest banks/assets of all banks in sample. ***, ** and * denotes significant at the 1%, 5% and 10% level respectively. The standard errors in parenthesis are White heteroskedasticity consistent.

Furthermore, management efficiency (measured by costs-to-income ratio) has a regression coefficient that is statistically significant and negatively related to banks' profits. The result suggests that costs have not been efficiently managed, which could explain the reason for the decline in bank profits as management efficiency increases. This result is inconsistent with findings of Molyneux and Thornton (1992) and Ben Naceur and Goaied (2003), whose results find a positive relationship between bank profits and management efficiency. Moreover, credit quality has a regression coefficient that is statistically significant and negatively related to banks' profits. The result suggests that there is no adequate provisioning for loan loss reserve, which could explain the reason for the negative relation between profits and credit quality. This result supports the findings of Athanasoglou et al. (2008) and Brock and Rojas-Suarez (2000) that find negative relation between profits and credit quality.

Turning to results of macroeconomic factors, the GDP regression coefficient is statistically significant and positively related to banks' profits. The result implies that as GDP growth increases, profit increases, which supports the importance of macroeconomic factors in banking research.

This result is consistent with findings of Demurguc-Kunt and Huizinga (1999) that report a positive relation between profits and GDP growth. Moreover, the concentration regression coefficient is statistically significant and positively related to bank profits. This result reveals that concentration increases bank profits in crisis-hit Asian countries. This result supports the findings of Bourke (1989), Molyneux and Thornton (1992) and Demirguc-Kunt and Huizinga (1999) that find evidence that profit is positively related to concentration. Conversely, our results do not support the findings of Park and Weber (2006) and Berger (1995b) that find evidence that profit is negatively related to concentration. Also, the regression coefficient of size is insignificant, but negatively related to banks' profits. This result suggests that size may not be a determinant of banks' profits in East Asia, which is contrary to what we expected. The result is inconsistent with findings of Kosmidou (2008) that find significant positive relation between profits and size.

Moreover, Table 12.5 shows that the capital adequacy regression coefficient is statistically significant and positively related to net interest

Table 12.5 Dependent variable – net interest margin

Variable	**Panel fixed effects results**
C	5.8480*** (1.4757)
Capital adequacy	0.1205*** (0.0311)
Management efficiency	−0.0150**
Liquidity	0.0099*** (0.0033)
Credit quality	−0.0250
Size	−0.3124**
GDP	−0.0149
Inflation	0.0126 (0.0249)
Concentration	−0.0011
N	78
Observation	468
R^2	0.8691
Adjusted R^2	0.8400
F-statistics	29.8474
Probability (F-statistics)	0.0000

Notes: NIM = Net interest margins; Capital adequacy = Equity/Total assets; Management efficiency = Cost/Income; Liquidity = Net loans/Customers and Short-term funding; Credit quality = Loan loss reserves/Gross loans; Size = LN Size; GDP = Real gross domestic product annual growth rate; Inflation = Consumer price index; Concentration = Assets of 3 largest banks/assets of all banks in sample. ***, ** and * denotes significant at the 1%, 5% and 10% level respectively. The standard errors in parenthesis are White heteroskedasticity consistent.

margin (NIM). The result implies banks that are adequately capitalized would increase their net interest margin. The result supports findings of Demirguc-Kunt and Huizinga (1999) that report a positive relation between net interest margin and capital adequacy ratio. The liquidity regression coefficient is statistically significant and positively related to net interest margin. This result indicates that as liquidity increases, net interest margin increases, which suggests that banks that are more liquid would have a better chance of increasing their net interest margin.

Conversely, the management efficiency (costs-to-income ratio) regression coefficient is statistically significant and negatively related to net interest margin. This indicates that costs have not been efficiently managed, which could explain the decline in net interest margin. The result contradicts findings of Angbazo (1997) who find a positive relation between net interest margin and management efficiency (costs-to-income ratio). Similarly, the size regression coefficient is statistically significant and negatively related to net interest margin. The significant negative relation between net interest margin and size may suggest scale inefficiencies, which may explain the decline in net interest margin. This result is inconsistent with findings of Demirguc-Kunt and Huizinga (1999) and Kosmidou (2008) that find bank size is positively related to net interest margins.

Finally, GDP growth has a negative, but insignificant, relationship with net interest margin. Our result is inconsistent with findings of Demirguc-Kunt and Huizinga (1999) that report a significant negative relation between net interest margin and GDP. Also, inflation has a positive, but insignificant, relationship with net interest margin. These results indicate that macroeconomic factors (GDP growth and inflation) may not be determinants of net interest margin in crisis-hit Asian countries. Similarly, the concentration has a negative, but insignificant, relationship with net interest margin, which suggests that concentration may not be an important determinant of net interest margin in crisis-hit Asian countries.

5 Conclusion

The objective of this chapter is two-fold. First, it investigates the determinants of bank profits in the post-crisis era in Asia using panel regression analysis. Second, this chapter investigates the determinants of bank net interest margins using panel regression analysis. Four countries, namely Malaysia, Thailand, Indonesia and South Korea, are selected because they successfully revamped after the Asian financial crisis. Also, the selected countries are emerging economies and, prior to 2000, had undergone a period of liberalization, restructuring and recapitalization as well as privatization.

Bank-unique characteristics rather than external factors consistently explain a substantial part of the variation in banks' profits and net interest margins in crisis-hit Asian countries. Amongst the variables, capital adequacy (measured by equity to total assets ratio) has significant positive effects on bank profitability in crisis-hit Asian countries, which suggest that capital adequacy is an important determinant of banks' profits. Indeed, a well-capitalized bank is better able to withstand external shocks, and face a lower risk of going bankrupt. Furthermore, our results indicate that increased bank size does not necessarily translate into more profits for banks, given that the sign of the coefficient for size variable is mixed.

The banking literature asserts that cost is one of the main contributing factors to high net interest margins. In this paper, we find evidence of a negative relationship between net interest margins and management efficiency (costs-to-income ratio). This result is inconsistent with findings in the literature that report a positive relationship between net interest margin and management efficiency. The reason for the negative relation between net interest margins and management efficiency could be that costs have not been efficiently managed, which leads to a decline in net interest margins. Similarly, we find evidence of a negative relationship between banks' profits and management efficiency, which implies that costs have not been efficiently managed to reduce them and increase profit. Concentration is a subject of interest in much research in the banking literature, relating to the structure-conduct performance (or market power) and efficient market hypothesis. In this chapter, we find mixed results. Concentration has a significant positive relationship with bank profits. The significant positive relationship between bank profits and concentration suggests banks that have market power could increase their profit. Conversely, concentration has a negative, but insignificant, relationship with net interest margins in crisis-hit Asian countries.

Furthermore, the results show that GDP growth has a significant positive relationship with banks' profits, while GDP growth has insignificant effects on net interest margins. The reasons for these inconsistent results may be due to the period used in this study (2003–08), which coincides with the period when banks experienced privatization, liberalization and recapitalization. There is little empirical research on net interest margins in the literature, which suggests more research is needed that uses bank data from other countries in order to add clarity to the main determinants of net interest margins.

The implication of this study are as follows: First, the negative relationship between management efficiency and banks' profits as well as the net interest margin implies that bank management in crisis-hit Asian countries should manage costs efficiently in other to reduce them and generate more profits in the future. Second, the positive relationship between the capital adequacy ratio and banks' profits as well as net interest margins imply that bank regulators should further strengthen the capital requirements of the banks in crisis-hit Asian countries in order to ensure uninterrupted stability of the banking sector. In addition, our study implies that bank-specific factors, rather than macroeconomic factors, are consistent determinants of banks' profits and net interest margins in crisis-hit Asian countries.

Finally, we contribute to the banking literature in East Asia by using broad samples as well as using both internal and external factors that determine bank profits and net interest margins in the post–financial-crisis era in Asia. Future research could extend the study period in this paper to uncover the effects of the business cycle (proxy by GDP growth) on banks' profits. Perhaps the panel Generalized Method of Moments (GMM) could be used to control for profits persistence observed in the East Asia banking industry.

Acknowledgement

The authors gratefully acknowledge the contribution of Low Mun Tin, the MBA student of Dr. Rubi Ahmad.

References

Abreu, M. and Mendes, V. (2001) 'Commercial Bank Interest Margins and Profitability: Evidence for Some EU Countries'. Paper Presented at the Proceedings of the Pan-European Conference, Jointly Organized by the IEFS–UK and the University of Macedonia Economic and Social Sciences, Thessaloniki, Greece, in May, 2001.

Afanasieff, T., Lhacer, P. M. and Nakane, M. (2002) 'The Determinants of Bank Interest Spread in Brazil', *Banco Central di Brazil Working Papers*.

Angbazo, L. (1997) 'Commercial Bank Net Interest Margins, Default Risk, Interest-Rate Risk, and Off-Balance Sheet Banking', *Journal of Banking and Finance*, 21, 55–87.

Athanasoglou, P. P., Brissimis, S. N. and Delis M. (2008) 'Bank-Specific, Industry-Specific and Macroeconomic Determinants of Bank Profitability', *Journal of International Financial Markets, Institutions & Money*, 18, 121–36.

Baltagi, B. H. (2005) 'Econometric Analysis of Panel Data', West Sussex: John Wiley and Sons.

Barajas, A., Steiner, R. and Salazar, N. (1999) 'Interest Spreads in Colombia, 1974–1996', *International Monetary Fund, IMF Staff Papers*, 46 (2), 196–224.

Ben Naceur, S. and M. Goaied (2003) 'The Determinants of the Tunisian Banking Industry Profitability: Panel Evidence', Paper Presented at the Proceedings of the Economic Research Forum (ERF) 10th Annual Conference, Marrakesh, Morocco, 16–19 December 2003.

Berger, A. (1995a) 'The Relationship between Capital and Earnings in Banking', *Journal of Money, Credit and Banking*, 27 (2), 433–56.

Berger, A. (1995b) 'The Profit-Structure Relationship in Banking: Tests of Market Power and Efficiency Structure Hypothesis', *Journal of Money, Credit and Banking*, 27, 404–31.

Biker, J. A. and Hu, H. (2002) 'Cyclical Patterns in Profits, Provisioning and Lending of Banks', *DNB (De Nederlandsche Bank NV)* Staff Reports No. 86/2002.

Bourke, P. (1989) 'Concentration and Other Determinants of Bank Profitability in Europe, North America and Australia', *Journal of Banking and Finance*, 13, 65–79.

Boyd, J. H., Levine, R. and Smith, B. D. (2001) 'The Impact of Inflation on Financial Sector Performance', *Journal of Monetary Economics*, 47, 221–28.

Brock, P. and Rojas-Suarez, L. (2000) 'Understanding the Behavior of Bank Spreads in Latin America', *Journal of Development Economics*, 63, 113–34.

Caprio, G. and Klingebile, D. (2003) 'Episodes of Systemic and Borderline Financial Crisis, World Bank. Retrieved 24 February 2010', http://econ.worldbank.org/view.php?type=18& id=23456

Demirguc-Kunt, A., Laeven, L. and Levine, R. (2004) 'Regulations, Market Structure, Institutions, and the Cost of Financial Intermediation', *Journal of Money, Credit and Banking*, 36(3), 593–622.

Demirguc-Kunt, A. and Huizinga, H. (2000) 'Financial Structure and Bank Profitability', *Working Paper*, Washington, D.C: World Bank.

Demirguc-Kunt, A. and Huizinga, H. (1999) 'Determinants of Commercial Bank Interest Margins and Profitability: Some International Evidence', *The World Bank Economic Review*, 13, 379–408.

Garcia-Herrero, A., Gavila, S. and Santabarbara, D. (2007) 'What Explains the Low-Profitability of Chinese Banks?' The American University of Paris, *Working Paper No. 30*.

Guru, B., Staunton, J. and Balashanmugam, B. (2002) 'Determinants of Commercial Bank Profitability in Malaysia', University Multimedia, *Working Paper*.

Ho, S. Y. and Saunders, A. (1981) 'The Determinants of Bank Interest Margins: Theory and Empirical Evidence', *Journal of Financial and Quantitative Analysis*, 16 (4), 159–75.

Kosmidou, K. (2008) 'The Determinants of Banks' Profits in Greece During the Period of EU Financial Integration', *Managerial Finance*, 34 (3), 146–59.

Kosmidou, K., Pasiouras, F. and Tsaklanganos, A. (2007) 'Domestic and Multinational Determinants of Foreign Bank Profits: The Case of Greek Banks Operating Abroad', *Journal of Multinational Financial Management*, 17, 1–15.

Kosmidou, K., Tanna, S. and Pasiouras, F. (2005) 'Determinants of Profitability of Domestic UK Commercial Banks: Panel Evidence from the Period 1995–2002', in Proceedings of the 37th Annual Conference of the Money Macro and Finance (MMF) Research Group, Rethymno, Greece, 1–3 September.

Molyneux, P. and Thornton, J. (1992) 'Determinants of European Bank Profitability: A Note', *Journal of Banking and Finance*, 16, 1173–78.

Park, K. H. and Weber, L. (2006) 'Profitability of Korean Banks: Test of Market Structure Versus Efficient Structure', *Journal of Economics and Business*, 58, 222–39.

Pasiouras, K. and Kosmidou, K. (2007) 'Factors Influencing the Profitability of Domestic and Foreign Commercial Banks in the European Union'. *Research in International Business and Finance*, 21, 222–37.

Rosly, S. A. and Bakar, M. A. (2003) 'Performance of Islamic and Mainstream Banks in Malaysia', *International Journal of Social Economics*, 30 (12), 1249–65.

Studenmund, A. H. (2006) *Using Econometrics, A Practical Guide*, Fifth Edition. Pearson Addison Wesley.

Unite, A. A. and Sullivan, M. J. (2003) 'The Effect of Foreign Entry and Ownership Structure on the Philippine Domestic Banking Market', *Journal of Banking and Finance*, 27, 2323–45.

Index

The manufacturer's authorised representative in the EU is Springer Nature Customer Service Centre GmbH, Europaplatz 3, 69115 Heidelberg, Germany. If you have any concerns regarding our products, please contact ProductSafety@springernature.com

Printed and bound by CPI Group (UK) Ltd, Croydon, CR0 4YY
14/10/2026
02233137-0007